ENCYCLOPEDIA OF ENVIRONMENTAL ISSUES

WATER AND
WATER POLLUTION

ENCYCLOPEDIA OF ENVIRONMENTAL ISSUES
WATER AND WATER POLLUTION

Editor

Craig W. Allin
Cornell College

SALEM PRESS
A Division of EBSCO Publishing, Ipswich, Massachusetts

Cover photo:
Tire Among Skunk Cabbage. (© Joel W. Rogers/Corbis)

ISBN: 978-1-42983-673-9

Table of Contents

Contributors vii

Acid mine drainage 1
Amoco Cadiz oil spill 1
Aqueducts 2
Aquifers. 4
Argo Merchant oil spill 5
Ashio, Japan, copper mine 6

Best available technologies 7
Black Sea 8
BP *Deepwater Horizon* oil spill 9
Braer oil spill 12
Brent Spar occupation. 13

Chesapeake Bay. 14
Chlorination 15
Clean Water Act and amendments 16
Coastal Zone Management Act 18
Colorado River 18
Continental shelves. 20
Cultural eutrophication 22
Cuyahoga River fires 22

Dams and reservoirs 23
Danube River 27
Desalination. 28
Dredging 29
Drinking water 30

Environment Canada. 31
Environmental Protection Agency. 32
Eutrophication 35
Experimental Lakes Area 36
Externalities. 38
Exxon Valdez oil spill. 38

Flood Control Act 40
Floodplains 41
Floods 43
Fluoridation. 45

Ganges River 47
Great Lakes International Joint
    Commission 48

Groundwater pollution. 49
Gulf War oil burning 50

Irrigation 52

Kesterson Reservoir 54
Klamath River. 55

Lake Baikal 56
Lake Erie 58
Leachates 59
London Convention on the Prevention of
    Marine Pollution 61
Los Angeles Aqueduct 62

Mediterranean Blue Plan 64
Mississippi River 65
Mono Lake 68
Monongahela River tank collapse 69

Nile River 71
North American Free Trade Agreement 72

Ocean currents. 74
Ocean dumping 76
Ocean pollution 78
Oil spills. 81

Pacific Islands. 84
PEMEX oil well leak 86
Polluter pays principle 87

Rain gardens 88
Rainwater harvesting 89
Rhine River 91
Riparian rights 91
Rocky Flats, Colorado, nuclear plant
    releases 92
Runoff, agricultural 94
Runoff, urban. 95

Sacramento River pesticide spill 97
Safe Drinking Water Act 98
Santa Barbara oil spill 99
Sea Empress oil spill 100

Sea-level changes 101
Seabed disposal 103
Sedimentation 104
Sludge treatment and disposal 105
Soil salinization 106
Stormwater management 107

Teton Dam collapse 109
Tobago oil spill 110
Torrey Canyon oil spill 111

United Nations Convention on the
    Law of the Sea 112
U.S. Geological Survey 113

Wastewater management 114
Water conservation 116

Water pollution 118
Water-pollution policy 121
Water quality 123
Water rights 125
Water-saving toilets 127
Water treatment 127
Water use 129
Watershed management 131
Wells 133
Wolman, Abel 134

Zebra mussels 135

Bibliography 137
Category Index 139
Index 141

Contributors

Richard Adler
University of Michigan-Dearborn

Craig W. Allin
Cornell College

Emily Alward
College of Southern Nevada

Alvin K. Benson
Utah Valley University

Cynthia A. Bily
Macomb Community College

Josephus J. Brimah
Fourah Bay College

Byron Cannon
University of Utah

Robert E. Carver
University of Georgia

Frederick B. Chary
Indiana University Northwest

Daniel J. Connell
Boston College

Mark Coyne
University of Kentucky

Greg Cronin
University of Colorado at Denver

Robert L. Cullers
Kansas State University

Roy Darville
East Texas Baptist University

C. R. de Freitas
University of Auckland

René A. De Hon
Northeast Louisiana University

Dennis R. DeVries
Auburn University

Joseph Dewey
University of Pittsburgh

John P. DiVincenzo
Middle Tennessee State University

John M. Dunn
Ocala, Florida

Sohini Dutt
Kansas State University

Howard C. Ellis
Millersville University of Pennsylvania

Jack B. Evett
*University of North Carolina
at Charlotte*

Wendy C. Hamblet
North Carolina A&T State University

Thomas E. Hemmerly
Middle Tennessee State University

Charles E. Herdendorf
Ohio State University

Joseph W. Hinton
Portland, Oregon

Robert M. Hordon
Rutgers University

Solomon A. Isiorho
*Indiana University-Purdue University
Fort Wayne*

Karen N. Kähler
Pasadena, California

Michael D. Kaplowitz
Michigan State University

Kyle L. Kayler
Kayler Geoscience, Ltd.

Christopher Kent
Pasadena, California

Grove Koger
Boise State University

Narayanan M. Komerath
Georgia Institute of Technology

Padma P. Komerath
SCV, Inc.

Thomas T. Lewis
Mount Senario College

Josué Njock Libii
*Indiana University-Purdue University
Fort Wayne*

Donald W. Lovejoy
Palm Beach Atlantic University

David F. MacInnes, Jr.
Guilford College

Louise Magoon
Fort Wayne, Indiana

Sergei A. Markov
Austin Peay State University

Laurence W. Mazzeno
Alvernia College

G. Padmanabhan
North Dakota State University

Ronald J. Raven
State University of New York at Buffalo

Donald F. Reaser
University of Texas at Arlington

Raymond U. Roberts
Oklahoma Department of Environmental Quality

Gene D. Robinson
James Madison University

Charles W. Rogers
Southwestern Oklahoma State University

Carol A. Rolf
Rivier College

Neil E. Salisbury
University of Oklahoma

Elizabeth D. Schafer
Loachapoka, Alabama

Alexander Scott
Pasadena, California

Martha A. Sherwood
Kent Anderson Law Office

Courtney A. Smith
Parks and People Foundation

Roger Smith
Portland, Oregon

Daniel L. Smith-Christopher
Loyola Marymount University

Robert J. Stewart
California Maritime Academy

Mary W. Stoertz
Ohio University

Nicholas C. Thomas
Auburn University at Montgomery

Lisa A. Wroble
Redford Township District Library

Robin L. Wulffson
Faculty, American College of Obstetrics and Gynecology

Acid mine drainage

CATEGORY: Water and water pollution

DEFINITION: The flow of acidified waters from mining operations and mine wastes

SIGNIFICANCE: Acid mine drainage can pollute groundwater, surface water, and soils, producing adverse effects on plants and animals.

During mining, rock is broken and crushed, exposing fresh rock surfaces and minerals. Pyrite, or iron sulfide, is a common mineral encountered in metallic ore deposits. Rainwater, groundwater, or surface water that runs over the pyrite leaches out sulfur, which reacts with the water and oxygen to form sulfuric acid. In addition, if pyrite is present in the mining waste materials that are discarded at a mine site, some species of bacteria can directly oxidize the sulfur in the waste rock and tailings, forming sulfuric acid. In either case, the resulting sulfuric acid may run into groundwater and streams downhill from the mine or mine tailings.

Acid mine drainage (AMD) pollutes groundwater and adjacent streams and may eventually seep into other streams, lakes, and reservoirs to pollute the surface water. Groundwater problems are particularly troublesome because the reclamation of polluted groundwater is very difficult and expensive. Furthermore, AMD dissolves other minerals and heavy metals from surrounding rocks, producing lead, arsenic, mercury, and cyanide, which further degrade the water quality. Through this process, AMD has contributed to the pollution of many lakes.

AMD runoff can be devastating to the surrounding ecosystem. Physical changes and damage to the land, soil, and water from AMD directly and indirectly affect the biological environment. Mine water immediately adjacent to mines that are rich in sulfide minerals may be as much as 100,000 to 1,000,000 times more acidic than normal stream water. AMD water poisons and leaches nutrients from the soil so that few, if any, plants can survive. Animals that eat those plants, as well as microorganisms in the leached soils, may also die. AMD is also lethal for many water-dwelling animals, including plankton, fish, and snails. Furthermore, people can be poisoned by drinking water that has been contaminated with heavy metals produced by AMD, and some people have developed skin cancer as a result of drinking groundwater contaminated with arsenic generated by AMD leaching.

Alterations in groundwater and surface-water availability and quality caused by AMD have also had indirect impacts on the environment by causing changes in nutrient cycling, total biomass, species diversity, and ecosystem stability. Additionally, the deposition of iron as a slimy orange precipitate produces an unsightly coating on rocks and shorelines.

AMD was so severe in the Tar Creek area of Oklahoma that the U.S. Environmental Protection Agency designated the area as the nation's foremost hazardous waste site in 1982. The largest complex of toxic waste sites in the United States was produced by the mines and smelters in Butte and Anaconda, Montana, with much of the pollution attributed to direct and indirect effects of AMD. AMD is also a widespread problem in many coal fields in the eastern United States.

Alvin K. Benson

FURTHER READING

Bell, F. G. *Basic Environmental and Engineering Geology*. Boca Raton, Fla.: CRC Press, 2007.

Younger, Paul L., Steven A. Banwart, and Robert S. Hedin. *Mine Water: Hydrology, Pollution, Remediation*. Norwell, Mass.: Kluwer Academic, 2002.

Amoco Cadiz oil spill

CATEGORIES: Disasters; water and water pollution

THE EVENT: Grounding of the tanker *Amoco Cadiz* off the coast of Brittany, France, resulting in the spilling of its cargo of crude oil into the sea

DATE: March 16, 1978

SIGNIFICANCE: The *Amoco Cadiz* oil spill resulted in the deaths of thousands of fish and seabirds and the pollution of coastal waters important to France for the harvest of marine life and for the tourism industry.

The four-year-old very large crude carrier (VLCC) *Amoco Cadiz* had been built in Spain. At 331 meters (1,086 feet) long and 68.6 meters (225 feet) wide, and with a draft of 19.8 meters (65 feet), it was one of the largest ships afloat. The vessel was American owned (by Standard Oil of Indiana), Liberian flagged, and crewed by Italians.

The *Amoco Cadiz* was in the final stages of its voyage from the Persian Gulf to Rotterdam in the Netherlands with 223,000 tons of mixed Kuwaiti and Iraqi crude oil.

The vessel was northbound along the coast of Brittany, France, at about 10:00 A.M. when a steering failure occurred. The ship was about 24 kilometers (15 miles) off the French coast. Within two hours, the tugboat *Pacific* was alongside the *Amoco Cadiz* connecting a towline. The tug ran out about 914 meters (3,000 feet) of steel towing wire in an attempt to keep the large tanker off the rocks, but after only two hours of towing, the towline broke. During this time, shipboard engineers had attempted to fix the tanker's damaged rudder, but the system was beyond repair. The ship was 10.5 kilometers (6.5 miles) off the coast of France.

By 9:00 P.M., the tug had reattached a towline to the stern of the *Amoco Cadiz*, but shortly thereafter the large tanker grounded on the Roches de Portsall. It immediately began leaking its cargo of crude oil over the coast of Brittany. This area accounts for almost 40 percent of the marine life and 7 percent of the oysters harvested in France. Within three days, the oil slick covered almost 80 kilometers (50 miles) to the north of the ship and 32 kilometers (20 miles) to the south. The French government implemented its oil-spill cleanup plan. Within six days of the spill, all of the vessel's tanks were open to the sea, and the slick measured 129 kilometers (80 miles) by 29 kilometers (18 miles). The French were unable to pump oil off the grounded vessel because of both poor weather and poor charts of the area.

Ten days after the ship grounded, the highest tide of the period occurred, and beach cleaning began in earnest. By the beginning of April, the French had mustered almost six thousand military personnel, three thousand civilians, twenty-eight boats, and more than one thousand vehicles for the cleanup operation. By the end of May, 206,000 tons of material had been cleaned off the shores of Brittany. Only 25,000 tons of this was actually oil—the rest was sand, rock, seaweed, and other plant life. Those involved in rescue efforts found some ten thousand dead fish and twenty-two thousand dead seabirds.

The cleanup effort was declared a success even though many criticized the French government for a slow response and fragmented efforts. The bulk of the oil cleanup was attributed to the sea itself. The relatively deep water and fast current along the shore helped the sea to disperse and dissipate the 223,000 tons of crude oil that had spilled into it over a six-day period.

Robert J. Stewart

FURTHER READING

Clark, R. B. *Marine Pollution.* 5th ed. New York: Oxford University Press, 2001.

Fairhall, David, and Philip Jordan. *The Wreck of the Amoco Cadiz.* New York: Stein and Day, 1980.

Fingas, Merv. *The Basics of Oil Spill Cleanup.* 2d ed. Boca Raton, Fla.: CRC Press, 2001.

Aqueducts

CATEGORY: Water and water pollution

DEFINITION: Artificial waterways constructed to move water from one area to another

SIGNIFICANCE: Human beings' redirection of water from one area to another through aqueducts can have numerous environmental effects. Ecosystems on both ends of an aqueduct are influenced by the reduction or increase in available water, and the building of aqueducts often involves the disturbance of what was formerly pristine land.

Sufficient water is an absolute necessity for all forms of life on earth (both plants and animals); this fact dictates that life-forms in areas that receive insufficient precipitation or that are not near lakes or rivers must either migrate to more favored regions to survive or develop techniques to bring water in from more favored areas. Certain xerophytic plants (such as cactus) and animals (such as the kangaroo rat and the jackrabbit) manage to survive on minimal amounts of water, but they are exceptions; most species need abundant supplies of water. Over time, human societies have either adopted the migration alternative or developed techniques to import water into drier areas by building conveyance devices. The artificial waterways known as aqueducts date back several thousand years; they have allowed human settlement and agriculture to flourish in several regions.

ANCIENT WATER DELIVERY SYSTEMS

The Minoan civilization, with its capital of Knossus on the Greek island of Crete in the Mediterranean Sea, represents the earliest known record of the development of water-supply infrastructure. Aqueducts were used to bring water into the city about five thousand years ago, until a major earthquake sometime around 1450 B.C.E. destroyed the region. The next major development in the building of aqueducts occurred circa 1000 B.C.E., when underground tunnels called *qanats* were used in the Middle East and North Africa to bring water from upland sources to villages and local farms. Modern-day Iran has the largest number of *qanats* in the region (more than twenty-two thousand), with lengths that vary from 40 to 45 kilometers (25 to 28 miles) and depths approaching 122 meters (400 feet).

The ancient Romans were renowned for their extensive system of elevated stone aqueducts beginning about 312 B.C.E. By 300 B.C.E., Rome had fourteen major aqueducts in service, bringing to the city about 150 million liters (roughly 40 million gallons) of water per day. Major water-supply systems were also built in those parts of Europe that were within the Roman Empire at that time, including what are now Italy, France, Spain, the Netherlands, and England. In Segovia, Spain, an aqueduct that was presumably built in the first century C.E. by the Romans is still being used.

In North America in the ninth century C.E. the Hohokam built canals that were 9-18 meters (30-60 feet) wide to transfer water from the Salt River, near present-day Phoenix, Arizona, to local farms for irrigation. In the tenth century the Anasazi developed a similar type of irrigation scheme in what is now southwest Colorado. During the fifteenth century, the Aztecs used rock aqueducts to supply both drinking water and water for irrigation to the area of present-day Mexico City.

MODERN AQUEDUCT SYSTEMS

As might be expected, modern water-delivery systems use some of the same techniques that were used successfully in ancient times. For example, modern systems, like ancient ones, make use of gravity to move water along as much as possible. Increased populations and the accompanying increased demand for water, however, require modern designers of aqueducts to employ additional techniques. Modern aqueducts must often transport water over great distances from the sources to the consuming populations, and conflicts sometimes arise when water is withdrawn from one area to serve another. Electricity or turbines are used to power huge pumps that can move water long distances. In some areas, the use of underground conduits is necessary to avoid interference with street traffic.

In 1825 the completion of the Erie Canal between Buffalo, New York, and New York City encouraged the export of agricultural products from the American Midwest to Europe and led to an increase in population for New York City. Since the Hudson River was too salty to use as a supply source, the city started work on a reservoir and aqueduct in the Croton River watershed in Westchester and Putnam counties. The project was finished in 1842 with a capacity of 341,000 cubic meters (90 million gallons) per day, an amount that the planners thought would be sufficient for a future city population of one million. New York continued to grow, however, necessitating expansion during the early twentieth century into the Catskill and Delaware watersheds and the construction of six new reservoirs and connecting aqueducts. The overall system now serves some nine million people with an average daily consumption of 4.5 million cubic meters (1.2 billion gallons) per day.

In contrast to New York, which receives average annual precipitation of 1,067 millimeters (42 inches), the Los Angeles metropolitan area receives about 381 millimeters (15 inches) of precipitation per year. The first project to bring in outside water to Los Angeles began in 1907 with the construction of an aqueduct 375 kilometers (200 miles) long, from the Owens Valley in east-central California, a project that was met initially with stiff resistance from Owens Valley residents. The next major undertaking for Los Angeles was the Colorado River Aqueduct Project, which was started in 1928 under the sponsorship of thirteen cities in Southern California that formed the Metropolitan Water District (MWD). By 2010 the MWD consisted of twenty-six water districts and cities and was responsible for supplying drinking water to an estimated population of eighteen million, with an average delivery of 7 million cubic meters (1.8 billion gallons) of water per day.

Other major projects to transfer water in arid to semiarid regions of the United States include the Central Arizona Project, which was authorized in 1968 by the U.S. Bureau of Reclamation. Construction started in 1973 to convey water from the Colorado River at Lake Havasu on the Arizona-California border to central and southern Arizona. The delivery system is 540 kilometers (336 miles) long and includes fourteen pumping plants and three tunnels. This is one prominent instance where huge amounts of power are required to overcome gravity, as the elevations at Lake Havasu, Phoenix, and Tucson are 136 meters (447 feet), 458 meters (1,503 feet), and 875 meters (2,870 feet), respectively.

Robert M. Hordon

FURTHER READING

Cech, Thomas V. *Principles of Water Resources: History, Development, Management, and Policy.* 3d ed. New York: John Wiley & Sons, 2010.

Hillel, Daniel. *Rivers of Eden: The Struggle for Water and the Quest for Peace in the Middle East.* New York: Oxford University Press, 1994.

Koeppel, Gerald T. *Water for Gotham: A History.* Princeton, N.J.: Princeton University Press, 2000.

Powell, James L. *Dead Pool: Lake Powell, Global Warming, and the Future of Water in the West.* Berkeley: University of California Press, 2008.

Strahler, Alan. *Introducing Physical Geography.* 5th ed. Hoboken, N.J.: John Wiley & Sons, 2011.

Aquifers

CATEGORY: Water and water pollution

DEFINITION: Water-bearing geological formations that can store and transmit significant amounts of groundwater to wells and springs

SIGNIFICANCE: Aquifers are important because groundwater supplies a substantial amount of the water available in many localities. The contamination of aquifers is thus a matter of concern, and so a variety of aquifer restoration techniques have been developed.

All rocks found on or below the earth's surface can be categorized as either aquifers or confining beds. An aquifer is a rock unit that is sufficiently permeable to allow the transportation of water in usable amounts to a well or spring. (In geologic usage, the term "rock" also includes unconsolidated sediments such as sand, silt, and clay.) A confining bed is a rock unit that has such low hydraulic conductivity (or poor permeability) that it restricts the flow of groundwater into or out of nearby aquifers.

There are two major types of groundwater occurrence in aquifers. The first type includes those aquifers that are only partially filled with water. In those cases, the upper surface (or water table) of the saturated zone rises or declines in response to variations in precipitation, evaporation, and pumping from wells. The water in these formations is then classified as un-

confined, and such aquifers are called unconfined or water-table aquifers. The second type occurs when water completely fills an aquifer that is located beneath a confining bed. In this case, the water is classified as confined, and the aquifers are called confined or artesian aquifers. In some fractured rock formations, such as those that occur in the west-central portions of New Jersey and eastern Pennsylvania, local geologic conditions result in semiconfined aquifers, which, as the name indicates, have hydrogeologic characteristics of both unconfined and confined aquifers.

Wells that are drilled into water-table aquifers are simply called water-table wells. The water level in these wells indicates the depth below the earth's surface of the water table, which is the top of the saturated zone. Wells that are drilled into confined aquifers are called artesian wells. The water level in artesian wells is generally located at a height above the top of the confined aquifer but not necessarily above the land surface. Flowing artesian wells occur when the water level stands above the land surface. The water level in tightly cased wells in artesian aquifers is called the potentiometric surface of the aquifer.

Water flows very slowly in aquifers, from recharge areas in interstream zones at higher elevations along watershed boundaries to discharge areas along streams and adjacent floodplains at lower elevations. Aquifers thus function as pipelines filled with various types of earth material. Darcy's law governing groundwater flow was developed in 1856 by Henry Darcy, a French engineer. In brief, Darcy's law states that the amount of water moving through an aquifer per unit of time is dependent on the hydraulic conductivity

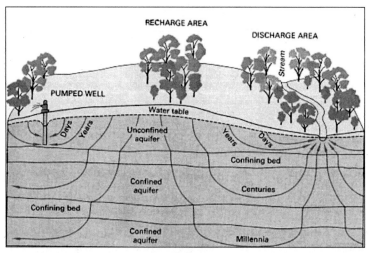

A standard aquifer system, featuring the flow times of different paths. (USGS)

(or permeability) of the aquifer, the cross-sectional area (which is at a right angle to the direction of flow), and the hydraulic gradient. The hydraulic conductivity depends on the size and interconnectedness of the pores and fractures in an aquifer. It ranges through an astonishing twelve orders of magnitude. Very few other physical parameters exhibit such a wide range of values. For example, the hydraulic conductivity ranges from an extremely low 10^7 to 10^8 meters per day in unfractured igneous rock such as diabase and basalt to as much as 10^3 to 10^4 meters per day in cavernous limestone and coarse gravel. Typical low-permeability earth materials include unfractured shale, clay, and glacial till. High-permeability earth materials include lava flows, coarse sand, and gravel.

In addition to this wide range of values, hydraulic conductivity varies widely in place and directionality within the same aquifer. Aquifers are isotropic if the hydraulic conductivity is about the same in all directions and anisotropic if the hydraulic conductivity is different in different directions. As a result of all of these factors, groundwater yield is extremely variable both within the same aquifer and from one aquifer to another when they are composed of different rocks.

Because groundwater flows slowly in comparison with surface water, any contaminant that gets into the groundwater could be around for a long time, perhaps hundreds or thousands of years. It is thus simpler and much more cost-effective to prevent groundwater contamination than it is to try to correct a problem that has been in existence for years.

Restoration of a contaminated aquifer may be accomplished, albeit at a price, through one or more of the following procedures: inground treatment or containment, aboveground treatment, or removal or isolation of the source of contamination. The first approach involves natural treatment based on physical, chemical, or biological means, such as adding nutrients to existing subsurface bacteria to help them break down hazardous organic compounds into nonhazardous materials. The second approach uses engineered systems such as pumping wells or subsurface structures, which create hydraulic gradients that make the contaminated water stay in a specified location, facilitating removal for later treatment. Regardless of the restoration method selected, the source that is continuing to contaminate the aquifer must be removed, isolated, or treated.

Robert M. Hordon

FURTHER READING

Ahmed, Shakeel, R. Jayakumar, and Abdin Salih. *Groundwater Dynamics in Hard Rock Aquifers: Sustainable Management and Optimal Monitoring Network Design.* New York: Springer, 2008.

Fetter, Charles W. *Applied Hydrogeology.* 4th ed. Upper Saddle River, N.J.: Prentice Hall, 2001.

Kuo, Jeff. *Practical Design Calculations for Groundwater and Soil Remediation.* Boca Raton, Fla.: CRC Press, 1998.

Nonner, Johannes C. *Introduction to Hydrogeology.* 2d ed. Boca Raton, Fla.: CRC Press, 2010.

Todd, David K. *Groundwater Hydrology.* 3d ed. Hoboken, N.J.: John Wiley & Sons, 2005.

Argo Merchant oil spill

CATEGORY: Disasters

THE EVENT: Grounding of the tanker *Argo Merchant* off the coast of Rhode Island, resulting in the spilling of heavy fuel oil into the sea

DATE: December 15, 1976

SIGNIFICANCE: A northwesterly wind helped to prevent extensive environmental damage to the New England shoreline when the *Argo Merchant* grounded.

The *Argo Merchant* was built as the *Arcturus* in Hamburg, Germany, in 1953 and renamed the *Permina Samudia III* in 1968. It was then renamed the *Vari* in 1970 and finally the *Argo Merchant* in 1973. Regardless of the name or the owners, the ship had a long history of accidents. The *Argo Merchant* was not an extremely large vessel. It was 195 meters (641 feet) in length and 25.6 meters (84 feet) wide and had a draft of 10.7 meters (35 feet). It was owned by the Thebes Shipping Company of Greece, was chartered to Texaco, and carried a crew of Greek officers and Filipino crewmen under the Liberian flag.

The vessel departed Puerto la Cruz in Venezuela bound for Salem, Massachusetts, with a cargo of 7.6 million gallons of heavy fuel oil in its thirty cargo tanks. The *Argo Merchant*'s problems began the evening before the grounding, as the onboard gyrocompass had broken, and the officers were unable to determine the ship's position.

At 6:00 A.M. on December 15, 1976, the *Argo Merchant* grounded on the southern end of Fish Rap Shoal in 5.5 meters (18 feet) of water. The ship was 48 kilometers (30 miles) north of the Nantucket light-ship station, 24 kilometers (15 miles) outside the normal shipping lanes, and 39 kilometers (24 miles) off its charted track line. When the crew of the *Argo Merchant* called the U.S. Coast Guard to report the grounding, they had no idea of their position; the position they gave turned out to be 48 kilometers (30 miles) from where the tanker was located.

The Coast Guard, however, responded quickly and soon located the grounded vessel. Attempts were made to float the ship and to tow it, but neither method worked. The sea continued to batter the grounded ship, which began to bend and twist on the reef until oil started leaking from the cargo tanks. Within one week the *Argo Merchant* had broken in half and was leaking large amounts of oil. As in the case of the 1967 *Torrey Canyon* oil spill in the English Channel, attempts were made to ignite the oil, but no attempt was made to destroy the oil remaining in the ship's tanks.

Within ten days of the grounding, the oil slick from the *Argo Merchant* extended 160 kilometers (100 miles). Although the weather was rainy and windy, which made oil transfer and salvage operations difficult, the wind blew predominantly from the northwest, and this drove the oil offshore, so that very little oil came ashore in the rich fishing and shellfish areas along the coast of New England. The northwesterly wind did drive the slick across Georges Bank, which is one of the richest fishing areas in the Atlantic Ocean, but the short-term effects of the windblown oil were marginal, and only a limited number of birds and marine mammals were killed. The long-term effects of the oil spill in the water column and the oil's impact on bottom-dwelling creatures have not been documented.

Robert J. Stewart

FURTHER READING

Clark, R. B. *Marine Pollution.* 5th ed. New York: Oxford University Press, 2001.

Fingas, Merv. *The Basics of Oil Spill Cleanup.* 2d ed. Boca Raton, Fla.: CRC Press, 2001.

Wang, Zhendi, and Scott A. Stout. *Oil Spill Environmental Forensics: Fingerprinting and Source Identification.* Burlington, Mass.: Academic Press, 2007.

Ashio, Japan, copper mine

CATEGORY: Human health and the environment

IDENTIFICATION: Copper mine that operated at the headwaters of the Watarase River from the seventeenth century to 1972

SIGNIFICANCE: Development of the Ashio copper mine propelled Japan's industrial revolution and also set the stage for the nation's first conflict over environmental quality. Hazardous runoff from the mine caused tension between agriculture and industry and dramatized the human and environmental costs of industrial pollution.

The Ashio copper mine, located 110 kilometers (68 miles) north of Tokyo, first operated during the seventeenth century, but private ownership spurred development of the mine in 1877. By 1890, it was the largest copper mine in Asia. Production expanded in 1950 because of the Korean War.

As copper production increased, the Ashio mine's impacts on the surrounding area also increased. Located at the headwaters of the Watarase River, the mine caused environmental damage by depositing waste products in the river. By 1880 fish were beginning to die, and people who ate fish from the river became ill. Almost all marine life in the river had died by 1890. Deforestation compounded the pollution problem. The operation of the mine required timber to shore up the mine shafts, for railroad ties, for the construction of buildings, and as fuel for steam engines. This timber was obtained through the deforestation of 104 square kilometers (40 square miles) of surrounding land, which destroyed the watershed at the head of the Watarase River. As a consequence, flooding became a serious problem in the Watarase Valley and the surrounding rice fields.

Although natural flooding had occurred before the development of the mine, such flooding had brought layers of rich silt that contributed to abundant crops. Later floods, however, produced vastly different results: Vegetation did not survive contact with the contaminated floodwaters. Floods became more frequent, more severe, and more damaging because they left poisons in the soil. Soil samples revealed concentrations of sulfuric acid, ammonia, magnesium, iron, arsenic, copper, and chlorine. These substances poisoned the rice fields, and new seeds would not grow. Earthworms, insects, birds, and animals succumbed to the contamination.

Although the Japanese government ordered pollution-control measures, they were ineffective. In 1907 the government forced the evacuation and relocation of the inhabitants of a contaminated village. The collapse of a slag pile in 1958 introduced 2,000 cubic meters (71,000 cubic feet) of slag into the Watarase River, contaminating 6,000 hectares (14,820 acres) of rice fields. The Japanese government set limits on the amount of copper that could be deposited in the river water and the soil, but the damage had already been done. In 1972 the mine was shut down. That year, soil samples from 3 meters (9.8 feet) down still contained excessive amounts of copper as well as significant amounts of lead, zinc, and arsenic. The government ordered the destruction of all rice that had been grown in the area.

Thousands of fishermen, rice farmers, and valley citizens suffered severe economic losses. Serious health problems in the area included a high infant mortality rate, the failure of new mothers to produce milk for their infants, sores on those who worked in the fields, and a high death rate. In 1973 the Japanese Environmental Agency's Pollution Adjustment Committee began to review farmers' claims. The mine was required to admit to being the source of the contamination, and the farmers were awarded a sum equivalent to five million U.S. dollars in 1974. Attempts to reforest the area have failed.

Louise Magoon

FURTHER READING

Tsuru, Shigeto. *The Political Economy of the Environment: The Case of Japan.* Vancouver: University of British Columbia Press, 1999.

Wilkening, Kenneth E. *Acid Rain Science and Politics in Japan: A History of Knowledge and Action Toward Sustainability.* Cambridge, Mass.: MIT Press, 2004.

Best available technologies

CATEGORY: Atmosphere and air pollution

DEFINITION: The most efficient control and treatment techniques that are economically achievable by various industries to limit adverse environmental impacts

SIGNIFICANCE: As concerns regarding all forms of pollution have increased around the world, many governments—including those of the United States and many European nations—have responded with environmental laws requiring industries to employ the best available techniques to reduce polluting emissions and discharges.

Major U.S. industries receiving national permits, usually from the Environmental Protection Agency (EPA), for new or modified emissions and point source discharges regulated by the Clean Air Act and the Clean Water Act are required to use the best available technologies to reduce environmental pollution. Best available technologies, also known as best available control technologies and best available techniques, include state-of-the-art controls on emissions and discharges into environmental media such as air, water, and soil. The term "available" means that the technology exists or is capable of being developed. A best available technology, however, must be affordable based on a cost-benefit analysis.

In addition to best available technology standards, the environmental laws in the United States include requirements for best conventional technologies. The best available technology mandates generally apply to pollutants that are considered to be toxic or are labeled as nonconventional because no determination has yet been made concerning their toxicity. However, once the EPA determines that a pollutant is toxic, an industry has three years to meet the best available technology standards that apply to that pollutant. Conventional pollutants, such as agricultural chemicals that have the ability to accumulate in body fat but have not been deemed toxic, are governed by the best conventional technology standards.

The permitting agency reviews each major industrial application for a stationary source permit to allow emissions into the air or discharges into the water on a case-by-case basis. Environmental, energy, and economic impacts are all considered in determining which processes and techniques an industry can afford while still protecting the environment. A variance from a best available technology standard may be granted as part of the permitting process to an industry that has agreed to use the best technology that is financially achievable, even if the technology is not the latest available. The technology used, however, must not create further pollution. For example, an industry will not receive a waiver to the best available technology requirements under the Clean Water Act unless it can show that the discharge controls and techniques it will utilize will not interfere with the quality of public water supplies, recreational activities, or wildlife, fish, and shellfish populations.

Under the Clean Air Act some of the best available technology standards include production and treatment techniques and fuel cleaning and combustion systems for various regulated air pollutants. Under the Clean Water Act effluent guidelines are based on best available technologies to achieve the goal of eliminating the discharge of all pollutants into the waters of the United States. Some of the factors considered in the cost-benefit analysis to determine if the effluent technologies are economically feasible include assessment of existing equipment, facilities, and techniques used in effluence reduction; the cost to achieve further effluent reduction; and other environmental impacts that are not related to water quality but that may occur if new technologies are employed, such as increased energy requirements. In addition to effluent guidelines, the Clean Water Act requires the use of best available technologies to minimize environmental impacts for cooling water intake structures that might be used in industries that produce heated water, such as nuclear power plants and food and beverage manufacturing facilities employing pasteurization.

Carol A. Rolf

FURTHER READING

Malone, Linda A. *Emanuel Law Outlines: Environmental Law.* 2d ed. Frederick, Md.: Aspen, 2007.

Morag-Levine, Noga. *Chasing the Wind: Regulating Air Pollution in the Common Law State.* Princeton, N.J.: Princeton University Press, 2005.

Revesz, Richard L. *Environmental Law and Policy: Statutory and Regulatory Supplement.* 2009-2010 ed. New York: Foundation Press, 2009.

Black Sea

CATEGORIES: Places; ecology and ecosystems

IDENTIFICATION: Large inland sea bounded by the Eurasian nations of Turkey, Bulgaria, Romania, Ukraine, Russia, and Georgia

SIGNIFICANCE: Because of a lack of oxygen, the lower levels of the Black Sea are virtually lifeless, and the abundant life of the sea's upper levels has been gravely endangered by pollution, overharvesting, and the introduction of destructive nonnative spe-

cies. Progress has been made in addressing these problems, however, as the result of dedicated international efforts.

It is believed that the Black Sea was formed when the rising waters of the Mediterranean Sea swamped a freshwater lake about 7,500 years ago. The sea has a surface area of approximately 448,000 square kilometers (173,000 square miles) and reaches a maximum depth of approximately 2,200 meters (7,200 feet). Five important rivers—the Kuban, Don, Dnieper, Dniester, and Danube—flow into it, and in turn its brackish surface water flows out into the Mediterranean through the Bosporus strait, the Sea of Marmara, and the Dardanelles strait. Colder, saltier water flows in beneath this current from the Mediterranean to fill the Black Sea's depths. Within the Black Sea itself, circulation between the two layers is poor.

Because the Black Sea's lower levels do not contain enough dissolved oxygen to enable bacteria to decompose the organic matter carried into the sea by the rivers, the water has grown increasingly eutrophied (saturated with nutrients) and anoxic (oxygen-depleted), creating the largest "dead zone" of virtually lifeless water on the planet. Bacteria have evolved under these conditions, to react with naturally occurring sulfate ions in the seawater to produce the world's largest concentration of deadly hydrogen sulfide gas. Significant deposits of ammonia and methane are also present.

Fish and shellfish such as anchovy, mullet, tuna, mussels, and oysters were once found in abundance in the upper levels of the Black Sea, but in the latter decades of the twentieth century their numbers fell dramatically. This decline was caused in part by overfishing, but pollution from agriculture, industry, and shipping (particularly of crude oil) played a more important role. Cultural (human-caused) eutrophication of the sea's shallower waters contributed to a precipitous decline in fields of *Cystoseira* and *Phyllophora* algae, species essential to the survival of the food chain. In 1982 the alien carnivorous sea jelly *Mnemiopsis leidyi* was found for the first time in the Black Sea, and within a few years its rapidly growing numbers had destroyed a large proportion of the native species' eggs and larvae. During the 1990's radioactive substances resulting from nuclear power generation and the Chernobyl nuclear accident of 1986 began to enter the Black Sea as well.

By the end of the twentieth century, however, the Black Sea's ecology began to show a partial recovery owing to the region's economic slowdown and a resulting decrease in pollution. The sea had been recognized as a major environmental disaster area, and the six nations on its shores had drafted the Convention for the Protection of the Black Sea Against Pollution in 1992. This convention was succeeded by a number of other international efforts focusing on specific environmental problems, including the Black Sea Ecosystem Recovery Project of 2004-2007, which dealt primarily with eutrophication and hazardous waste.

In the future the Black Sea's deposits of ammonia and methane may be utilized to produce fertilizer and to generate electricity, and its hydrogen sulfide may be tapped as a source of hydrogen gas for fuel. The extraction technologies involved are expected to have the added advantage of returning purified water to the sea.

Grove Koger

FURTHER READING

Ascherson, Neal. *Black Sea.* New York: Hill & Wang, 1995.

Kostianoy, Andrey G., and Aleksey N. Kosarev, eds. *The Black Sea Environment.* Berlin: Springer, 2008.

Land, Thomas. "The Black Sea: Economic Developments and Environmental Dangers." *Contemporary Review* 278 (March, 2001): 144-151.

BP *Deepwater Horizon* oil spill

CATEGORY: Disasters

THE EVENT: Explosion and fire on the *Deepwater Horizon* drilling platform in the Gulf of Mexico that claimed eleven lives and triggered the largest accidental marine oil spill in history and the largest oil spill of any kind in the United States

DATES: April 20-July 15, 2010

SIGNIFICANCE: The oil spill that began with an explosion on British Petroleum's *Deepwater Horizon* drilling platform raised questions about the safety of deepwater drilling, the adequacy of the corporate response to the disaster and of governmental regulation of offshore oil drilling, and the possibility of long-term damage to the Gulf of Mexico's ecosystem.

The *Deepwater Horizon* was a semisubmersible drilling platform owned by Transocean and under lease to British Petroleum (BP). In April, 2010, it was located in the Gulf of Mexico approximately 84 kilometers (52 miles) southeast of Venice, Louisiana, where it was completing work on the exploratory Macondo 252 well. Oil had been found 5.5 kilometers (18,000 feet) below the seafloor and 7 kilometers (23,000 feet) below the drilling platform. The drill hole had been—or was being—cemented to seal the well so that the drill pipe could be removed and the *Deepwater Horizon* could be moved to a new location. The cement failed, allowing gas and oil under high pressure to escape the reservoir and rise through the drill pipe casing and up the riser pipe to the drilling platform. A blowout preventer located on top of the wellhead was designed to cut through the drill casing and seal the wellhead in cased of an emergency. The blowout preventer also failed, and about 11:00 P.M. central daylight time on April 20 the escaping gas reached the surface and exploded, setting the *Deepwater Horizon* on fire. Most of the workers on the platform were evacuated without serious injury, but eleven who had been in close proximity to the explosion died.

Without any mechanism to stop the flow of oil to the platform, fireboats were unable to extinguish the flames. The drilling platform burned for about thirty-six hours and then sank, twisting and breaking the riser pipe that had connected the platform to the wellhead some 1.5 kilometers (5,000 feet) beneath the sea surface.

MAGNITUDE OF THE SPILL

On April 24, unmanned submarines working for BP detected oil flow from the wellhead and the collapsed riser pipe. The magnitude of the flow was estimated to be about 1,000 barrels per day (BPD), a figure repeated by both company and governmental officials. (One barrel of oil equals 42 gallons, or approximately 159 liters.) On April 26 a scientist with the National Oceanic and Atmospheric Administration (NOAA) estimated the flow at roughly 5,000 BPD based on satellite imagery of the oil slick. Nongovernmental scientists using similar methodologies provided estimates as high as 26,500 BPD.

After BP released video images of the underwater leak on May 12, independent experts reported estimates of up to 50,000 BPD. Despite the existence of potentially better methodologies, government officials adhered to their estimate of 5,000 BPD until May 27, when a government task force, the Flow Rate Group (FRG), released its first estimate: 12,000 to

25,000 BPD. FRG estimates were increased to 20,000 to 40,000 BPD on June 12 and to 35,000 to 60,000 BPD on June 15. By that time oil was being washed up on the shores of the coasts of Louisiana, Mississippi, Alabama, and Florida.

In the aftermath of the spill, both government and independent scientists appeared to agree that the actual flow rate was approximately 60,000 BPD and that the total release of oil into the Gulf was approximately 5 million barrels, roughly twenty times the volume of the 1989 *Exxon Valdez* oil spill in Prince William Sound. This was the largest oil spill in the history of the Gulf of Mexico, exceeding the 3 million gallons discharged into the Gulf after the 1979 explosion and fire on a PEMEX semisubmersible drilling platform off the coast of Mexico.

EMERGENCY RESPONSE

Within one week of the initial explosion, oil had reached the Mississippi Delta, and the nation became aware that the "Gulf oil spill" threatened serious economic and environmental damage. The event was better described as a discharge, a blowout, a flow, or a leak, but the term "spill" was almost universally adopted. In the space of a few days, President Barack Obama announced that the United States would use all available resources to contain the spill. Fishing was prohibited in the affected areas, and a moratorium was declared on further deepwater drilling in the Gulf of Mexico pending an investigation. President Obama announced that British Petroleum was responsible for the spill and that it would be held responsible for the cleanup. The U.S. Coast Guard commandant, Admiral Thad Allen, was named incident commander for the federal response, and it was announced that a national commission would be formed to study the disaster and make recommendations. BP chief executive officer Tony Hayward declared that BP would take full responsibility; he pledged to stop the leak, repair the damage to the Gulf, and pay all legitimate claims for damages.

From the beginning experts agreed that the permanent solution would be a relief well that would intersect the drill hole below the lowest level of drill pipe casing and above the top of the petroleum reservoir. Cement pumped through the relief well would

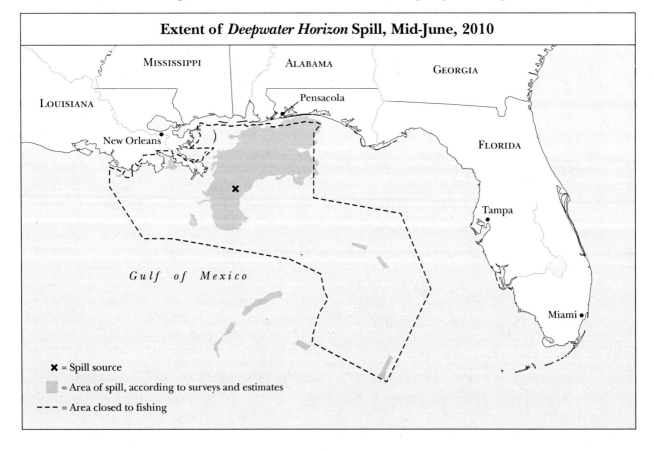

Extent of *Deepwater Horizon* Spill, Mid-June, 2010

MISSISSIPPI   ALABAMA   GEORGIA

LOUISIANA

Pensacola

New Orleans

FLORIDA

Tampa

Gulf of Mexico

Miami

✖ = Spill source

▨ = Area of spill, according to surveys and estimates

- - - = Area closed to fishing

seal the reservoir permanently. BP began drilling such a relief well on May 2. It was anticipated that the relief well would be completed in August, but waiting that long to stop the flow of oil was not a viable option.

BP pursued multiple strategies to stanch the flow. Several attempted quick fixes were relatively unsuccessful. Remotely controlled underwater vehicles working for the company failed to close valves on the blowout preventer. Surface oil slicks were burned on several occasions, but the volume of oil consumed was relatively small. U.S. Air Force planes were enlisted to spray chemical dispersants on surface slicks while BP injected dispersants underwater in an effort to break up the oil flow at the source. More than 1.8 million gallons of dispersants were used—almost 800,000 gallons near the wellhead. Local fishing boats were hired to skim floating oil, and miles of booms were deployed in an effort to prevent slicks from contaminating ecologically sensitive coastlines. In many areas wind and waves rendered these strategies ineffective. Efforts were also undertaken to construct artificial barrier islands to protect fragile coastlines. Every strategy was controversial, and some worked at cross-purposes. Chemical dispersants, for example, made the use of booms and skimming less effective but also arguably less necessary. At the height of the crisis thousands of people and hundreds of vessels were employed in efforts to mitigate the environmental damage of the spill.

By early May it was apparent that at least three significant leaks were coming from a section of broken riser pipe that lay crumpled on the ocean floor still attached to the failed blowout preventer on the wellhead. On May 4 remotely controlled underwater vehicles successfully sawed off the free end of the leaking riser pipe and installed a shutoff valve, reducing the number of leaks to two, but without significantly diminishing the flow of oil. On May 7 and 8 one of three custom-built coffer dams was lowered over the largest leak on the ocean floor. This concrete and metal box, 12 meters (40 feet) high, was designed to capture the plume of escaping oil so that it could be pumped to the surface. The coffer dam failed, however, when a frozen mixture of gas and water clogged the system. A smaller version, dubbed "top hat," was lowered on May 11 but never deployed. Instead, BP chose to insert a 15.2-centimeter (6-inch) pipe directly into the leaking 53.3-centimeter (21-inch) riser pipe.

On May 16 BP announced that it was capturing most of the leaking oil, but the following day the estimate of oil captured was reduced to 1,000 BPD, ap-

proximately one-fifth of BP's estimated leak rate. Plans were announced for a "junk shot" to plug the leak by injecting the well with a high-pressure mixture of cement and solids such as shredded tires. It was never executed, however; instead BP chose the "top kill," which was designed to stop the flow by pumping drilling mud into the blowout preventer. This procedure failed to stop the flow, even after "junk shot" solids were added to the mixture.

By June 1 BP was working to saw off the broken riser pipe just above the blowout preventer and attach a cap connected to a new riser pipe. This strategy entailed significant risk because cutting off the bent riser pipe would increase the flow of oil into the Gulf. The cap was connected, but the fit was loose. Over time the fraction of escaping oil that was recovered slowly increased, approaching 50 percent. A significant fraction of the captured oil was burned at the surface. After about a month, while efforts continued to drill relief wells, BP removed the cap and replaced it with what amounted to a blowout preventer on top of the previous blowout preventer. After eighty-seven days, the flow of oil was stopped on July 15.

In August, as work on the relief wells continued, BP announced a successful "static kill." Tons of drilling mud followed by cement were pumped into the wellhead, providing increased assurance that the flow would not resume. The first relief well intersected Macondo 252 on September 16, and crews cemented the blown-out well from the bottom. The federal incident commander declared Macondo 252 officially sealed on September 19.

CONSEQUENCES

The economic damage associated with the BP oil spill is difficult to quantify. One study estimated the short-term damage to the Gulf fishing industry at $115 to $172 million. Severe economic impacts were also associated with the deepwater drilling moratorium and the spill's damage to the "Louisiana brand." Perhaps the clearest economic indicator of damage done was reduced investor confidence in BP. Between April 21 and June 25, 2010, the value of BP stock declined by 55 percent, representing a reduction of $67 billion in market capitalization. By the time the well was sealed, BP had reportedly spent more than $11 billion on the capping and cleanup operations, and it had created a $20 billion escrow account for payment of damages. In the autumn of 2010 BP announced that it had taken a pretax charge of $32.2 billion and had plans to sell up to $30 billion in assets. It had canceled its stock dividend. It is likely that BP, and possibly other companies involved, will eventually face penalties that could amount to billions of dollars under the Clean Water Act and other federal statutes.

BP's long-term liability will depend in part on the environmental damage caused by the spill, which is even more difficult to measure than economic damage. Studies are expected to continue for years if not decades. The fate of the spilled oil remains the subject of scientific controversy. No one knows with any degree of certainty what fraction evaporated, sank to the bottom of the Gulf, or remained suspended in the water column. The environmental consequences of the unprecedented intensive use of chemical dispersants remain unclear, but preliminary analyses by the Environmental Protection Agency indicated that the environmental benefits of dispersant use outweighed the environmental cost.

The totality of environmental damage to the Gulf of Mexico from the *Deepwater Horizon* spill will certainly be significant, but the ecological significance of a major oil spill may depend significantly on the location. The ecological damage done by the *Exxon Valdez* grounding in Prince William Sound was disproportionate to the size of the spill. By contrast, the vastly larger PEMEX spill in the Gulf of Mexico is generally regarded as having caused relatively little environmental damage. Despite the attention given to the acute BP spill, the chronic damage from agricultural runoff throughout the Mississippi River basin probably remains the most significant ecological threat to the Gulf.

The BP oil spill raised important questions about the safety of deepwater drilling, the industry's preparedness for spills, and the government's supervision of industry behavior. Early reports by the national commission studying the spill indicated that the industry and the government were both poorly prepared for a spill of such magnitude. BP and its contractors had bypassed safety measures, and government agencies had routinely approved work that did not meet legal standards.

Craig W. Allin

FURTHER READING

Barstow, David, et al. "Between Blast and Spill, One Last, Flawed Hope." *New York Times,* June 1, 2010, A1.

Fausset, Richard. "Oil Spill's Legacy." *Los Angeles Times,* September 19, 2010, A1.

Jernelöv, Arne. "The Threats from Oil Spills: Now, Then, and in the Future." *AMBIO: A Journal of the Human Environment* 39, no. 6 (2010): 353-366.

Jonsson, Patrik. "Gulf Oil Spill: Where Has the Oil Gone?" *Christian Science Monitor,* July 27, 2010.

Ornitz, Barbara E., and Michael A. Champ. *Oil Spills First Principles: Prevention and Best Response.* New York: Elsevier, 2002.

Braer oil spill

CATEGORY: Disasters

THE EVENT: Grounding of the oil tanker *Braer* at the Shetland Islands, resulting in the spilling of its cargo of crude oil into the sea

DATE: January 5, 1993

SIGNIFICANCE: The oil spilled when the *Braer* ran aground killed or sickened thousands of shellfish

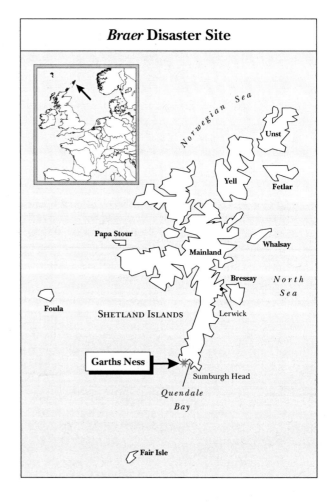

Braer Disaster Site

and led to severe economic setbacks for the local fishing industry.

When the oil tanker *Braer* ran aground at the southern tip of the Shetland Islands, located about 210 kilometers (130 miles) north of the Scottish mainland, more than one million barrels of crude oil were spilled into the Atlantic Ocean. Under the severe wind and wave conditions that prevailed around the Shetland Islands at the time, the spilled oil thoroughly mixed into the turbulent seawater and rapidly dispersed. Ten days after the spill, the concentrations in the vicinity of the wreck had fallen from several hundred parts per million (ppm) to 4 ppm, still about two thousand times the normal level.

Being less dense than water, most of the oil floated. The lightest, most volatile hydrocarbons started to evaporate, decreasing the volume of the spill but polluting the air. Subsequently, a slow decomposition process occurred, caused by sunlight and bacterial action. After several months, the oil mass was reduced by approximately 80 percent.

Shortly after the *Braer* oil spill, all fishing activities were prohibited in the surrounding areas. For most shellfish species, this ban remained in effect for more than two years, until the spring of 1995, when they were judged to be free of any significant levels of oil contamination. Shortly after fishing resumed, however, the catches of lobsters and queen scallops were found to be very poor, and the proportion of young lobsters and scallops was abnormally low.

Supported by the Shetland Fishermen's Association, the North Atlantic Fisheries College carried out a number of laboratory trials in 1996 and 1997 to determine what effects crude oil may have on lobsters and scallops and to investigate whether the *Braer* oil spill could have had adverse effects on these stocks. During the experiments, researchers used Norwegian Gullfaks crude oil, the same type as the *Braer*'s cargo, to simulate the spill conditions. Results of the study showed that in the short term, adult scallops and lobsters could survive exposure to relatively high concentrations of oil, but lobster eggs and larvae suffered high mortality rates. Although the oil did not kill the adult lobsters, it did cause major behavioral abnormalities, including significant reductions in feeding, movement, responsiveness to stimuli, and aggression.

In May, 1997, the Scottish Office Fisheries Department released a document indicating that the *Braer* oil spill polluted a much wider area than previously thought. The report showed that levels of oil in prawns and mussels from a 1,036-square-kilometer (400-square-mile) zone of excluded fishing were still rising in 1996, and there were indications that the tides had spread the oil underwater all around the Shetland Islands' 1,450-kilometer (900-mile) coastline. Fishermen reported that their fishing grounds were ruined, with nothing replacing what was being caught. Into the late 1990's, considerable work was still being undertaken to rectify the damage done by the *Braer* oil spill, particularly by the large quantities of oil that had become incorporated into subtidal sediments.

Alvin K. Benson

FURTHER READING

Burger, Joanna. *Oil Spills.* New Brunswick, N.J.: Rutgers University Press, 1997.

Clark, R. B. *Marine Pollution.* 5th ed. New York: Oxford University Press, 2001.

National Research Council. *Oil in the Sea III: Inputs, Fates, and Effects.* Washington, D.C.: National Academies Press, 2003.

Brent Spar occupation

CATEGORY: Activism and advocacy

THE EVENT: Occupation of an abandoned oil storage platform by Greenpeace protesters

DATES: April 30-May 23, 1995

SIGNIFICANCE: As the result of their occupation of the *Brent Spar*, which Royal Dutch Shell had planned to sink, Greenpeace protesters were able to influence the company to adopt alternative disposal methods.

On April 30, 1995, fourteen Greenpeace volunteers boarded the abandoned oil storage platform *Brent Spar*, which was anchored off the western coast of Norway in the North Sea. The *Brent Spar*, a floating cylinder moored to the sea bottom, had been built in 1976, but it had been taken out of commission in 1991. Its owner, Royal Dutch Shell, intended to lower the platform into the Atlantic Ocean and then sink it under more than six thousand feet of water.

Greenpeace had engaged in months of negotiations with Shell prior to the occupation. Representatives of the environmental activist group had urged Shell officials to develop a plan for dismantling the platform on land, citing studies that had concluded that on-land disposal and recycling of oil rigs is environmentally preferable to sea dumping. Shell replied with studies of its own asserting that deep-sea disposal is the more environmentally sound option.

When it became clear that Shell planned to proceed with the ocean dumping, Greenpeace sent fourteen volunteers to the platform. It also stepped up its publicity campaign, drawing support from the European Union (EU) commissioner for the environment, Denmark's minister for environment and energy, and other important sources. In May, the European Parliament passed a resolution opposing the dumping of the *Brent Spar.*

On May 22, Shell dispatched a team to the *Brent Spar* to remove the protesters, but bad weather delayed the evacuation. The volunteers ended their occupation the next day but vowed to continue the fight in the courts. However, an English judge refused to hear the Greenpeace case, stating that the English courts had no jurisdiction over the North Sea matter.

In June, German chancellor Helmut Kohl raised the question of the *Brent Spar* with British prime minister John Major. By then, Germany had joined the list of nations opposing the dumping of oil platforms in the sea. Shell nevertheless proceeded with its plan. In late June, therefore, Greenpeace activists again boarded the platform by helicopter. Meanwhile, demonstrations against Shell took place in Great Britain, Denmark, the Netherlands, Germany, and Switzerland. In Germany, a Shell gas station was firebombed, and the company's sales fell more than 15 percent.

On June 20, Shell announced that it would not dump the *Brent Spar* in the sea. Nine days later, the member nations of the Oslo Paris Commission (OSPAR), in a vote of eleven to two (Norway and the United Kingdom opposing), decided to impose a moratorium on sea disposal of oil platforms. The following month, Shell received permission from the Norwegian government to store the *Brent Spar* in an inlet on Norway's west coast while working out plans for its dismantling. The platform was finally dismantled in 1999, with parts of it repurposed as the foundation for a new ferry terminal at Mekjarvik, Norway.

Christopher Kent

FURTHER READING

Chasek, Pamela S., et al. *Global Environmental Politics.* 4th ed. Boulder, Colo.: Westview Press, 2006.
Entine, Jon. "Shell, Greenpeace, and *Brent Spar:* The Politics of Dialogue." *Case Histories in Business Ethics,* edited by Chris Megone and Simon J. Robinson. New York: Routledge, 2002.
Jordan, Grant. *Shell, Greenpeace, and the Brent Spar.* New York: Palgrave, 2001.

Chesapeake Bay

CATEGORIES: Places; ecology and ecosystems
IDENTIFICATION: Atlantic Ocean inlet bordered by the states of Maryland and Virginia
SIGNIFICANCE: Since the 1970's the health of the Chesapeake Bay and its marine inhabitants has been threatened increasingly by pollution related to environmental stressors in the surrounding watershed. By the early years of the twenty-first century, efforts to reverse the problems were under way.

The Chesapeake Bay, the largest estuary in the United States, spans from northeastern and central Maryland down to southeast Virginia, where it meets the Atlantic Ocean. The rivers and streams that feed the bay extend into the surrounding states of New York, Delaware, Pennsylvania, Virginia, and West Virginia, as well as Washington, D.C. The largest rivers flowing directly into the Chesapeake Bay include the Susquehanna, the Chester, the Potomac, the Rappahannock, and the James.

The bay includes habitats of sandy beaches, intertidal flats, piers, rocks and jetties, shallow waters, sea grass meadows, wetlands, oyster bars, and open waters, all of which house a wide array of animals, plants, and aquatic life. Additionally, its surrounding watershed is home to a number of land-dwelling animals that feed on organisms that live in the bay. More than 3,600 species live within the Chesapeake Bay and its surrounding watershed, including approximately 350 species of fish, 173 species of shellfish, and numerous species of birds, mammals, reptiles and amphibians, bay grasses, and lower-food-web species, including both bottom-dwelling and free-floating plant and animal communities.

The Chesapeake Bay is widely known for its thriving seafood industry, which focuses primarily on the harvest of blue crabs, eastern oysters, clams, and rockfish (also known as striped bass). Since the 1970's, however, overfishing and deteriorating environmental conditions in the bay have caused decreases in the populations of fish, other wildlife, and plants in the watershed.

The Chesapeake Bay has experienced environmental pressures related to population growth, land-use policies, air and water pollution, overfishing, invasive species, and climate change. Approximately 17 million people live within the Chesapeake Bay watershed, and this large population contributes to environmental stress through the development of homes, businesses, and infrastructure, which adds impervious surfaces that contribute to stormwater runoff, destroys habitat, and increases the pollutants entering the bay. Excess nutrients and sediment from agricultural and industrial runoff have contributed to marine dead zones in the bay, areas where oxygen has been depleted and vital sunlight cannot reach bottom-dwelling organisms. Efforts have been undertaken to improve the health of the Chesapeake Bay by restoring water quality through more careful management of land use and reduction of harmful pollutants in agriculture and development, restoring bay grass and wetland habitats, improving fishery management, establishing stewardship and education programs, and enacting protective legislation.

Courtney A. Smith

FURTHER READING

Ernst, Howard R. *Chesapeake Bay Blues: Science, Politics, and the Struggle to Save the Bay.* Lanham, Md.: Rowman & Littlefield, 2003.

Lippson, Alice Jane, and Robert L. Lippson. *Life in the Chesapeake Bay.* 3d ed. Baltimore: The Johns Hopkins University Press, 2006.

Chlorination

CATEGORY: Water and water pollution
DEFINITION: Practice of disinfecting water by the addition of chlorine
SIGNIFICANCE: Although the chlorination of public water in the United States has helped reduce outbreaks of waterborne disease, it has raised concerns about the possible formation of chloro-organic compounds in treated water.

Drinking water, wastewater, and water in swimming pools are the most common water sources where chlorination is used to kill bacteria and prevent the spread of diseases. Viruses are generally more resistant to chlorination than are bacteria, but they can be eliminated with an increase in the chlorine levels needed to kill bacteria. Common chlorinating agents include elemental chlorine gas and sodium or calcium hypochlorite. In water these substances generate hypochlorous acid, which is the chemical agent responsible for killing microorganisms by inactivating bacteria proteins or viral nucleoproteins.

Public drinking water was chlorinated in most large U.S. cities by 1914. The effectiveness of chlorination in reducing outbreaks of waterborne diseases in the early twentieth century was clearly illustrated by the drop in typhoid deaths: 36 per 100,000 in 1920 to 5 per 100,000 by 1928. Chlorination has remained the most economical method of purifying public water, although it is not without potential risks. Chlorination has also been widely used to prevent the spread of bacteria in the food industry.

In its elemental form, high concentrations of chlorine are very toxic, and solutions containing more than 1,000 milligrams per liter (mg/l) are lethal to humans. Chlorine has a characteristic odor that is detectable at levels of 2-3 mg/l of water. Most public water supplies contain chlorine levels of 1-2 mg/l, although the actual concentration of water reaching consumer faucets fluctuates and is usually around 0.5 mg/l. Consumption of water containing 50 mg/l has produced no immediate adverse effects.

The greatest environmental concern regarding chlorination has less to do with the chlorine itself than it does with the potential toxic compounds that may form when chlorine reacts with organic compounds present in water. Chlorine, which is an extremely reactive element, reacts with organic material associated with decaying vegetation (humic acids), forming chloro-organic compounds. Trihalomethanes (THMs) are one of the most common chloro-organic compounds. At least a dozen THMs have been identified in drinking water since the 1970's, when health authorities in the United States came under pressure to issue standards for the identification and reduction of THM levels in drinking water.

Major concern has focused on levels of chloroform because of this compound's known carcinogenic properties in animal studies. Once used in cough syrups, mouthwashes, and toothpastes, chloroform in consumer products is now severely restricted. A 1975 study of chloroform concentrations in drinking water found levels of more than 300 micrograms per liter (μg/l) in some water, with 10 percent of the water systems surveyed having levels of more than 105 μg/l. In 1984 the World Health Organization set a guideline value of 30 μg/l for chloroform in drinking water.

Although there are risks associated with drinking chlorinated water, it has been estimated that the risk of death from cigarette smoking is two thousand times greater than that of drinking chloroform-contaminated water from most public sources. However, as water sources become more polluted and require higher levels of chlorination to maintain purity, continual monitoring of chloro-organic compounds will be needed.

Nicholas C. Thomas

FURTHER READING

Bull, Richard J. "Drinking Water Disinfection." In *Environmental Toxicants: Human Exposures and Their Health Effects*, edited by Morton Lippmann. New York: John Wiley & Sons, 2000.

Gray, N. F. *Drinking Water Quality: Problems and Solutions.* 2d ed. New York: Cambridge University Press, 2008.

Clean Water Act and amendments

CATEGORY: Treaties, laws, and court cases

THE LAWS: Federal legislation designed to improve the quality of surface water throughout the United States

DATES: Enacted on October 18, 1972; major amendments in 1977, 1981, and 1987

SIGNIFICANCE: The legislation now called the Clean Water Act was largely shaped by the 1972 amendments to the Federal Water Quality Act of 1965, itself an amendment to 1948 legislation. The complex law was further strengthened by later amendments as the American public became increasingly aware of the importance of clean water supplies to the public health.

Before the mid-1960's government regulation of water pollution in the United States was mostly left up to individual states. The earliest U.S. federal environmental law was the Rivers and Harbors Act of 1899, which prohibited the dumping of debris into navigable waters. Although the law was intended to protect interstate navigation, it became an instrument for regulat-

ing water quality sixty years after its passage. The Oil Pollution Act of 1924 prohibited the discharge of oil into interstate waterways, with criminal sanctions for violations. The first Federal Water Pollution Control Act (FWPCA), passed in 1948, authorized the preparation of federal pollution-abatement plans, which the states could either accept or reject, and provided some financial assistance for state projects. Although the FWPCA was amended in 1956 and 1961, it still contained no effective mechanisms for the federal enforcement of standards.

By this period, however, many Americans were recognizing water pollution as a national problem that required a national solution. The Federal Water Quality Act of 1965 amended the 1948 legislation to introduce a policy of minimum water-quality standards that could be enforced in federal courts. The standards applied regardless of whether discharges could be proven to harm human health. The act also significantly increased federal funds for the construction of sewage plants. A 1966 amendment required the reporting of discharges into waterways, with civil penalties for failure to comply. Another amendment, the Water Quality Improvement Act of 1970, established federal licensing for the discharge of pollutants into navigable rivers and provided plans and funding for the detection and removal of oil spills.

THE ADVENT OF MODERN WATER-PROTECTION LEGISLATION

Congress and President Richard Nixon agreed that existing programs were ineffective in controlling water pollution. The resulting Federal Water Pollution Control Act Amendments of 1972 amended the Federal Water Quality Act to establish the basic framework for the Clean Water Act. The centerpiece of the landmark amendments was the National Pollutant Discharge Elimination System (NPDES), which utilizes the command-and-control methods earlier enacted in the Clean Air Act. The premise of the legislation was that polluting surface water is an unlawful activity, except for those exemptions specifically allowed in the act. The announced goal was to eliminate all pollutants discharged into U.S. surface waters by 1985.

In addition to standards of quality for ambient water, the amendments included technology-based standards. Industrial dischargers were given until 1977 to make use of the "best practicable technology" in their industries, and the standard was to be increased to the "best available technology" by 1983. The 1972 act also included stringent limitations on the release of toxic chemicals judged harmful to human health. For members of Congress, the most popular part of the act was the grant program for the construction of publicly owned treatment works (POTWs).

The U.S. Environmental Protection Agency (EPA), created just two years earlier, was assigned the primary responsibility for regulating and enforcing the legislation. The agency could issue five-year permits for the discharge of pollutants, and any discharge without a license or contrary to the terms of a license was punishable by either civil or criminal sanctions. When dealing with a discharge of oil or other hazardous substances, the EPA could go to court and seek a penalty of up to $50,000 per violation and up to $250,000 in the case of willful misconduct. In addition, a discharger might be assessed the costs of removal, up to $50 million. Because of the technical complexity of the law, the EPA for many years relied more on civil penalties than on criminal prosecutions.

The 1972 amendments prohibited the discharge of dredged or fill materials into navigable waters unless authorized by a permit issued by the U.S. Army Corps of Engineers (USACE). Based on the literal wording of the statute, the USACE at first regulated only actually, potentially, and historically navigable waters. In 1975, however, it revised its regulations to include jurisdiction over all coastal and freshwater wetlands, provided they were inundated often enough to support vegetation adapted for saturated soils. The Supreme Court endorsed the USACE's broad construction of the law. The USACE and the EPA later adopted a rule under which isolated waters that were actual or potential habitat for migratory birds that crossed state lines were subject to the provisions of the Clean Water Act.

The Clean Water Act amendments of 1977, which gave the legislation its current name, focused on a large variety of technical issues. They required industries to use the best available technology to remove toxic pollutants within six years. For conventional pollutants (such as ammonia, pathogens, phosphorus, and suspended solids), businesses could seek waivers from the technology requirements if the removal of the pollutants was not worth the cost. The act further required an environmental impact statement for any federal project involving wetlands, and it extended liability for oil-spill cleanups from 19 kilometers (12 miles) to 322 kilometers (200 miles) offshore.

LATER AMENDMENTS

The Municipal Wastewater Treatment Construction Grants Amendments of 1981, an important piece of environmental public works legislation, streamlined the municipal construction grants process. This allowed for municipalities to improve their sewage treatment capabilities.

The amendments of 1987, entitled the Water Quality Act, were passed by Congress over President Ronald Reagan's veto. In addition to increasing the powers of the EPA, the act significantly raised the criminal penalties for acts of pollution. Individuals who knowingly discharged certain dangerous pollutants could receive a fine of up to $250,000 and imprisonment for up to fifteen years. The maximum prison term for making false statements or tampering with monitoring equipment was increased from six months to two years. The most controversial part of the act was its authorization of $18 billion for the construction of wastewater treatment plants. In addition, the 1987 amendments phased out the earlier construction grants program, replacing it with the State Water Pollution Control Revolving Fund. Also called the Clean Water State Revolving Fund, the new program relied on EPA-state partnerships.

The 1987 Water Quality Act also provided state funds for managing and controlling nonpoint source pollution, such as stormwater runoff from urban areas, forests, agricultural lands, and construction sites. Earlier legislation had focused more on pollution from discrete sources, such as industrial plants and municipal sewage facilities, that could be more easily identified and regulated. Roughly half of the nation's remaining water pollution stemmed from nonpoint sources.

In the wake of the 1989 *Exxon Valdez* oil spill, Congress passed the Oil Pollution Act of 1990. This legislation strengthened cleanup requirements and penalties for oil discharges.

Ongoing points of contention regarding the Clean Water Act have been its wetlands protection program, the loose interpretation of "navigable waters," and the EPA/USACE "migratory bird rule." In a 2001 case, *Solid Waste Agency of Northern Cook County v. Army Corps of Engineers*, the U.S. Supreme Court found that federal protection under the Clean Water Act did not apply in the case of isolated wetlands such as the area that Cook County, Illinois, planned to use as a landfill. In 2006 the Court also determined that the act was inapplicable in the related cases *Rapanos v. United States* and *Carabell v. Corps of*

Engineers, which involved two Michigan landowners planning to develop on wetlands. In early 2010 a Clean Water Act amendment was proposed that would replace the phrase "navigable waters" with "waters of the United States."

Some of the worst causes of water pollution in the United States have been curtailed in the years since the Clean Water Act was overhauled in 1972, even though the act has manifestly failed to achieve its stated goals. The legislators who hoped to render all U.S. waters fishable and swimmable within a decade were clearly overly optimistic. It is probably inevitable that economic prosperity and population growth will mean that water in the United States will never be completely free of pollutants. Since 1972, nevertheless, the American public has become increasingly intolerant of dirty and unhealthful water, and Congress, reflecting public sentiment, has continued to strengthen the Clean Water Act.

Thomas T. Lewis
Updated by Karen N. Kähler

FURTHER READING

Copeland, Claudia. *Clean Water Act: A Summary of the Law.* Washington, D.C.: Congressional Research Service, 2008.

Finkmoore, Richard J. *Environmental Law and the Values of Nature.* Durham, N.C.: Carolina Academic Press, 2010.

Freedman, Martin, and Bikki Jaggi. *Air and Water Pollution Regulation: Accomplishments and Economic Consequences.* Westport, Conn.: Quorum Books, 1993.

Lazarus, Richard J. *The Making of Environmental Law.* Chicago: University of Chicago Press, 2004.

Milazzo, Paul Charles. *Unlikely Environmentalists: Congress and Clean Water, 1945-1972.* Lawrence: University Press of Kansas, 2006.

Ryan, Mark. *The Clean Water Act Handbook.* 2d ed. Chicago: American Bar Association, 2003.

Coastal Zone Management Act

CATEGORIES: Treaties, laws, and court cases; land and land use

THE LAW: U.S. federal law providing for the management of land and water uses in coastal areas, including the Great Lakes

DATE: Enacted on October 27, 1972

SIGNIFICANCE: The Coastal Zone Management Act has provided coastal zones with funding and research to create effective management programs to guide development. More than 153,000 kilometers (95,000 miles) of oceanic and Great Lakes coastlines are managed through these programs.

In 1970 the National Oceanic and Atmospheric Administration (NOAA) was created as an agency of the U.S. Department of Commerce. One of its charges was to develop a comprehensive plan to help guarantee the appropriate balance between the economic development of coastal and marine ecosystems and the protection of such ecosystems from pollution, overfishing, erosion, and invasive species. In 1972 the U.S. Congress passed the Coastal Zone Management Act (CZMA), creating a framework for local and federal partnerships to protect marine life and maintain clean water resources while permitting coastal economies to grow.

Under the CZMA, two new programs were created. The National Coastal Zone Management Program provides matching funds to coastal states that voluntarily submit management plans for conservation. More than half of the thirty-five eligible U.S. states and territories submitted approved plans by the end of 1979; by early 2010, Illinois was the only eligible state that had not yet joined the program. The National Estuarine Research Reserve System studies and protects the coastal zones where freshwater and saltwater bodies intersect. By early 2010, twenty-seven estuaries had been designated as sanctuaries.

Cynthia A. Bily

Colorado River

CATEGORY: Places

IDENTIFICATION: Large river that flows through the southwestern United States and northwestern Mexico

SIGNIFICANCE: The Colorado River is located in an arid region, and numerous disputes regarding rights to the river's water have arisen among the political entities that have land within the river basin: seven U.S. states and Mexico. All of these parties want to ensure that they will have continued access to the river's water for agricultural irrigation and urban-suburban expansion.

The Colorado River watershed has a drainage area of 637,000 square kilometers (246,000 square miles) and includes parts of seven western states (Colorado, Wyoming, Utah, Nevada, New Mexico, Arizona, and California) and parts of northwestern Mexico. The river begins in the Rocky Mountains of Colorado and flows for 2,330 kilometers (1,450 miles), to the Gulf of California.

Many dams were built on the Colorado River during the twentieth century for hydroelectricity and flood control, creating bodies of water that are also used for recreation. Together, these dams have the capacity to store more than 85 billion cubic meters (3,000 billion cubic feet) of water, a volume that is roughly four times the average annual flow of the entire river. The two largest dams are Hoover Dam, on the border between Nevada and Arizona, and Glen Canyon Dam, in north-central Arizona. These dams represent 80 percent of the total water-storage capacity in the watershed. Irrigation accounts for two-thirds of the water use, with much of the remaining portion going to cities (such as Phoenix, Tucson, and Las Vegas) and evaporation. Withdrawals from the river include not only water use within the Colorado River watershed basin but also major deliveries to areas outside the basin, such as the Los Angeles metropolitan area, the farms of the Imperial Valley in southeastern California, portions of Baja California, the Central

Utah Project, and the Colorado-Big Thompson Project to bring water to Denver and other areas east of the Rockies.

Over the years, numerous disputes have arisen over the rights to the water of the Colorado River. One attempt to resolve such disputes was the Colorado River Compact of 1922. That agreement made water allocations among states based on the water that had been available during the relatively limited period from 1896 to 1922, even though the river had been in existence for at least five million years. It was later understood that the period chosen was actually one of above-normal precipitation, as indicated by tree-ring analysis, which enabled scientists to extend the record back several centuries. The ten-year running mean for the annual flow of the Colorado River at Lee's Ferry below Glen Canyon Dam showed a downward trend from 1987 to 2007.

Problems with water quality in the Colorado River include high salinity levels that reflect the combination of an arid climate, the presence of saline soils, and the impacts of large amounts of surface-water runoff from irrigation return flows. Continuing population growth in the region is likely to add to problems of water demand and water quality. Environmentalists and others have suggested that those living in the region should take steps to conserve the water of the Colorado River through such practices as using

Colorado River Storage Project Act

The Colorado River Storage Project Act of 1956 was passed after a bitter battle between environmental groups and the U.S. government to prevent the construction of Echo Park Dam. The act's main points follow:

The Act authorizes the Secretary of the Interior to construct a variety of dams, reservoirs, powerplants, transmission facilities and related works in the Upper Colorado River Basin. The Act also authorizes and directs the Secretary to investigate, plan, construct and operate facilities to mitigate losses of, and improve conditions for, fish and wildlife and public recreational facilities. The Act provides authority to acquire lands and to lease and convey lands and facilities to state and other agencies. . . .

The Act provides for the comprehensive development of the water resources of the Upper Colorado River Basin to: regulate the flow of the Colorado River; store water for beneficial consumptive use; make it possible for states of the Upper Basin to use the apportionments made to and among them in the Colorado River Compact and the Upper Colorado River Basin Compact, respectively; provide for the reclamation of arid and

semiarid land, the control of floods, and the generation of hydroelectric power. . . .

By authorizing construction and prioritizing planning of specified projects, Congress does not intend to interfere with comprehensive development providing for consumptive water use apportioned to and among the Upper Colorado River Basin states or preclude consideration and authorization by Congress of additional projects. No dam or reservoir authorized by the Act shall be constructed within a national park or monument. . . .

Recreational, Fish and Wildlife Facilities. The Secretary is authorized and directed to investigate, plan, construct, operate and maintain: public recreational facilities on project lands to conserve scenery, the natural, historic and archaeologic objects, wildlife and public use and enjoyment; facilities to mitigate losses and improve conditions for the propagation of fish and wildlife. . . .

native drought-resistant vegetation in landscaping (xeriscaping) and using lower-quality water for irrigating certain kinds of properties, such as golf courses.

Climate change could be another important factor in the future of the Colorado River. According to estimates by the Intergovernmental Panel on Climate Change, global warming could result in a 20 percent reduction in runoff in the Colorado River watershed by the middle of the twenty-first century. The resultant environmental impacts on the river system would be substantial.

Robert M. Hordon

FURTHER READING

Cech, Thomas V. *Principles of Water Resources: History, Development, Management, and Policy.* 3d ed. Hoboken, N.J.: John Wiley & Sons, 2010.

Powell, James L. *Dead Pool: Lake Powell, Global Warming, and the Future of Water in the West.* Berkeley: University of California Press, 2008.

Continental shelves

CATEGORY: Ecology and ecosystems

DEFINITION: Nearly flat platforms of land that extend into the seas at the margins of continents

SIGNIFICANCE: Human activities have had many negative environmental impacts on the world's continental shelves, both directly and indirectly. These impacts include pollution of the waters of the shelves' ecosystems through runoff from land, the direct dumping of wastes, and oil extraction; the construction of artificial reefs and breakwaters; and the dredging of sand and gravel.

Continental shelves constitute the parts of the oceans most utilized by humans, but much of the environmental degradation that the shelves have undergone has resulted indirectly from human activities on land. The waters of the continental shelves in many parts of the world have become polluted by chemical fertilizers, industrial wastes, and sewage released into the seas from rivers and storm drains. Such pollution threatens the plants and animals present in coastal ecosystems.

During the early 1960's, for example, the brown pelican, a seabird species native to the coasts of the Americas, almost became extinct owing to coastal pollution. Scientists found that the brown pelican population was dying out because the birds were laying eggs with extremely thin shells that would break in the nest, so few hatchlings survived. The cause was determined to be the presence of the pesticide dichloro-diphenyl-trichloroethane (DDT) in coastal waters, which came from agricultural runoff that was deposited in the Gulf of Mexico by the Mississippi River. DDT had accumulated in the bodies of the fish on which the pelicans fed. After the dangers of DDT were recognized, use of the pesticide was eventually banned in the United States.

Chemical pollution of coastal waters remains a problem, however. In some areas, pollution of the continental shelves by agricultural runoff containing fertilizers has led to the creation of hypoxic (oxygen-deprived) areas known as dead zones. The nitrogen and phosphorus in fertilizers are nutrients that cause algae to grow at accelerated rates. When the algae die and sink to the bottom, their decay depletes the dissolved oxygen in the water, and the fish and other marine life die. A seasonal hypoxic zone the size of the state of New Jersey forms during the summer months at the mouth of the Mississippi River in the Gulf of Mexico, and similar dead zones are found on continental shelves around the world.

Coral reefs, many of which develop along the edges of continental shelves, have been increasingly damaged by human activities, both indirectly and directly. Chemical pollution is thought to contribute to the discoloration of these reefs known as bleaching and white-band disease, and serious damage to reefs can result from the dragging of anchors across them and from shipwrecks. Other damaging human activities include the use of harmful chemicals and even dynamite to drive reef organisms out of their hiding places and the mining of reefs to collect coral for ornamental purposes. Policy makers and legislators have responded to increasing recognition among scientists that the ecosystems of coral reefs need to be protected. In the United States, for instance, the National Marine Sanctuaries Program protects the reefs of the Florida Keys as well as thirteen other pristine marine sites around North America, Hawaii, and American Samoa.

DUMPING OF WASTES

Various kinds of environmental damage to the continental shelves have resulted directly from human actions. For example, humans have intentionally changed coastal seabeds—and thus destroyed marine habitats and disrupted ecosystems—by building breakwaters, pilings for bridges, artificial reefs, and wind farms; in addition, in some cases, these areas have been used for the disposal of construction debris, municipal solid waste, and outdated military hardware.

An extreme example of the dumping of waste on a continental shelf is provided by New York City, which has always faced difficulty in the disposal of construction debris. Manhattan Island is only 21.6 kilometers (13.4 miles) long and 3.7 kilometers (2.3 miles) wide, and it represents some of the most expensive real estate in the world. In 1890 builders in Manhattan began the practice of dumping construction debris and other waste in the New York Bight, an indentation in the coastline between New York State and New Jersey. The mound formed on the continental shelf in this area was soon so large that it was jokingly called an underwater Mount Everest. Amendments made in 1986 to the Marine Protection, Research, and Sanctuaries Act of 1972 (also known as the Ocean Dumping Act) prohibited dumping in this area, and a new dump site was opened 170 kilometers (106 miles) offshore. Since that time, an even larger mound of waste materials has been accumulating on the seabed at a depth of 2,500 meters (8,200 feet).

The dumping of obsolete military hardware in coastal waters creates special problems because such hardware may contain materials that are hazardous. Two crewmen on a clam boat off the shore of Massachusetts had to be hospitalized in June, 2010, for example, after they hauled up World War I-era military shells filled with mustard gas along with a load of clams. It turned out that the U.S. military had been using the area as a dumping ground for munitions from after World War II through 1970.

DREDGING AND OIL SPILLS

In addition to building and dumping things on continental shelves, humans also take things out. Sand is routinely dredged from the continental shelf off southern Florida, for example, to "nourish" beaches that have lost their sand due to erosion, and some cities that are heavily dependent on tourist revenue, such as Delray Beach and Palm Beach, have had their beaches rebuilt several times. In countries that are highly industrialized and densely populated, con-

tinental shelves may be mined for the sand and gravel required for construction. It has been estimated that 25 percent of the sand and gravel needed for construction in southeastern England comes from offshore; the proportion is believed to be even higher for Japan. In addition to exploiting continental shelves for sand and gravel, humans also mine deposits of valuable minerals, such as diamonds and gold, on some of the world's continental shelves.

Oil spills represent another way in which humans degrade the shelves. Production platforms and drilling rigs jut up offshore in areas where oil and gas deposits are found, and the oil that can leak or spill from these rigs has the potential to foul the ocean and seabed for hundreds of miles around. Two examples of disastrous spills that resulted from such offshore oil extraction have taken place in the Gulf of Mexico. In 1979 a blowout in an exploratory well drilled by Petróleos Mexicanos (PEMEX), the Mexican state-owned oil company, in 50 meters (164 feet) of water off the coast of Mexico caused a spillage of oil that fouled the seabed and beaches as far away as Texas. An even greater tragedy was the blowout of BP's *Deepwater Horizon* rig off the coast of Louisiana in 2010. Heavy reddish-brown oil from this spill fouled the continental shelf and beaches as far away as Florida, even though the well was drilled 72 kilometers (45 miles) offshore in water 1,524 meters (5,000 feet) deep.

Donald W. Lovejoy

FURTHER READING

Ketchum, Bostwick H., ed. *The Water's Edge: Critical Problems of the Coastal Zone.* Cambridge, Mass.: MIT Press, 1972.

Porter, James W., and Karen G. Porter, eds. *The Everglades, Florida Bay, and Coral Reefs of the Florida Keys: An Ecosystem Sourcebook.* Boca Raton, Fla.: CRC Press, 2002.

Sverdrup, Keith A., and E. Virginia Armbrust. *An Introduction to the World's Oceans.* New York: McGraw-Hill, 2009.

Viles, Heather A., and Tom Spencer. *Coastal Problems: Geomorphology, Ecology, and Society at the Coast.* London: Arnold, 1995.

Walsh, John J. *On the Nature of the Continental Shelves.* San Diego, Calif.: Academic Press, 1988.

Cultural eutrophication

CATEGORY: Water and water pollution

DEFINITION: Unwanted increase in nutrient concentrations in sensitive waters caused by human activities

SIGNIFICANCE: Cultural eutrophication causes the degradation of productive aquatic environments, which has prompted state and federal governments to regulate point and nonpoint source pollution in surrounding watersheds.

Eutrophication (from the Greek term meaning "to nourish") is the sudden enrichment of natural waters with excess nutrients, such as nitrogen, phosphorus, and potassium, which can lead to the development of algae blooms and other vegetation. In addition to clouding otherwise clear water, some algae and protozoa (namely, *Pfiesteria*) release toxins that harm fish and other aquatic wildlife. When the algae die, their decomposition produces odorous compounds and depletes dissolved oxygen in these waters, which causes fish and other organisms to suffocate.

Eutrophication is a naturally occurring process as an environment evolves over time. Cultural eutrophication is a distinct form of eutrophication in which the process is accelerated by human activities, including wastewater treatment disposal, runoff from city streets and lawns, deforestation and development in watersheds, and agricultural activities such as farming and livestock production. These activities contribute excessive amounts of available nutrients to otherwise pristine waters and promote rapid and excessive plant growth.

Eutrophication of the Great Lakes, particularly Lake Erie, was one of the key factors that prompted passage of the Clean Water Act and various amendments during the 1970's. This act specifically addressed the disposal of sewage into public waters, a major contributor to cultural eutrophication. However, it did not specifically address nonpoint source pollution, which comes from sources that are not readily identifiable. Agricultural activities such as farming, logging, and concentrated livestock operations all contribute to nonpoint source pollution through fertilizer runoff, soil erosion, and poor waste disposal practices that supply readily available nutrients to surrounding watersheds and lead to eutrophication in these environments.

The Chesapeake Bay is an excellent case study in cultural eutrophication. As development surrounding the bay dramatically increased, wetland and riparian buffers that helped reduce some of the impact of additional nutrients were destroyed. Eutrophication in the bay during the 1980's threatened the crabbing and oyster industry. Consequently, in 1983 and 1987, Maryland, Pennsylvania, and Virginia, the three states bordering the Chesapeake Bay, agreed to a 40 percent reduction of nutrients by the year 2000 from point and nonpoint sources in all watersheds contributing to the bay. These reductions were to be accomplished through such actions as the banning of phosphate detergents, the implementation of management plans to control soil erosion, the protection of wetlands, and the institution of controls on production and management of animal wastes. Although these steps reduced phosphorus levels in the Chesapeake Bay and kept nitrogen levels constant, regulators remained unsure how much nutrient reduction must take place for the bay and its surroundings to resemble their original condition.

Mark Coyne

FURTHER READING

Grady, Wayne. *The Great Lakes: The Natural History of a Changing Region.* Vancouver: Greystone Books, 2007.

Laws, Edward A. "Cultural Eutrophication: Case Studies." In *Aquatic Pollution: An Introductory Text.* 3d ed. New York: John Wiley & Sons, 2000.

McGucken, William. *Lake Erie Rehabilitated: Controlling Cultural Eutrophication, 1960's-1990's.* Akron, Ohio: University of Akron Press, 2000.

Cuyahoga River fires

CATEGORY: Disasters

THE EVENT: Burning of oil slicks on the surface of the Cuyahoga River near Cleveland, Ohio

DATES: November, 1952, and June 22, 1969

SIGNIFICANCE: The fire that occurred on the oil-slicked Cuyahoga River in 1969 demonstrated the poor environmental condition of the Great Lakes and sparked a major media event that served to sway public opinion toward supporting the cleanup of Lake Erie.

The Cuyahoga River divides the city of Cleveland into east and west sides. Originating on the Appalachian Plateau 56 kilometers (35 miles) east of Cleveland, the river meanders 166 kilometers (103 miles) to Lake Erie. About 8 kilometers (5 miles) from its mouth, it becomes a sharply twisting but navigable stream that forms part of Cleveland's harbor. Industrial development took place along the river in the early nineteenth century, and by 1860 docks and warehouses lined the ship channel. Industry had claimed virtually all of Cleveland's riverfront by 1881, when, according to Cleveland mayor Rensselaer R. Herrick, the discharge from factories and oil refineries made it an open sewer running through the center of the city.

In 1951 the Ohio Department of Natural Resources reported that the Cuyahoga River was heavily polluted with industrial effluents at its mouth, creating conditions that were unsatisfactory for the existence of aquatic life. In September of that year, thousands of dead fish were washed ashore just west of the river's mouth, and observers noted that the area gave off strong river odors.

An oil slick burned on the Cuyahoga River for days in November, 1952, causing an estimated $1.5 million in damage, without attracting national attention. Almost seventeen years later, at approximately noon on Sunday, June 22, 1969, the Cuyahoga River again caught fire. The fire was brought under control by approximately 12:20 P.M., but not before it had done some $50,000 worth of damage to two key railroad trestles over the river in the Flats area of Cleveland. An oil slick on the river had caught fire and floated under the wooden bridges, setting fire to both. Witnesses reported that the flames from the bridges reached as high as a five-story building. The fireboat *Anthony J. Celebrezze* rushed upstream and battled the blaze on the water while units from three fire battalions brought the flames on the trestles under control. Responsibility for the oil slick was placed on the waterfront industries, which used the river as a dumping ground for oil wastes instead of reclaiming the waste products.

The railroad trestles that burned were not all that sustained damage in the fire. Cleveland's reputation as "the best location in the nation" was severely damaged by the occurrence. The city became the brunt of numerous jokes, and the mass media across the country characterized it as the only city with a river so choked with pollution that it had burned. No river in the United States had a more notorious national reputation than the Cuyahoga River. Media coverage of the fire helped galvanize nationwide public support for efforts to clean up not only Lake Erie in particular but also the environment in general.

Charles E. Herdendorf

FURTHER READING

Adler, Jonathan A. "Fables of the Cuyahoga: Reconstructing a History of Environmental Protection." *Fordham Environmental Law Journal* 14 (2002): 89-146.

Grady, Wayne. *The Great Lakes: The Natural History of a Changing Region.* Vancouver: Greystone Books, 2007.

McGucken, William. *Lake Erie Rehabilitated: Controlling Cultural Eutrophication, 1960's-1990's.* Akron, Ohio: University of Akron Press, 2000.

Dams and reservoirs

CATEGORY: Preservation and wilderness issues

DEFINITION: Structures that obstruct the natural flow of water in rivers and streams, and the bodies of water created by the impoundment of water behind or upstream of such structures

SIGNIFICANCE: Because dams obstruct the natural flow of water, they have significant effects on stream and river ecosystems. Although dams provide benefits such as flood control and hydroelectric power generation, they also have a number of negative environmental impacts.

Dams are designed for a number of purposes, including conservation, irrigation, flood control, hydroelectric power generation, navigation, and recreation. Not all dams create reservoirs of significant size. Low dams, or barrages, have been used to divert portions of stream flows into canals or aqueducts since human beings' first attempts at irrigation thousands of years ago. Canals, aqueducts, and pipelines are used to change the direction of water flow from a stream to agricultural fields or areas with high population concentrations.

Dams and reservoirs provide the chief, and in most cases the sole, means of storing stream flow over time. Small dams and reservoirs are capable of storing water for weeks or months, allowing water use during local dry seasons. Large dams and reservoirs have the capacity to store water for several years. As urban populations in arid regions have grown and irrigation agriculture has dramatically expanded, dams and reservoirs have increased in size in response to demand. They are frequently located hundreds of kilometers from where the water is eventually used. The construction of larger dams and reservoirs has resulted in increasingly complex environmental and social problems that have affected large numbers of people. This has been particularly true in tropical and developing nations, where most of the large dam construction of the last three decades of the twentieth century was concentrated.

SIZES AND PURPOSES OF DAMS

Early dams and their associated reservoirs were small, and dams remained small, for the most part, until the twentieth century. The first dams were simple barrages constructed across streams to divert water into irrigation canals. Water supply for humans and animals undoubtedly benefited from these diversions, but the storage capacity of most dams was small, reflecting the limited technology of the period. The earliest dams were constructed some five thousand years ago in the Middle East, and dams became common two thousand years ago in the Mediterranean region, China, Central America, and South Asia.

The energy of falling water can be converted by water wheels into mechanical energy to perform a vari-

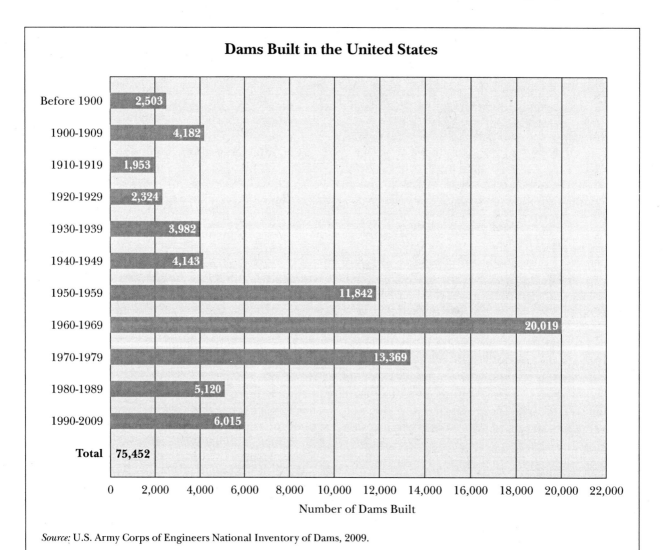

Dams Built in the United States

Period	Number of Dams Built
Before 1900	2,503
1900-1909	4,182
1910-1919	1,953
1920-1929	2,324
1930-1939	3,982
1940-1949	4,143
1950-1959	11,842
1960-1969	20,019
1970-1979	13,369
1980-1989	5,120
1990-2009	6,015
Total	75,452

Number of Dams Built

Source: U.S. Army Corps of Engineers National Inventory of Dams, 2009.

ety of tasks, including the grinding of grain. Dams create a higher "head" or water level, increasing the potential energy, and thus served as the earliest energy source for the beginnings of the Industrial Revolution during the nineteenth century. The most significant contribution of dams to industrialization occurred in 1882 with the development of hydroelectricity, which permitted energy to be transferred to wherever electric power lines were built rather than being confined to river banks.

During the nineteenth century, large-scale settlement of the arid regions of western North America and Asia soon exhausted the meager local supplies of water and prompted demands for both exotic supplies from distant watersheds and storage for dry years. Big dams for storage and big projects for transportation of the water were thought to be the answer. Small dam projects could be financed locally; grander schemes required the assistance of federal or national governments. To justify expenditures on larger dams, promoters of these projects touted the multiple uses for reservoir water as benefits that would offset the projects' costs. Benefit-cost ratios thus became the tool by which potential projects were judged. To raise the ratio of benefits to costs, promoters placed increasing importance on intangible benefits—those to which it is difficult to assign universally agreeable currency values. While dams in arid regions were originally justified chiefly for irrigation, public water supply, and power, decisions to build dams in wetter areas were usually based on projected benefits from flood control, navigation, and recreation in addition to power generation and public water supply.

Complicating the equation is the fact that multiple uses are frequently conflicting uses. While all dams are built to even out the uneven flow of streams over time, flood control requires an empty reservoir to handle the largest floods; conversely, power generation requires a high level of water in the reservoir to provide the highest head. Public water supply and navigation benefit most from supplies that are manipulated in response to variable demand. Recreation, fishing, and the increasingly important factor of environmental concerns focus on in-stream uses of the water.

By the last two decades of the twentieth century, environmental costs and benefits and the issue of Native American water rights in the American West dominated decisions concerning dam projects in the United States, and few dams were constructed. Most of the best sites for the construction of large dams in the developed nations had been utilized, and the industry turned its attention to the developing nations. Most of the large dam projects of the last quarter of the twentieth century were constructed in or proposed for developing nations and the area of the former Soviet Union.

HUMAN IMPACTS

Small dams have small impacts on the environment; they affect small watersheds and minor tributaries and usually have only a single purpose. Farm ponds and tanks, as they are known in many parts of the world, generally cover a fraction of 1 hectare (2.47 acres) in area and are only a few meters in height. These tiny ponds are designed to store water for livestock and occasionally for human supply. They frequently serve recreational purposes as well, such as fishing. During dry spells they become stagnant and subject to contamination by algae and other noxious organisms, which can threaten the health of humans and livestock. Otherwise, they have little negative impact on the environment or on nearby people and animals.

Large dams and reservoirs are responsible for environmental and social impacts that often appear to be roughly related to their size: The larger the dam or reservoir, the greater the impact. Geographical location is also important in assessing a project's impact. Scenic areas in particular, or those with endangered species of plants or animals or irreplaceable cultural or archaeological features, raise more controversy and litigation if they are chosen as potential sites for dam and reservoir projects.

People in tropical regions suffer proportionately greater health-related impacts from dams than do those in corresponding nontropical areas. The large numbers of workers required for the construction of big dams and associated irrigation projects can carry diseases into unprotected populations. Stagnant or slow-moving waters in reservoirs and irrigation canals, as well as fast-moving waters downstream of dams, are associated with particularly vicious tropical health risks. Snails in slow-moving water carry schistosomiasis, a parasitic disease that infects intestinal and urinary tracts, causing general listlessness and more serious consequences, including failure of internal organs and cancer. Estimates of the numbers of people infected range into the hundreds of millions. Malaria, lymphatic filariasis (including elephantiasis), and other diseases are carried by mosquitoes that breed in water; the incidence of such insect-borne diseases dramatically expands near irrigation projects and reservoirs. River blindness, which results from the bite of black flies, is associated with fast-flowing water downstream of dams and affects hundreds of thousands of humans.

The flooding of densely populated river valleys by reservoirs displaces greater numbers of people, with attendant health problems and social impacts, than similar projects in sparsely populated areas. Population displacement in developing countries, especially those in the Tropics, causes greater health and social problems than in developed nations, where remedial measures and compensation are more likely to assuage the loss of homestead and community.

ENVIRONMENTAL IMPACTS

Many of the environmental problems created by large dams are associated with rapid changes in water level below the dams or with the ponding of stream flow in the reservoirs, which replaces fast-flowing, oxygenated water with relatively stagnant conditions. Indigenous animal species, as well as some plant life, are adapted to seasonal changes in the natural stream flow and cannot adjust to the postdam regime of the stream. Consequently, the survival of these species may be threatened. In 1973 the Tennessee Valley Authority—the worldwide model for builders of many large, integrated river basin projects—found that the potential demise of a small fish, the snail darter, stood in the way of the completion of the Tellico Dam. After considerable controversy and litigation, the dam was completed in 1979, but few large projects have been proposed in the United States since then, particularly in the humid East. Since the early 1970's, the arguments for abandoning dam projects have been more likely to be backed up by laws, regulations, and court decisions.

Construction of the Hetch Hetchy Dam in the Sierra Nevada mountain range of California in the early twentieth century sparked vigorous dissent, which is said to have led to the growth of the Sierra Club and organized environmental opposition to dam building. This opposition successfully challenged the construction of the Echo Park Dam on the Green River in Colorado in the early 1950's but was unsuccessful in stopping the construction of the Glen Canyon Dam on the Colorado River, which was completed in 1963. Glen Canyon, however, was the last of the big dams constructed in the American West. The preservationists, whose arguments chiefly concerned scenic and wilderness values, with attendant benefits to endangered species, lost the Glen Canyon battle but won the war against big dams. The controversy surrounding the Glen Canyon Dam continued for more than three decades after its completion, pitting wilderness and scenic preservationists against powerboat recreationists, who benefit from the access accorded by the dam's reservoir to the upstream canyonlands.

All reservoirs eventually fill with silt from upstream erosion; deltas form on their upstream ends. Heavier sediments, mainly sands, are trapped behind the dam and cannot progress downstream to the ocean. The Atlantic coastline of the southeastern United States suffers from beach erosion and retreat because the sands are no longer replenished by the natural flow of nearby rivers. The Aswan High Dam on the Nile River in Egypt has had a similar impact on the Nile Delta. Moreover, the natural flow of sediments downstream has historically replenished the fertility of floodplain soils during floods. To the extent that the flood-control function of a dam is successful, new fertile sediment never reaches downstream agricultural fields. While irrigation water provided by the dam may permit the expansion of cropland, this water in arid regions is often highly charged with salts, which then accumulate in the soils and eventually become toxic to plant life.

Reservoir waters release methane from decaying organic matter into the atmosphere. Methane is a greenhouse gas that promotes global warming, and some estimates suggest that the effect of large reservoirs is roughly equal to the greenhouse gas pollution of large thermal-powered electrical generation plants. The weight of the water in large reservoirs has also been implicated in causing earthquakes, which may lead to the failure of a dam. Dam failure may also occur because of poor construction or poor design, or because the builders had inadequate knowledge of the geology of the site. Tens of thousands of lives have been lost as a consequence of such failures.

Neil E. Salisbury

FURTHER READING

Berga, L., et al., eds. *Dams and Reservoirs, Societies, and Environment in the Twenty-first Century.* New York: Taylor & Francis, 2006.

Billington, David P., and Donald C. Jackson. *Big Dams*

of the New Deal Era: A Confluence of Engineering and Politics. Norman: University of Oklahoma Press, 2006.

Cech, Thomas V. "Dams." In Principles of Water Resources: History, Development, Management, and Policy. 3d ed. New York: John Wiley & Sons, 2010.

Goldsmith, Edward, and Nicholas Hildyard. The Social and Environmental Effects of Large Dams. New York: Random House, 1984.

Leslie, Jacques. Deep Water: The Epic Struggle over Dams, Displaced People, and the Environment. New York: Farrar, Straus and Giroux, 2005.

McCully, Patrick. Silenced Rivers: The Ecology and Politics of Large Dams. Enlarged ed. London: Zed Books, 2001.

Stevens, Joseph E. Hoover Dam: An American Adventure. Norman: University of Oklahoma Press, 1988.

Danube River

CATEGORY: Places

IDENTIFICATION: European river originating in Germany and flowing generally eastward to the Black Sea

SIGNIFICANCE: The Danube, which passes through nine European countries, has suffered severe pollution from both natural and human sources. Maintenance of the river has been difficult because so many nations share its waters, but with the signing of the Danube River Protection Convention in 1994, improvements began to be made.

The source of the Danube is close to that of the Rhine, which flows north, making the pair of rivers a major waterway cutting through Central Europe. The Danube passes through or borders on nine countries: Germany, Austria, Slovakia, Hungary, Croatia, Serbia, Romania, Bulgaria, and Ukraine. Because the river's tributaries affect other areas as well, the International Commission for the Protection of the Danube River (ICPDR) includes representatives from the Czech Republic, Slovenia, Bosnia and Herzegovina, Montenegro, and Moldova, as well as the European Union. In addition, the Danube basin includes Poland, Italy, Albania, and Macedonia, but these nations do not take part in the ICPDR.

The ICPDR was formed to carry out the mandates of the Danube River Protection Convention of 1994: to conserve and improve both surface water and groundwater of the Danube in a rational manner and to oversee the use of the river's waters. According to the convention, the ICPDR constitutes the overall legal instrument for cooperation on transboundary water management in the Danube River basin. Its missions are to ensure the management of the waters of the river basin and the distribution of those waters in an equitable manner; to prevent hazards from ice and flooding; and to prevent dangerous materials and pollution from entering the Black Sea through the river. The parties to the convention have agreed to take all legal, administrative, and technical measures to maintain—or improve, if possible—the state of the water quality in the Danube and its basin and prevent any damage to the waters. The ICPDR also publishes the magazine Danube Watch, which is intended to inform the public about environmental issues concerning the Danube.

The members of the ICPDR and the members of the International Sava River Basin Commission (the Sava is a tributary of the Danube in southern Europe) issued a joint statement in October, 2007, addressing the topics of navigation on the river and the river basin's ecology. The statement noted both the positive and the negative effects that river navigation can have on the environment as shipping on the Danube replaces road transport. The commission members' observations fit into a general transportation statement by the European Union covering the ecological impacts of all modes of transportation: road, rail, air, and river.

In 2008 the results of a scientific survey conducted by the ICPDR showed that the river had undergone remarkable improvement since the first such survey was taken in 2001. While the results were positive, however, the commission's report on the survey findings emphasized that work still needed to be done. Swimming was possible in some areas of the river but not all. Fish taken from some parts were edible, but further investigation of mercury concentrations were still needed. Although significant populations of plants and animals still existed in the river, and the countries along the river had repaired many damaged areas, pollution of the river by waste plants in such major cities as Belgrade, Budapest, and Bucharest still needed attention.

Frederick B. Chary

FURTHER READING

Jansky, Libor. The Danube: Environmental Monitoring of an International River. New York: United Nations University Press, 2004.

Magris, Claudio. *Danube.* Translated by Patrick Creagh. 1989. Reprint. New York: Farrar, Straus and Giroux, 2008.

Murphy, Irene Lyons, ed. *Protecting Danube River Basin Resources: Ensuring Access to Water Quality Data and Information.* Norwell, Mass.: Kluwer Academic, 1997.

Desalination

CATEGORY: Water and water pollution

DEFINITION: Process of removing minerals from salty water to make the water fit for humans to drink or for use in irrigation

SIGNIFICANCE: More than eighty countries around the world have problems obtaining sufficient potable water to serve their populations. Desalination offers a way to provide water to people living where sources of fresh water are scarce, but the process is associated with a number of negative environmental impacts.

Water is abundant in the world, but only about 3 percent of all water is potable—that is, fit for humans to drink. It is possible to remove salts from seawater or brackish water to make potable water, but the desalination process uses large amounts of energy. The costs of desalination depend on the type of feed water (seawater or brackish water) and its temperature, the method being used (membrane filtration, distillation, or ion exchange), the type of energy used (nuclear, petroleum, or solar), and the amount of water to be processed. Producing potable water through desalination is expensive compared with taking potable water out of the ground or from streams, ranging from about 50 cents to 70 cents per cubic meter of potable water produced (1 cubic meter is equal to about 35 cubic feet, or 264 gallons).

The nations that have established large desalination plants are bordered by oceans, have little potable water on their land, and have large amounts of cheap energy, such as petroleum, available for use. Middle Eastern countries produce the greatest amounts of potable water produced in the world through the desalination of seawater. Up to 49 billion liters (13 billion gallons) of potable water are produced each day by more than fifteen thousand desalination plants located in such places as North Africa, Saudi Arabia,

the United Arab Emirates, Japan, Australia, and the United States.

The largest desalination plant in the world is the Jebel Ali plant in Dubai, in the United Arab Emirates, which is expected eventually to provide up to 250 million cubic meters (8.8 billion cubic feet, or 66 billion gallons) of water per year. The plant uses the common multiflash distillation process, in which seawater is boiled at low pressure so that relatively low amounts of energy are needed. Among the large desalination plants in the United States are one in Tampa Bay, Florida, and one in El Paso, Texas. The El Paso plant uses the popular method of reverse osmosis to process undrinkable brackish waters, generating about 25 percent of the water used by the city. In the reverse osmosis process, membranes gradually purify the water as less salty water moves out of the membranes, leaving much saltier water behind.

Several negative environmental impacts are associated with the operation of desalination plants. For one thing, the plants use high amounts of energy, usually electricity generated by the burning of fossil fuels, a process that produces carbon dioxide, one of the gases associated with global warming. Desalination plants can also have more direct effects on the environment. The intake of seawater into a plant can kill organisms such as fish larvae and plankton, and the disposal into the ocean of warm residual waters very high in dissolved solids after processing may harm some animals. Plants can be designed to avoid the latter problem, however. The warm, concentrated brine waters can be mixed with cooler and less concentrated waters so that the water returned to the ocean is more similar in temperature and concentration to seawater, or the concentrated brine water can be dispersed over a large area in the ocean so that it changes the seawater composition and temperature very little.

Robert L. Cullers

FURTHER READING

Chiras, Daniel D. "Water Resources: Preserving Our Liquid Assets and Protecting Aquatic Ecosystems." In *Environmental Science.* 8th ed. Sudbury, Mass.: Jones and Bartlett, 2010.

Eltawil, Mohamed A., Zhao Zhengming, and Liqiang Yuan. "A Review of Renewable Energy Technologies Integrated with Desalination Systems." *Renewable and Sustainable Energy Review* 13 (2009): 2245-2262.

Escobar, Isabel, and Andrea Schäfer, eds. *Sustainable*

Water for the Future: Water Recycling Versus Desalination. Oxford, England: Elsevier, 2010.

Karagiannis, Ioannis C., and Petros G. Soldatos. "Water Desalination Cost Literature: Review and Assessment." *Desalination* 223 (2008): 448-456.

National Research Council. *Desalination: A National Perspective.* Washington, D.C.: National Academies Press, 2008.

Dredging

CATEGORY: Water and water pollution

DEFINITION: Removal by excavation or suction of sedimentary materials from the bottoms of lakes, rivers, estuaries, and coastal areas

SIGNIFICANCE: Dredging is performed to maintain navigation systems, exploit mineral resources, or remove polluted bottom sediments. The activity of dredging disturbs bottom-dwelling organisms and has negative impacts on water quality. It also generates waste sediment, which must be used or disposed of in an environmentally responsible manner.

Natural erosion processes, sometimes enhanced or exacerbated by human activity, break down rock and soil into sediments that ultimately migrate downstream. When suspended sediments eventually sink to the bottom of a lake, river, estuary, or bay, they form deposits that can impede navigable waterways or increase the likelihood of flooding. Dredging, or removing underwater sediments with digging or suction equipment, keeps ports, harbors, and waterways open for commerce, security, flood-control, and recreational purposes.

Dredging also serves as a mining method. Where suspended sediments contain ore minerals, the dense ore particles sink more readily than nonore materials and form concentrated deposits. Diamonds, cassiterite (a major tin mineral), ilmenite (a titanium ore mineral), and gold are among the minerals mined by dredging. Other resources obtained through dredging include sand and gravel, which are used in construction. In areas where land is expensive, dredging river bottoms for these materials is an alternative to quarrying them on land. For example, dredging along the Kansas River in the Kansas City, Missouri, metropolitan area has provided a local source of sand and gravel for many years.

Another reason for dredging is to remove polluted bottom sediments from a body of water. Contaminant removal by dredging generates its own problems, as disturbing the sediments allows toxic materials that have settled out of suspension to reenter the overlying water, where they can affect aquatic life or be transported to another location. Maintenance dredging for navigation purposes is similarly problematic when it occurs in bodies of water where sewage or industrial pollutants have contaminated bottom sediments.

Large quantities of sediment are displaced during dredging operations. In the United States alone, maintenance dredging of navigable waters generates several hundred million cubic yards of sediment per year. In Southeast Asia, large dredges used to mine tin deposits handle more than 5 million cubic meters (177 million cubic feet) of sediment annually.

Dredging can mobilize existing contaminants but is not in itself a significant source of pollutants. However, dredging disrupts the habitats of bottom-dwelling organisms and can kill them outright. In addition, the dredging process and associated dumping of waste sediments in open waters causes turbidity (water cloudiness caused by suspended particles), which can harm or kill organisms that need clear water to survive. Oysters, for example, are detrimentally affected by turbid waters. Dredging can also affect erosion patterns, river flow, and ocean currents. In the Kansas River, dredging has removed far more sediment than can be replenished naturally. This has resulted in increased riverbank erosion, a wider and deeper river channel, a lowered water surface, a steeper bed gradient, and loss of vegetation and farmland along the river.

Clean dredged sediments can be employed for beneficial purposes, among them replenishing beaches and creating wetlands habitat. They can also be dried and used in construction materials or as fill dirt. Heavily polluted waste sediment must be sent to a secure disposal facility equipped to handle the contaminants in question.

In the United States, concerns about environmental degradation and watershed management issues related to dredging led to the adoption of a national dredging policy in 1995. The National Dredging Team (NDT), a multidisciplinary group made up of representatives from several governmental agencies and cochaired by the Environmental Protection Agency and the Army Corps of Engineers, serves as a forum for implementation of the policy. The NDT works to ensure that timely dredging operations keep navigable waterways open while protecting, conserving, and restoring the coastal environment. A priority of the NDT is the beneficial use of waste sediments.

Robert L. Cullers
Updated by Karen N. Kähler

FURTHER READING

Bray, R. N., ed. *Environmental Aspects of Dredging*. London: Taylor & Francis, 2008.

National Dredging Team. *Dredged Material Management: Action Agenda for the Next Decade*. Washington, D.C.: U.S. Environmental Protection Agency, 2003.

Palermo, Michael R., et al. *Technical Guidelines for Environmental Dredging of Contaminated Sediments*. Vicksburg, Miss.: U.S. Army Corps of Engineers, Environmental Laboratory, 2008.

Drinking water

CATEGORY: Water and water pollution

DEFINITION: Water supplies that are safe for human consumption

SIGNIFICANCE: Many areas of the world lack sufficient safe drinking water to support their populations. International, national, and local efforts have been undertaken to conserve existing water supplies, to clean up polluted water supplies with appropriate treatment, and to find new ways of distributing safe drinking water to those who need it.

In many parts of the world human beings lack access to safe drinking water. More than one million people die each year because of a lack of drinking water or because their water supplies are contaminated owing to unsanitary conditions. Even in developed countries where water supplies are sufficient, drinking water may contain dangerous contaminants, including such toxic chemicals as lead and arsenic, harmful microorganisms, and even radioactive compounds such as radon.

QUALITY, ACCESSIBILITY, AND REGULATION

Most problems with water quality involve contamination with disease-causing (pathogenic) microorganisms. Safe, clean drinking water is free of all pathogenic microbes. A number of dangerous microorganisms can be transmitted by water, including viruses (for example, hepatitis A), bacteria (*Salmonella* and *Vibrio cholera*), protozoa (*Giardia*, *Cryptosporidium*, and *Entamoeba*), and parasitic worms, or helminths (*Ascaris lumbricoides*). Pollution and microbial contamination make the waters of most rivers, lakes, and ponds (surface water) unfit for human consumption without prior purifying treatment. The most common method of treating surface water to produce safe drinking water is disinfection by chlorination. Chloramines and ultraviolet light are also used for treatment.

A sufficient quantity of good-quality drinking water exists to satisfy the needs of all human beings on the planet, but the water is not distributed in such a way that it reaches populations in all parts of the world. Population growth also has impacts on drinking-water resources, even in regions with large supplies of water. In many developing countries people have no choice but to use water that is polluted with various wastes—including human sewage, animal excrement, and a variety of pathogenic microorganisms—because no water treatment systems are in place. The United Nations estimates that one billion people around the world do not have access to unpolluted drinking water.

In many locations, drinking water is obtained from groundwater sources. Groundwater—water found beneath the ground surface in soil and rock spaces—can generally be used for drinking with minimal treatment because it has already been purified by passing through soil. Wells must be dug to reach this water. More than one and one-half billion people in the world use groundwater as a source of drinking water. In the United States, about 60 percent of drinking water comes from rivers and lakes and about 40 percent from groundwater sources. In many parts of the world, groundwater usage is increasingly outpacing the rate of groundwater replacement.

Several countries have introduced regulations intended to ensure the good quality of drinking water. In the United States, the Environmental Protection Agency (EPA) sets standards for drinking water under the 1974 Safe Drinking Water Act. These standards cover some ninety-four possible contaminants, including biological and chemical substances. For example, the EPA sets the acceptable number of microorganisms per 1 milliliter (0.034 ounce) of water at fewer than 10, and water that is considered drinkable can contain no coliform bacteria.

DESALINATION AND CONSERVATION

The need to obtain more drinking water in some regions has led to increased use of desalination technologies as well as increasing emphasis on the conservation of existing water supplies. The desalination of ocean water produces billions of gallons of drinking water per day around the world, but this process can have some negative environmental impacts, such as thermal pollution and damage to shoreline ecosystems.

Water conservation is the most cost-effective way to reduce demand for drinking water. Both local and national governments in many nations have introduced regulations and programs aimed at encouraging water conservation on the level of individual households; among the areas targeted for reduced usage of drinking-water supplies have been lawn maintenance and toilet flushing. The practice of rainwater harvesting is encouraged in some areas, and some governments have instituted strict compulsory water metering to raise awareness of the need to conserve water.

Another option for increasing supplies of drinking water is the restoration of municipal and industrial wastewater to drinkable quality. Using technologies such as membrane bioreactor treatment (which involves treating wastewater with certain types of microorganisms and then putting it through microfiltration, followed by disinfection with ultraviolet light), communities can turn their own wastewater into drinking water.

Sergei A. Markov

FURTHER READING

Hammer, Mark J. *Water and Wastewater Technology.* Upper Saddle River, N.J.: Pearson, 2004.

Shannon, Mark A., et al. "Science and Technology for Water Purification in the Coming Decades." *Nature* 452 (March, 2008): 301-310.

Sigee, David. *Freshwater Microbiology.* New York: John Wiley & Sons, 2005.

Wright, Richard T. *Environmental Science: Toward a Sustainable Future.* 10th ed. Upper Saddle River, N.J.: Pearson, 2008.

Environment Canada

CATEGORIES: Organizations and agencies; human health and the environment; atmosphere and air pollution

IDENTIFICATION: Department of the Canadian federal government responsible for environmental policies and programs

DATE: Established on June 11, 1971

SIGNIFICANCE: Environment Canada serves as a model for best practices in monitoring, public education, and action in protection of the environment. The department works to develop, implement, and enforce policies that can prevent future damage to the environment and repair damage already done.

Environment Canada (officially the Department of the Environment) was created in 1971 through the combination of various existing elements of the Canadian federal government, including the Meteorological Service (established in 1871) and the Wildlife Service (established in 1947). The first five services established by the new department were the Atmospheric Environment Service, the Environmental Protection Service, the Fisheries Service, the Water Management Service, and the Land, Forest, and Wildlife Service. In 1979, organizational changes were made, and the Fisheries Service left Environment Canada to form the Department of Fisheries and Oceans.

Environment Canada's stated mandate includes the following elements: preservation and enhancement of the quality of the natural environment, including water, air, soil, flora, and fauna; conservation of Canada's renewable resources; conservation and protection of Canada's water resources; the forecasting of weather and environmental changes; enforcement of rules relating to boundary waters; and coordination of environmental policies and programs for the Canadian federal government. The various services and programs of Environment Canada are concerned with protecting, conserving, and enhancing the environment by shaping how Canadians think about the environment, developing and supporting partnerships, and establishing economic incentives for industries and individuals to make sound environmental decisions.

The department uses scientific research and technologies to track and manage wildlife populations, improve understanding of ecosystems and support the recovery of degraded ecosystems, and assess environmental risk. The department also supports policy and legislative action aimed at promoting environmental health and sustainable practices. It is a participant in several United Nations organizations, including the United Nations Environment Programme, the World Meteorological Organization, and the Commission on Sustainable Development, and is involved in joint efforts with international organizations such as the Arctic Council and the Inter-American Institute for Global Change. In addition, the department works with industries, businesses, farmers, municipalities, customs officials, hunters, the U.S. Environmental Protection Agency, and the Royal Canadian Mounted Police to enforce legislation related to areas of environmental concern, including the import and export of harmful substances, the protection of migratory birds and endangered species, and the protection and trade of both domestic and internationally shared waters.

Wendy C. Hamblet

FURTHER READING

Biggs, David, et al. *Life in 2030: Exploring a Sustainable Future for Canada.* Vancouver: University of British Columbia Press, 1996.

Boyd, Susan C., Dorothy E. Chunn, and Robert Menzies, eds. *Toxic Criminology: Environment, Law, and the State in Canada.* Halifax, N.S.: Fernwood, 2002.

Fafard, Patrick C., and Kathryn Harrison, eds. *Managing the Environmental Union: Intergovernmental Relations and Environment Policy in Canada.* Kingston, Ont.: School of Policy Studies, Queen's University, 2000.

Holland, Kenneth M., F. L. Morton, and Brian Galligan, eds. *Federalism and the Environment: Environmental Policymaking in Australia, Canada, and the United States.* Westport, Conn.: Greenwood Press, 1996.

Environmental Protection Agency

CATEGORIES: Organizations and agencies; human health and the environment; atmosphere and air pollution

IDENTIFICATION: U.S. government agency responsible for enforcing many federal environmental laws

DATE: Established on December 2, 1970

SIGNIFICANCE: The U.S. Environmental Protection Agency administers federal laws that protect natural resources such as air, water, and land. Among its many duties, the agency enforces regulations regarding air and water pollutants, oversees programs that promote energy efficiency and conservation, and participates in the cleanup of sites where toxic materials have polluted the natural environment.

The U.S. Environmental Protection Agency (EPA) is responsible for protecting the public health and ensuring a clean environment by safeguarding natural resources, controlling air and water pollution, and regulating the disposal of solid waste in the United States. The agency carries out its mission through its rule-making and enforcement authority granted by the U.S. Congress. The EPA also conducts scientific research, provides environmental education to the public and to private companies, and utilizes the best available scientific information in its quest to reduce environmental risk. States and tribal nations throughout the United States follow the national standards set by the EPA in enforcing their own environmental regulations. The EPA provides grants to states, nonprofit entities, and academic institutions to carry out environmental and human public health research, often related to the cleanup of toxic waste sites. The EPA also works with other nations to protect the global environment.

HISTORY

After World War II the growth of industrialization in the United States led to serious air and water pollution and environmental deterioration, which in turn spurred a movement that demanded the adoption of federal laws to protect the public health and clean up the environment. In 1969, President Richard Nixon created a White House committee to consider the existing environmental laws and enforcement agencies in the United States. In addition, Congress passed the National Environmental Policy Act of 1969, which was signed into law on January 1, 1970.

A public policy of achieving harmony between humankind and the environment by assessing the environmental impacts of various federal projects was the impetus behind the National Environmental Policy Act and eventually the establishment of the EPA. The president's committee recommended the creation of an independent environmental agency that would not be influenced by the goals and mandates of other agencies for the purpose of enforcing environmental laws. The Environmental Protection Agency became a reality when Congress consolidated the duties of several federal agencies into one entity in December, 1970. William D. Ruckelshaus became the agency's first administrator.

The EPA was established for the purpose of enforcing many of the environmental laws adopted and amended by the federal government during the

U.S. Environmental Protection Agency

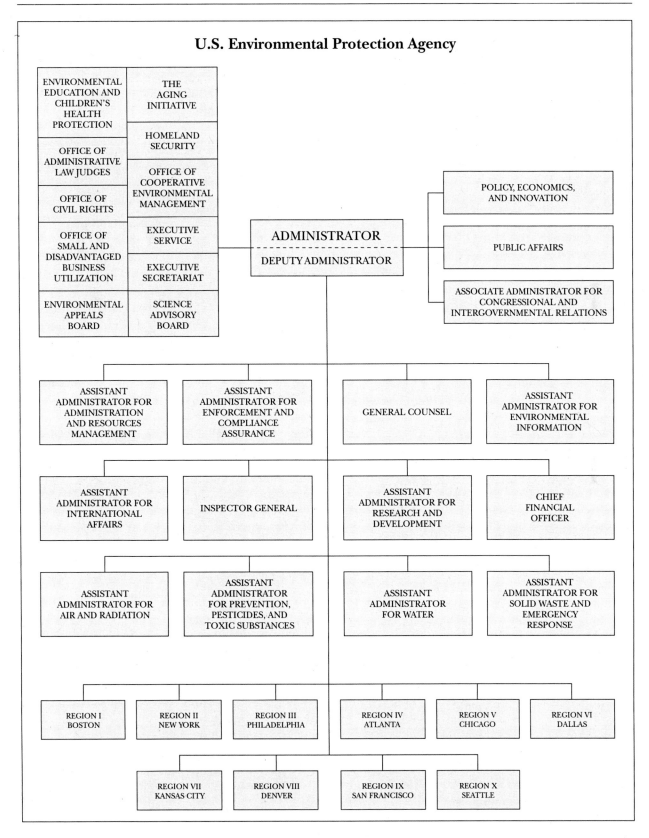

1970's and 1980's as the result of public pressure to clean up the environment. These early laws included the 1970 Clean Air Act amendments, which authorized the EPA to adopt vehicular controls to reduce emissions, set national air-quality standards and attainment goals, and regulate point source air emissions through a permitting and enforcement process. In 1972 the EPA worked in tandem with the U.S. Army Corps of Engineers to set standards for water quality and to regulate discharges into national water resources under the Clean Water Act.

The EPA was named as the primary agency for enforcement of the Federal Insecticide, Fungicide, and Rodenticide Act of 1947, including the act's 1972 and later amendments, which resulted in the ban of the toxic pesticide dichloro-diphenyl-trichloroethane (DDT) in the U.S. In addition, the EPA was made responsible for regulating the manufacture, distribution, import, and processing of specific toxic substances through the Toxic Substances Control Act of 1976. The EPA, however, was not given authority over all environmental laws; the U.S. Fish and Wildlife Service remains responsible for enforcement of the Endangered Species Act, and nuclear wastes are regulated by the Department of Energy.

RCRA AND SUPERFUND

Before the adoption of federal environmental laws in the 1970's, the dumping of toxic materials in the United States, mostly illegal, took place with little government control. When the degradation of natural resources became a major concern, the federal government realized that it needed to step in and help to prevent the contamination of the environment with hazardous substances and to clean up old, abandoned toxic waste sites. In 1976 Congress passed the Resource Conservation and Recovery Act (RCRA) to prohibit future dumping of toxic and hazardous substances and granted the EPA authority for legal management of the disposal of such wastes "from cradle to grave." Under the act, the EPA is re-

---

Federal-Level Environmental Protection

On July 9, 1970, U.S. president Richard M. Nixon delivered the following message to Congress about establishing the Environmental Protection Agency and the National Oceanic and Atmospheric Administration:

To the Congress of the United States:

As concern with the condition of our physical environment has intensified, it has become increasingly clear that we need to know more about the total environment—land, water, and air. It also has become increasingly clear that only by reorganizing our Federal efforts can we develop that knowledge, and effectively ensure the protection, development and enhancement of the total environment itself.

The Government's environmentally-related activities have grown up piecemeal over the years. The time has come to organize them rationally and systematically. As a major step in this direction, I am transmitting today two reorganization plans: one to establish an Environmental Protection Agency, and one to establish, with the Department of Commerce, a National Oceanic and Atmospheric Administration. . . .

The Congress, the Administration and the public all share a profound commitment to the rescue of our natural environment, and the preservation of the Earth as a place both habitable by and hospitable to man. With its acceptance of the reorganization plans, the Congress will help us fulfill that commitment.

---

sponsible for regulating the generation, transportation, treatment, storage, and disposal of toxic and hazardous substances. Congress later passed several amendments to RCRA that gave the EPA the power to set standards for nonhazardous solid waste disposal and for the installation and maintenance of underground storage tanks containing hazardous substances such as petroleum products.

By 1980 Congress recognized that contaminated toxic waste sites throughout the United States had become a serious threat to public health and enacted the Comprehensive Environmental Response, Compensation, and Liability Act. The act, known as Superfund, provides for retroactive liability for those deemed to be the parties responsible for the hazardous waste dumping, usually the property owners, even if the dumping took place before passage of the law in 1980. In addition, the law established a trust fund through a tax on the petrochemical industry to cover costs of cleanup not covered by the responsible parties. Superfund provides for short-term toxic waste removal from the most dangerous hazardous waste sites in the United States, which are listed by the EPA on the agency's National Priorities List. In addition, the EPA often employs long-term remedial actions to reduce public health dangers posed by the continuing release of buried hazardous substances at some of the highest-priority sites. In 1986 Congress passed the Superfund Amendments and Reauthorization Act (SARA) to clarify liability issues. Many U.S. states followed suit and adopted their own environmental dumping, enforcement, and cleanup laws.

CHALLENGES AND FUTURE OPPORTUNITIES

Since its establishment, the EPA has demanded compliance with federal environmental laws from private businesses, from states, and from individual cities, such as Cleveland, Ohio; Detroit, Michigan; Los Angeles, California; and Atlanta, Georgia. The EPA has met its enforcement challenges by adopting and imposing strict regulations and often seeking assistance from the courts to obtain compliance. Moreover, the EPA has been in the forefront of cleanup after natural and human-caused environmental disasters, including those related to the hazardous wastes buried under the Love Canal residential development in Niagara Falls, New York; the Three Mile Island nuclear plant core meltdown near Harrisburg, Pennsylvania; the *Exxon Valdez* oil spill in Alaska; the destruction of the World Trade Center towers by terrorists in New York City on September 11, 2001; and the 2010 BP *Deepwater Horizon* oil spill in the Gulf of Mexico.

In addition to its enforcement and cleanup functions, the EPA works in many areas to encourage the protection of the environment. Aside from its Energy Star program, which promotes energy efficiency in household appliances and other consumer products, the EPA has undertaken initiatives concerned with the reduction of greenhouse gases and the adoption of air-quality visibility rules. The agency has also conducted risk and peer-review assessments to ensure the safety of high-concern chemicals found in products and in the environment, developed new strategies to protect the quality of public drinking-water supplies, and supported the revitalization and reuse of abandoned and contaminated inner-city brownfields.

The EPA must carry out its responsibilities of protecting the environment, natural resources, and public health while attempting to avoid negative impacts on economic growth, industrial development, energy production, agriculture, transportation, and international trade—a balance that at times seems impossible to achieve. In its efforts to keep that balance, the EPA has partnered with both public and private companies and institutions to find new and innovative approaches to environmental protection that can satisfy competing goals.

Carol A. Rolf

FURTHER READING

Andrews, Richard N. L. *Managing the Environment, Managing Ourselves: A History of American Environmental Policy.* 2d ed. New Haven, Conn.: Yale University Press, 2006.

Carson, Rachel. *Silent Spring.* 40th anniversary ed. Boston: Houghton Mifflin, 2002.

Collin, Robert W. *The Environmental Protection Agency: Cleaning Up America's Act.* Westport, Conn.: Greenwood Press, 2006.

Landy, Marc K., Marc J. Roberts, and Stephen R. Thomas. *The Environmental Protection Agency: Asking the Wrong Questions—From Nixon to Clinton.* Expanded ed. New York: Oxford University Press, 1994.

McBrewster, John, Frederic P. Miller, and Agnes F. Vandome, eds. *United States Environmental Protection Agency: Federal Government of the United States, National Environment, Environmental Policy of the United States, Energy Star, WaterSense, Safe Drinking Water Act.* Phoenix, Ariz.: Alphascript, 2009.

Scheberle, Denise. *Federalism and Environmental Policy: Trust and the Politics of Implementation.* 2d ed. Washington, D.C.: Georgetown University Press, 2004.

Eutrophication

CATEGORY: Water and water pollution

DEFINITION: Overenrichment of a water body with nutrients

SIGNIFICANCE: The process of eutrophication, in which a body of water receives an excessive amount of nutrients that accelerates aquatic plant growth, leads to a reduction in the oxygen in the water that fish need to survive. Continued enrichment can lead to excessive algal growth, which in turn impairs fisheries, limits recreational uses of the water, and can create major problems for water-supply purveyors.

From a geologic perspective, lakes are relatively temporary features of a landscape. For example, the Great Lakes were formed over the last two million years by four or more major advances of huge ice sheets. Only relatively recently (about twelve thousand years ago) did these lakes develop into their current shapes.

Most lakes go through a series of trophic (nutrition-related) states that can take thousands of years before the lake basins eventually fill in with sediment. Oligotrophy is the first trophic stage; it is characterized by clear water, low plant productivity because of limited nutrient inputs, and high levels of dissolved oxygen throughout the water column. Crater Lake in Oregon is a good example of an oligotrophic lake. The next stage is mesotrophy, which has moderately clear water and moderate plant productivity and lower levels of oxygen in the hypolimnion, which is the lowest level in a lake. In the third stage, eutrophy, excess nutrients are present, transparency is reduced, algal scums start to appear, and oxygen (which fish need) is not present in the summer in the hypolimnion. Hypereutrophy is the final stage; in this stage algal scums dominate in the summer, few macrophytes (plants that can be seen without magnification) exist, and the hypolimnion is devoid of oxygen.

Anthropogenic (human-caused) changes in lakes result from excessive inputs of sediment, fertilizers (such as nitrates and phosphates), pesticides from agricultural practices, runoff from urban sewage, and industrial effluents such as lead and mercury. The inevitable result is accelerated or cultural eutrophication, which can occur in decades as compared to the thousands of years seen under natural conditions.

Reservoirs that are used for water-supply purposes are particularly sensitive to algal blooms. If sufficient light and warmth are present, which is common in the high sun season, thermal stratification occurs, and the lower zone of the reservoir (where the hypolimnion is located) becomes anaerobic. This lack of oxygen enables algal nutrients, such as silica, phosphorus, and ammonia, to come from bottom sediments, which in turn increases more algal growth, and the cycle continues. The reservoir surface becomes covered with algae, which then requires either physical removal or large applications of copper sulfate, which in itself can cause problems.

Eutrophication can occur in streams and marine environments as well as in lakes and reservoirs. Coastal waters, bays or estuaries that are partially enclosed, and shallow seas provide excellent opportunities for unbridled nutrient enrichment. For example, excess nutrients emanating from the extensive agricultural area in the midwestern United States flow down the Mississippi and Missouri rivers to where the rivers empty into the Gulf of Mexico. As a result, a hypoxic (depleted of oxygen) area known as a dead zone appears on a fairly regular basis off the mouth of the Mississippi River in the gulf. Although it varies in size, this dead zone has been known to cover an area of approximately 21,000 square kilometers (8,000 square miles), which is larger than the entire state of Massachusetts.

Robert M. Hordon

FURTHER READING
Cech, Thomas V. *Principles of Water Resources: History, Development, Management, and Policy.* 3d ed. New York: John Wiley & Sons, 2010.
Cunningham, William P., and Mary Ann Cunningham. *Principles of Environmental Science: Inquiry and Applications.* 4th ed. New York: McGraw-Hill, 2008.
Gray, N. F. *Drinking Water Quality: Problems and Solutions.* 2d ed. New York: Cambridge University Press, 2008.
Laws, Edward A. "Cultural Eutrophication: Case Studies." In *Aquatic Pollution: An Introductory Text.* 3d ed. New York: John Wiley & Sons, 2000.
North American Lake Management Society and Terrene Institute. *Managing Lakes and Reservoirs.* Madison, Wisc.: Author, 2001.

Experimental Lakes Area

CATEGORY: Water and water pollution
IDENTIFICATION: Research facility that studies environmental problems, especially acidification, in lakes in eastern Canada
DATE: Established in 1968
SIGNIFICANCE: The research conducted at the Experimental Lakes Area sheds light on the causes of water pollution and suggests ways of maintaining the health of freshwater lakes.

Increasing acidification of the water in lakes in Ontario and Nova Scotia led to significant declines of fish populations in those lakes during the 1960's through the 1980's. As a result, Canadian environmentalist David Schindler founded the Experimental Lakes Area (ELA) research facility in 1968 in order to investigate acidification and other environmental problems that were affecting the lakes of eastern

Canada. The goals of the ELA are fourfold: to develop better understanding of global threats to the environment through knowledge gained from ecosystem, experimental, and scientific research; to monitor and demonstrate the impacts of human activities on watersheds and lakes; to develop appropriate responsibility for the preservation, restoration, and enhancement of ecosystems; and to promote environmental protection and conservation for ecosystems through education. The ELA includes fifty-eight small lakes and their drainage basins, plus three additional stream segments.

The ELA is operated by the Central and Arctic Region of the Canadian Department of Fisheries and Oceans from its Freshwater Institute in Winnipeg. Because the ELA research facility is located in a sparsely inhabited region of southern Ontario, it is relatively unaffected by external human influences and industrial activities. As such, it serves as a natural laboratory for the study of physical, chemical, and biological processes and interactions operating on an ecosystem over a large area and a multiyear time scale.

With renewed operating support in the late 1990's, the ELA took on several new experimental studies in addition to whole-lake acidification experiments and eutrophication recovery studies. For example, one ELA ecosystem study investigated additions of trace amounts of mercury to one of the ELA lakes. It is generally believed that high concentrations of methylmercury, the most toxic form of mercury, in fish in remote lakes is caused by elevated inputs of atmospheric inorganic mercury deposited directly into lakes and indirectly through their watersheds. The ELA has provided researchers with the opportunity to investigate this hypothesis as well as an alternative that suggests that geologic mercury is the most important source of mercury to remote lakes; such mercury originates from the weathering of mineral deposits in lake basins.

ELA scientists have also examined the effects of climate change, dissolved organic carbon, and ultraviolet radiation on lakes. One study investigated the effects of experimentally deepening the mixed layer of a lake, thereby exposing more of the lake water and organisms to surface radiation and simulating the effects observed in natural ELA lakes during two decades of warming between 1970 and 1990. Another area of research has involved reducing the natural color of an ELA lake to investigate the effects of increased ultraviolet radiation on lake life-forms. Other projects have included studies of the effects of persistent toxic substances—such as cadmium and hydrocarbons—in lakes, contributions of forest materials to lake nutrient inputs, and the alteration of food-chain processes caused by human intervention.

Alvin K. Benson

Experimental Lakes Area

FURTHER READING

Laws, Edward A. *Aquatic Pollution: An Introductory Text.* 3d ed. New York: John Wiley & Sons, 2000.

O'Sullivan, P. E., and Colin S. Reynolds, eds. *The Lakes Handbook.* 2 vols. Malden, Mass.: Blackwell, 2004-2005.

Resetarits, William J., Jr., and Joseph Bernardo, eds. *Experimental Ecology: Issues and Perspectives.* New York: Oxford University Press, 1998.

Externalities

CATEGORY: Atmosphere and air pollution
DEFINITION: Effects that are imposed on third parties who were not voluntarily involved in the activity or transaction creating them
SIGNIFICANCE: Parties who voluntarily engage in market transactions expect to benefit from them, but if a transaction imposes costs on unwilling third parties, the transaction might be unfair to those parties and might create a net loss for society.

When one resident of an apartment building has a party, his neighbors may be bothered by the noise. If an office building is built next to a resort hotel, shading the latter's swimming pool, the hotel may lose much of its business. If a pig farm is close to a housing development, the noise, smells, and flies that go along with the farming operation may reduce the property value of the houses. These are examples of externalities.

Consider a manufacturer of automobiles, who must pay for the land, equipment, materials, labor, utilities, advertising, and myriad other costs that are necessary for the production process. Pollution is also a cost that results from the manufacturing process. Suppose the manufacturer is able to avoid paying the cost of disposing of the pollutants by dumping them into the air or water near the plant, so that the costs are instead borne by the surrounding community or downstream landowners. The manufacturer would be externalizing the pollution cost—that is, making someone else pay for it.

A rational manufacturer will maximize profit by increasing the level of production so long as each unit can be sold for more than its cost. Suppose an automaker calculates that producing one additional car will add $20,000 to costs, but the car can be sold for $20,200. It makes sense to make that additional car. The manufacturer should, in fact, increase production until it is no longer possible to make a profit by making additional units. However, what if the external cost caused by pollution amounts to $500 of harm to the environment for each unit produced? If the manufacturer can externalize that cost by allowing others to absorb it, the calculation of the profit-maximizing number of units is not affected. The social cost (manufacturing cost plus harm caused by pollution) for the marginal units actually exceeds the value of the automobile, as measured by its purchase price. The manufacturer thus has incentive to produce more than the socially optimal amount of pollution and more than the optimal number of automobiles.

If forced to "internalize" the pollution cost—that is, to pay for it—the manufacturer would reduce the amount of pollution and the number of units produced to the socially optimal level. One way in which governments force manufacturers to internalize pollution costs is by compelling specific pollution controls. For example, governments may mandate cleaner production processes or the safe disposal of liquid effluents. Another approach governments take is to impose taxes on effluents equal to the amount of harm the pollution causes. If manufacturers can find ways to reduce the pollution at costs lower than the taxes, they will do so.

In many externality cases it is not obvious who should absorb the costs. In the case of the pig farm, should the farmer have to compensate the home owners or move the farming operation to another location? Should home owners who knew they were moving in next to a pig farm have the right to complain about the negative environmental impacts of the farm? Courts are commonly asked to resolve such conflicts. They often decide the issue by requiring the party who can solve the problem at lowest cost to do so.

Howard C. Ellis

FURTHER READING

Friedman, David D. *Law's Order: What Economics Has to Do with Law and Why It Matters*. Princeton, N.J.: Princeton University Press, 2001.

Winston, Clifford. *Government Failure Versus Market Failure: Microeconomic Policy Research and Government Performance*. Washington, D.C.: Brookings Institution Press, 2006.

Exxon Valdez oil spill

CATEGORY: Disasters
THE EVENT: Grounding of the supertanker *Exxon Valdez* in a shallow stretch of Prince William Sound off the coast of Alaska, resulting in the largest oil spill in U.S. history
DATE: March 24, 1989

SIGNIFICANCE: The *Exxon Valdez* spill caused enormous environmental damage to coastal areas in southeastern Alaska and to marine life in Prince William Sound. Populations of both large and small marine mammals, birds, fish, and mollusks were devastated, as was plant life.

Oil spills are common occurrences in U.S. waters. According to a U.S. Coast Guard report, about ten thousand oil spills occur in and around U.S. waters each year, totaling 15 million to 25 million gallons of oil. These oil spills may result from drilling accidents, as was the case with the major spill that took place in Santa Barbara, California, in 1969, or they may be related to problems associated with supertankers such as the *Exxon Valdez*.

The *Exxon Valdez* was a single-hulled supertanker operated by the Exxon Corporation. The ship was 300 meters (987 feet) long and cost about $125 million to build. It was equipped with state-of-the-art instruments for depth sounding, guidance, and navigation. On March 23, 1989, the vessel was loaded with more than ten million barrels, or approximately 420 million gallons, of North Slope crude. The oil had been transported about 1,300 kilometers (800 miles) from Prudhoe Bay near the Arctic Circle to the Port of Valdez in southern Alaska. Shortly after midnight on Friday, March 24, the ship left port and traveled west and southwest down the Valdez fjord to the vicinity of Bligh Island in Prince William Sound, where it ran aground on Bligh Reef.

At the time the ship left port, conditions for sailing were ideal: light winds, calm seas, and good visibility. However, because of miscalculations by the officers in charge, the ship hit a chain of rocks about 4 kilometers (2.5 miles) west of Bligh Island. The rocks tore a gash in the tanker hull and allowed an estimated 10 million to 11 million gallons of crude oil to escape before noon. The oil spread across 4,600 square kilometers (1,776 square miles) of water in Prince William Sound and the Gulf of Alaska. Approximately 5,100 kilometers (3,169 miles) of shoreline received some oiling. The oiled areas included a number of fishing villages, a national forest, state and national parks, national wildlife refuges, critical habitat areas, and a state game sanctuary.

The damage to coastal areas in southeastern Alaska and to marine life in Prince William Sound was enormous. The spill affected the livelihoods of villagers along the west side of the sound, the Alaska and Kenai peninsulas, the Kodiak Archipelago, and part of Cook Inlet. Populations of both large and small marine mammals, birds, fish, and mollusks were devastated, as was plant life. Thousands of dolphins, sea lions, sea otters, and harbor seals died or were otherwise adversely affected by the fouling of their environment. An estimated 250,000 to 300,000 seabirds were also killed by the oil spill. These included harlequin ducks, pigeon quillemotes, common murres, and marbled murrelets. A significant number of bald eagles (more than one hundred), Canadian geese, and cormorants also perished. Economically important fish, such as pink and sockeye salmon and Pacific herring, as well as a large number of small forage fish (capelin, pollock, sandlance, and smelt), died as a result of the spill. Shellfish, such as clams, crabs, oysters, and shrimp, were also killed or threatened.

According to G. Tyler Miller, Jr., and Scott Spoolman, writing in *Environmental Science* (2010), "Many forms of marine life recover from exposure to large amounts of crude oil within about 3 years." For the marine life in Prince William Sound, this proved to be generally true; an exception was the area's population of harbor seals, which did not recover and stabilize until the mid-1990's.

RECOVERY EFFORTS

Immediately after the spill, various techniques were used to consume or disperse the oil slick and the oil coating surrounding beaches. Attempts to ignite the oil met with limited success because they occurred after most of the lighter, more volatile components of the oil had evaporated, leaving behind emulsified, pancakelike layers of crude oil. Boat skimmers, which are designed to confine and collect oil with floating booms, recovered less than 5 percent of the oil. Such booms are most effective when wave height is below 1 meter (3.28 feet). The application of chemical dispersants to the oil slick also was not effective. In cold water, the mousselike layers of oil residue are almost impossible to break up chemically.

The techniques used to wash beach rocks ranged from hand-applied cold water to steam cleaning. The latter was effective in some areas. Exxon workers substantially reduced the oil coating on beach rocks at some islands in the northern part of Prince William Sound. This method may have done more harm than good, however, because most of the small, beneficial organisms along the beach and in the tidal zone were killed by the hot waters. Meanwhile, tons of oiled gravel underlying mussel beds were removed from Prince William Sound and the Kenai Peninsula by recovery team workers and local residents. The oiled gravel was replaced with clean sediment.

Perhaps the most effective technique used to clean the oil was bioremediation. Workers sprayed a fertilizer solution along miles of the cobbled beaches in Prince William Sound in an effort to promote the growth of naturally occurring, oil-eating microbes. Such microorganisms consist primarily of spiral-type bacteria that can rapidly develop under ideal conditions. Most of these encapsulated cells reproduce asexually by splitting in half, a process known as fission. These oil-metabolizing bacteria can double their number in less than twenty-four hours.

As a result of the *Exxon Valdez* spill, both criminal charges and civil damage claims were filed against Exxon by the state of Alaska and the United States. In the civil settlement, Exxon was required to pay $900 million over a ten-year period. A state-federal trustee council consisting of six members was designated to administer the settlement and coordinate studies of the spill's effects on wildlife and the environment. In an agreement concerning the criminal charges, Exxon was originally required to pay a fine of $250 million. However, because of Exxon's cooperation with governmental agencies during the cleanup and its quick payment of most private claims, $125 million of the fine was forgiven.

Donald F. Reaser

FURTHER READING

Fingas, Merv. *The Basics of Oil Spill Cleanup.* 2d ed. Boca Raton, Fla.: CRC Press, 2001.

Keeble, John. *Out of the Channel: The Exxon Valdez Oil Spill in Prince William Sound.* 2d ed. Cheney: Eastern Washington University Press, 1999.

Kvenvolden, Keith, et al. "Ubiquitous Tar Balls with a California-Source Signature on the Shorelines of Prince William Sound, Alaska." *Environmental Science and Technology* 29 (October, 1995): 2684-2694.

Loughlin, Thomas R., ed. *Marine Mammals and the Exxon Valdez.* San Diego, Calif.: Academic Press, 1994.

Miller, G. Tyler, Jr., and Scott Spoolman. *Environmental Science: Problems, Concepts, and Solutions.* 13th ed. Belmont, Calif.: Brooks/Cole, 2010.

Ornitz, Barbara E., and Michael A. Champ. *Oil Spills First Principles: Prevention and Best Response.* New York: Elsevier, 2002.

Ott, Riki. *Not One Drop: Betrayal and Courage in the Wake of the Exxon Valdez Oil Spill.* White River Junction, Vt.: Chelsea Green, 2008.

Flood Control Act

CATEGORIES: Treaties, laws, and court cases; resources and resource management

THE LAW: U.S. federal law designed to direct and coordinate significant water development projects in the Missouri River basin

DATE: Enacted on December 22, 1944

SIGNIFICANCE: To help control chronic flooding along the Missouri River and to help irrigate the Great Plains, the Flood Control Act of 1944 provided a sweeping vision for reconceiving the river basin and a practical apparatus for the federal construction of dams and levees to achieve that reconstruction.

Although the Dust Bowl of the southern plains received far more national attention during the economic catastrophe of the 1930's, chronic flooding along the Missouri River was responsible for disastrous property losses in the same period (the river drains more than one-sixth of the continental United States). Navigation on the river was unreliable, and the unpredictable depth of the river (at different points it was a meandering stream, at others a broad and swift river) meant that it generated little hydropower. Further, despite its considerable length (more than 4,000 kilometers, or 2,500 miles), the river was largely neglected as an irrigation source for the arid northern plains states.

The Flood Control Act of 1944, passed in the second session of the Seventy-eighth Congress, was breathtaking in its scope even among the numerous large-scale public works projects authorized by Franklin D. Roosevelt's presidential administration. Never had river management on such a scale been undertaken by the federal government. The act envisioned nothing less than the redesign of the Missouri River; it aimed to develop the river's considerable commercial potential for hydroelectric energy and for the agriculture industry while at the same time protecting both the river itself and its wildlife and fish resources. It was known as the Pick-Sloan Act, named for two men largely responsible for proposing the enormous reach of the legislation: General Lewis Pick, who directed the U.S. Army Corps of Engineers, and William Glenn Sloan, who served in the Department of the Interior.

The Flood Control Act authorized the Army Corps of Engineers, in consultation with specific cabinet officers and the governors of affected states, to direct water development projects along the broad reach of the Missouri: irrigation projects through the Department of the Interior, flood-control projects with direct impacts on navigation through the Department of the Army, and projects designed to protect against soil erosion and river sedimentation through the Department of Agriculture. In addition, the Corps of Engineers would develop and maintain public parks and recreational facilities along the river.

The most immediate impacts of the act were realized in dozens of dams (and modifications of existing dams), as well as in miles of levees erected along the main stem of the Missouri. Those dams, in turn, created more than fifty lakes that continue to be used as recreational facilities (for boating, fishing, and swimming) as well as reservoirs for generating hydroelectric power. As public works legislation, the Flood Control Act was responsible for creating thousands of jobs, particularly among veterans returning from World War II. The act in turn authorized the Pick-Sloan Missouri River Basin Program to coordinate river projects.

Although the water-control projects authorized by the act provided long-term control of flooding in the Missouri basin as well as improved navigation on the river, the legislation also raised significant questions concerning the reach of the federal government into local development. Thousands of Native Americans were displaced from their homes by the projects, and hundreds of thousands of hectares of tribal lands were flooded, most notably those of the Lakota and Dakota tribes.

Joseph Dewey

FURTHER READING

Andrews, Richard N. L. *Managing the Environment, Managing Ourselves: A History of American Environmental Policy.* 2d ed. New Haven, Conn.: Yale University Press, 2006.

O'Neill, Karen M. *Rivers by Design: State Power and the Origins of U.S. Flood Control.* Durham, N.C.: Duke University Press, 2006.

Schneiders, Robert Kelley. *Unruly River: Two Centuries of Change Along the Missouri.* Lawrence: University Press of Kansas, 1999.

Thorson, John E. *River of Promise, River of Peril: The Politics of Managing the Missouri River.* Lawrence: University Press of Kansas, 1994.

Floodplains

CATEGORY: Land and land use
DEFINITION: Low-lying areas adjacent to river channels that become partially or completely covered with water when the rivers overflow their banks
SIGNIFICANCE: Floodplains occupy an important part of landforms around rivers covering large areas, especially within humid and tropical climatic settings. They also house riparian wetlands, acting as buffers to flooding. Floodplains provide habitat for many land and aquatic life-forms.

Floodplains filter water and provide silt and nutrients that make them fertile places. Perhaps the most famous examples are the fertile floodplains of Egypt's Nile Valley region, which have supported civilizations for several millennia. Floodplains also provide fresh water and backwaters to wetlands, and they also dilute salts, thereby improving the health of the habitat for fish, bird, and plant populations.

Floodplains are good for food production such as rice cultivation. Farmers graze their livestock on the grasslands in floodplains, and fresh fruits and cash crops are grown in floodplains, which are often very fertile and easy to cultivate. In tropical settings, timber is harvested on floodplains, and nontimber forest resources such as animals and plants are used for foods and medicines as well as construction materials.

TYPES AND ECOLOGY

Riverine flooding can cover vast areas, many of which are among the most diverse biologically productive ecosystems on earth. Three types of floodplains are identified based on temperature: temperate stochastic, temperate seasonal, and tropical seasonal. Within floodplains, algae appear to provide the most important source of primary production within the grazer web. The flow regime is very important in determining the physical habitat for biotic composition. The shape, size, and the formation of features such as deltas, riffles, runs, pools, and backwaters that tend to shift are linked to the flow regimes of rivers. Certain aquatic life-forms have their early life stages in floodplains, and the types of fauna and flora within floodplains can be as diverse as in any other ecosystems. Owing to the highly dynamic nature of floodplain terrains, varied species may be seen on the same floodplains over the course of years.

Floodplains contain several kinds of geomorphologic features, including oxbow lakes, point bars, areas of dead water, and braided channels. Swamps, among other types of riparian wetlands, can also be found in floodplains. Floodplains can be classified into different types depending on their morphology. Several methods of classification are used, but the simplest and most common is based on the fluvial styles: gravel-dominated, sand-dominated with high sinuosity, and sand-dominated with low sinuosity.

ENVIRONMENTAL THREATS

As global warming increases, some floodplains may see more flooding, which will greatly affect local populations because of land subsidence and increases in water level. For example, Bangkok, the capital of Thailand, is sinking at a rate of 2 to 5 centimeters (0.79 to 1.97 inches) per year because of sediment

compression and compaction owing to increased human activities. The elevation of New Orleans, Louisiana, is also dropping at a rate of about 5 centimeters per year.

Urbanization affects the hydrology of floodplains, either by reducing water through withdrawal or by adding to it through importation. It also alters the water chemistry by introducing chemicals, sediments, and other form of pollutants, including increases in temperature, all of which affect the biotic richness of floodplains. The nutrients brought into play through flood activities can also be altered through changes in land-use patterns. Changes within a drainage basin (watershed) affect the production and supply of organic materials in floodplains. High levels of biodiversity can provide stability to floodplain ecosystems and help protect them from human-caused impairments.

The expansion of urban areas into floodplains and wetlands alters the onset, duration, distribution, speed, quantity, and quality of floodwaters. Among the human activities that lead to increases in flooding are deforestation and the removal of stabilizing vegetation along riverbanks. Human-built structures along or near rivers affect the flow direction, resulting in deflection of the water, or reduce storage. Storm drains, housing developments, and pavements increase the rate of rainfall runoff to rivers, thereby increasing the rate of flooding. The straightening of river channels increases the rate at which water is transported. Another human activity that affects floodplains is the dumping of sediment loads from farms or construction sites into rivers, which decreases channel depth and increases the area covered by floodwaters. With increasing changes in land use, a watershed approach to floodplain management becomes imperative.

Impairment of floodplain waters can have adverse effects on coastal ecosystems, as these waters end up in lakes or oceans. The quality of the water in rivers has a great impact on the quality of the water in nearby coastal areas; the waters of the Amazon, for example, can be traced sev-

---

Rivers

Roughly 70 percent of Earth's surface is covered with water. About 97 percent of this water is salt water in oceans, and 2 percent is fresh water in glaciers and groundwater. Only 1 percent is fresh water in rivers, lakes, and water vapor. Fresh water is recycled again and again by evaporation and condensation in a hydrologic cycle that creates and maintains rivers and lakes.

When water vapor condenses and falls as rain, it seeps into the ground, filling pores in soil and rocks. After all pores fill, excess water pools on the surface, flowing downhill due to gravity. Then it becomes streams that coalesce into rivers. Each river is a large body of water, regenerated over and over by the hydrologic cycle, flowing through low ground areas that become channels (river courses) and valleys. Because Earth's oceans are lower than the land, rivers flow down into them.

A river and the composition of its banks change as movement toward the ocean both creates and destroys land. A river's course has upper, middle, and lower parts. The upper course, near the river's source, flows downhill and carves deep valleys, as well as waterfalls wherever tough rock resists erosion. Next, the river flows onto plains in its middle course, and the gently sloping land slows it, leading to sideways erosion and snakelike bends. The last part of a river, its lower course, near entry to an ocean, is often an estuary. Here, the slow flow of the river across virtually flat land causes settling of sediment, forming mud flats and sandbanks.

eral miles into the Atlantic Ocean. Contaminants carried in such waters ultimately affect large biological populations.

Solomon A. Isiorho

FURTHER READING

Bridge, John S. *Rivers and Floodplains: Forms, Processes, and Sedimentary Record.* Malden, Mass.: Blackwell, 2003.

Millius, Susan. "Losing Life's Variety." *Science News*, March 13, 2010, 20-25.

Richards, Keith, James Brasington, and Francine Hughes. "Geomorphic Dynamics of Floodplains: Ecological Implications and a Potential Modelling Strategy." *Freshwater Biology* 47, no. 4 (2002): 559-579.

Tockner, Klement, and Jack A. Stanford. "Riverine Flood Plains: Present State and Future Trends." *Environmental Conservation* 29, no. 3 (2002): 308-330.

Floods

CATEGORY: Weather and climate

DEFINITION: High water flows that usually emanate from rivers, streams, or drainage ditches whose waters overtop their normal confines and spill out over lands that are normally dry

SIGNIFICANCE: Floods are among the most common and widespread natural disasters in terms of human hardship and economic loss. Almost all countries of the world are subject to annual flooding of different magnitudes.

Floods are primarily caused by heavy rainfall. Several hydraulic factors exacerbate the problem of discharging the enormous volume of water that collects in catchment areas. These factors include very low gradient of a river, the loss of channel capacity because of siltation, inadequate dredging of riverbeds, and the disruption of existing drainage systems by road construction without adequate culverts and by the building of unplanned houses. Unplanned urbanization, rapid population growth, and conversion of agricultural lands to other uses also contribute to flooding. Other causes of floods include melting of snow, the greenhouse effect and global warming, tides, elevated sea levels, storm surges, and tsunamis.

Floods account for one-third of all global disasters involving geophysical hazards. Occurrences of severe floods in human-occupied regions often involve loss of human life and property along with disruption of ongoing activities in affected rural and urban communities. In remote, unpopulated regions, natural floodplains can be significantly changed though not damaged by floods.

In the United States, floods represent the most costly extreme natural events. Since 1900 floods have been responsible for the deaths of more than ten thousand persons in the United States, and the economic consequences of floods are estimated to be in the billions of dollars per year. Despite the implementation of numerous flood mitigation measures to reduce the adverse impacts of these events, U.S. flood fatalities and losses have consistently increased over time.

TYPES OF FLOODS

Floods are classified into three major types based on their origins: river floods, flash floods, and coastal floods. River floods occur when runoff from heavy or prolonged rainfall or melting of mountain snow causes rivers to rise high enough to overflow their banks or levees and spread water to floodplain zones. The extent of influence of such floods varies with distance from the river and depends on the type and amount of sediment load the river carries. In cold regions where there is a lot of accumulation of snow, river flooding often occurs as a result of snow melting or when ice or floating debris causes a jam. Such debris flows tend to occur primarily in the summer. Floods also sometimes occur when the water table rises above ground level; such flooding often leads to overspill flooding of rivers and streams.

Flash floods, which are localized extreme events, occur suddenly under a broad range of climatological and geographical conditions. They can occur within a few minutes or hours and may involve excessive rapid rainfall, a dam failure, a sudden release of water that had been held by an ice jam, slow-moving thunderstorms, or heavy rains such as those from hurricanes or tropical storms. Flash floods normally occur when the ground has become completely saturated with water, making further absorption impossible. The resultant overflow causes flooding. Flash floods can be very violent; the heavy, rapid flows of water can move boulders, tear out trees, destroy buildings and bridges, and trigger catastrophic mudslides. Flash floods are frequently associated with other events, such as riverine floods on larger streams and mudslides. Areas prone to flash flooding include steep canyons, urbanized areas, and arid and semiarid regions.

Coastal floods are divided into two subtypes. Tidal floods occur twice a day in low-lying areas adjacent to estuaries and tidal waters; the areas affected by tidal flooding vary seasonally. Storm-surge floods are associated with tropical cyclones or hurricanes; flooding occurs when strong offshore winds push water from an ocean onto the land. Such floods are season-specific.

All types of flood events lead to inundations of water that carries solids, either in suspension or in solution. The depth and velocity of the water in such inundations vary. The impacts that floods have, through erosion or deposition of soil and through social and economic losses, depend on a combination of factors, including the quality, depth, and velocity of the water; seasonality and frequency of the flooding; and the type of flooding.

Low-lying plains in close proximity to rivers and coastal areas are commonly considered flood-prone zones. Generally, coastal areas and river valleys have large human populations, and these residents may be particularly vulnerable to damage from flooding. The level of a population's vulnerability to flood risk is often dependent on the level of development of the economy in the country affected. In case of developed countries, the risk of flooding depends on the amount of urban development in flood-prone zones rather than population density. In less developed regions, persons who live in flood-prone areas often have a high risk of exposure to floods.

POSITIVE ASPECTS

Outside the Western world, floods are not always viewed negatively and regarded as natural disasters. The people of Bangladesh, for example, perceive flooding as both a resource and a hazard. In that country, a normal flood (*barsha*) resulting from typical monsoon rainfall is considered a resource. It is beneficial in the sense that it makes the land productive by providing necessary moisture and fresh fertile silt to the soil. Moreover, fish caught during flood season constitute the main source of protein for many. Millions of Bangladeshis depend on fisheries in the floodplains for their livelihood, and the life cycles of some key fish species depend on the species' ability to migrate between the rivers and the seasonal floodplains.

Abnormal flooding (*bonna*), which occurs once every few years and results from excessive rainfall, is regarded by Bangladeshis as an undesirable and damaging phenomenon. It causes widespread damage to standing crops and property and costs animal and human lives. An analysis of crop production in Bangladesh found that despite considerable crop damage from flooding, there can be compensatory increases in rice production in areas not affected by the floods. Moreover, affected areas can experience increases in rice production in the following dry season; these increases can be attributed to the extra moisture resulting from the year of high floods as well as deposits of fertile silt on the floodplains.

STRATEGIES FOR DAMAGE REDUCTION

To reduce the loss of lives and property, people who live in flood-prone areas often undertake a host of measures, known as flood adjustments, at the household level. For example, in Bangladesh farmers resow or replant crops immediately after receding floods. They also sell land or other assets at distress prices to buy food or other necessary items. In the United States, people in flood-prone zones place sandbags along riverbanks and around homes to protect their property from flooding. They also take steps to protect their possessions from flood damage, such as moving important materials from the basement to the first or second floor and relocating electrical circuits and outlets from floor level to waist or ceiling level. Structures that are generally impermeable to water may be modified with watertight barriers or closures at openings to keep out floodwaters. Waterproofing sealants may be applied to walls or floors to reduce permeability.

Other effective measures that are taken to prevent structures from being damaged by floods are known as property relocation, property elevation, and walling. In property relocation, an existing structure is physically moved to land that is unlikely to flood. Property elevation involves the retrofitting of existing buildings in flood-prone areas so that they are raised above the likely flood level. Constructing walls high enough to keep floodwaters out around individual buildings or small clusters of buildings can also be an effective way of keeping flood damage to a minimum.

The measures that communities and governments undertake to modify the hazards associated with flooding include the control of flood flows through reservoir storage, levees, and channel improvement. Dikes, levees, and flood walls are all structures that hold the water off the land and confine it within a main channel of flow. Dikes are the most commonly used method of flood protection around the world. Extensive levee systems tend to raise flood levels because they block off flood channels, decreasing the channels' conveyance of water. Dams are widely used in the United States to minimize the damage caused by floods. Although dams are a good mitigation measure against flooding, they do not necessarily prevent flooding from occurring.

Often local governments adopt regulatory measures aimed at reducing flood damage, such as land-use zoning and building codes. Other flood preparedness and mitigation measures taken by governments include providing flood warnings to potential victims, evacuating people to safer places, and encouraging people to buy flood insurance. Such measures, however, have not been widely and effectively introduced in developing countries that are prone to severe flooding.

Sohini Dutt

FURTHER READING

Few, Roger, and Franziska Matthies, eds. *Flood Hazards and Health: Responding to Present and Future Risks.* Sterling, Va.: Earthscan, 2006.
Miller, G. Tyler, Jr., and Scott Spoolman. "Water Resources." In *Living in the Environment: Principles, Connections, and Solutions.* 16th ed. Belmont, Calif.: Brooks/Cole, 2009.
Smith, Keith, and David N. Petley. "Hydrological Hazards: Floods." In *Environmental Hazards: Assessing Risk and Reducing Disaster.* 5th ed. New York: Routledge, 2009.
Smith, Keith, and Roy Ward. *Floods: Physical Processes and Human Impacts.* New York: John Wiley & Sons, 1998.
Wescoat, James L., Jr., and Gilbert F. White. *Water for Life: Water Management and Environmental Policy.* New York: Cambridge University Press, 2003.

Fluoridation

CATEGORY: Water and water pollution
DEFINITION: The treatment of community water-supply systems with fluoride as a public health measure
SIGNIFICANCE: The issue of whether it is a safe practice for communities to add fluoride to water supplies to prevent tooth decay remains controversial among some environmentalists.

Fluoridation of water supplies was first introduced in the United States in the 1940's as a preventive measure to reduce tooth decay, which was a serious and widespread problem in the early twentieth century. Since that time, many cities have taken the step of adding fluoride to their public water-supply systems, but the merits and drawbacks of fluoridation have long been subjects of debate. Proponents of fluoridation claim that it has dramatically reduced tooth decay in Americans, but opponents of the practice have not been entirely convinced of its effectiveness, and some are concerned about possible health risks that may be associated with fluoridation. The decision to fluoridate drinking water generally rests with local governments and communities.

Fluoride is the water-soluble, ionic form of the element fluorine. It is present naturally in most water supplies at low levels, generally less than 0.2 part per million (ppm), and nearly all food contains traces of fluoride. Tea contains more fluoride than most foods, and fish and vegetables also have relatively high levels. The findings of many scientific studies suggest that water containing a concentration of about 1 ppm fluoride, in contrast with water containing less fluoride, dramatically reduces the incidence of tooth decay.

Tooth decay occurs when acids in the mouth dissolve the protective enamel outer coating of a tooth, creating a hole, or cavity. These acids are present in food and can also be formed by bacteria that convert sugars into acids. The American diet has long included large quantities of sugar, which is a significant factor in the high incidence of tooth decay. By contrast, studies reveal that tooth decay is less common among people in primitive cultures; these findings have been attributed to these cultures' more natural diets.

Early fluoridation studies conducted between 1930 and 1950 demonstrated that fluoridation of public water systems produced a 50 to 60 percent reduction in tooth decay and that no immediate health risks were associated with increased fluoride consumption. Consequently, many communities quickly moved to fluoridate their water, and fluoridation was endorsed by most major health organizations in the United States.

OPPOSITION TO FLUORIDATION
Strong opposition to fluoridation began to emerge in the 1950's, as some people asserted that the possible side effects of consuming fluoride had not been adequately investigated. This concern was not unreasonable, given that high levels of ingested fluoride

can be lethal. It is not unusual, however, for a substance that is lethal at high concentration to be safe at low levels, as is the case with most vitamins and trace elements. Opponents of fluoridation were also concerned on moral grounds; they argued that fluoridation represents compulsory mass medication.

Since the 1960's, heated debates have arisen over the issue of fluoridation across the United States. Critics have pointed to the harmful effects of large doses of fluoride, including bone damage, and the special risks fluoride may pose for some people, such as those with kidney disease and others who are particularly sensitive to toxic substances. Between the 1950's and the 1980's, some scientists suggested that fluoride may have a mutagenic effect—that is, it may be associated with human birth defects, including Down syndrome.

Controversial claims that fluoride can cause cancer were also raised in the 1970's, most notably by biochemist John Yiamouyiannis, who asserted that U.S. cities with fluoridated water had higher rates of death from cancers than did cities with unfluoridated water. Fluoridation proponents were quick to discredit his work by pointing out that he had failed to take other factors into consideration, such as the levels of known environmental carcinogens. Most scientific opinion suggests that the link between cancer and fluoride is a tenuous one. Nevertheless, it is a link that cannot be ignored completely, and a number of respected scientists continue to argue that the benefits of fluoridation are not without potential health risks.

A 1988 article in the American Chemical Society publication *Chemical and Engineering News* gained considerable attention with its suggestion that scientists opposing fluoridation were more credible than had previously been acknowledged. By the 1990's even some fluoridation proponents began suggesting that observed reductions in tooth decay as a result of water fluoridation may have been at levels of only around 25 percent. Other factors—such as education, improvements in dental hygiene, and the addition of fluoride to some foods, salt, toothpastes, and mouthwashes—may also contribute to the overall reduction in levels of tooth decay.

While there is little doubt that fluoride does reduce tooth decay, the exact degree to which fluoridated water contributes to the reduction remains unanswered. It also remains unclear what, if any, side effects are associated with the ingestion of fluoride in water at the level of 1 ppm over many years. Whether or not any risks associated with fluoridation are small, any risk level may not be acceptable to everyone.

Since the 1960's and 1970's, Americans' concerns about environmental and health issues have been growing, and it has often been difficult, if not impossible, for scientists to measure—and to explain to the complete satisfaction of the public—the potential hazards posed by small amounts of chemical substances in the environment. The fact that, as of 2006, only about 69 percent of U.S. residents were living in communities with fluoridated water supplies is indicative of the continuing caution regarding this issue. In 1993 the National Research Council published a report on the health effects of ingested fluoride that included information on an attempt to determine whether the Environmental Protection Agency's maximum recommended level of 4 ppm for fluoride in drinking water should be modified. The report concluded that this level is appropriate but stated that further research may indicate a need for revision. The report also noted inconsistencies in the scientific studies of fluoride toxicity and recommended further research in this area.

The development of the fluoridation issue in the United States has been closely observed by other countries. Dental and medical authorities in Australia, Canada, New Zealand, and Ireland have endorsed fluoridation of water supplies, although not without considerable opposition from various groups. In Western Europe fluoridation has been greeted less enthusiastically, and scientific opinion in some countries, such as France, Germany, and Denmark, has concluded that it is unsafe. As a result, few Europeans drink fluoridated water.

Nicholas C. Thomas

FURTHER READING

De Zuane, John. *Handbook of Drinking Water Quality.* 2d ed. New York: John Wiley & Sons, 1997.

Martin, Brian. *Scientific Knowledge in Controversy: The Social Dynamic of the Fluoridation Debate.* Albany: State University of New York Press, 1991.

National Research Council. *Health Effects of Ingested Fluoride.* Washington, D.C.: National Academy Press, 1993.

Reilly, Gretchen Ann. "The Task Is a Political One: The Promotion of Fluoridation." In *Silent Victories: The History and Practice of Public Health in Twentieth-Century America,* edited by John W. Ward and Christian Warren. New York: Oxford University Press, 2007.

Stewart, John Cary. *Drinking Water Hazards.* Hiram, Ohio: Envirographics, 1989.

Weinstein, L. H., and A. W. Davison. *Fluorides in the Environment.* Cambridge, Mass.: CABI, 2004.

Ganges River

CATEGORY: Places

IDENTIFICATION: River that flows from west to east across the plains of north India from headwaters at Gangotri in the Himalayas to the Bay of Bengal

SIGNIFICANCE: Bringing life to a fertile plain that has hosted human habitation since the dawn of humanity, the Ganges is prominent in Indian lore. With Himalayan snowmelt and rains from both the southwest and northeast monsoons, the Ganges remains a viable waterway and irrigation source year-round, sustaining more than 400 million people, despite the fact that it is highly polluted.

The Ganges, also known as the Ganga, originates from an ice cave at the foot of the Gangotri glacier in the western Himalayas and drains an area of more than 1 million square kilometers (386,000 square miles) into the Bay of Bengal, more than 2,500 kilometers (1,550 miles) away. The Ganges and its Himalayan tributaries—Bhagirathi, Alaknanda, Mandakini, Gandak, Ghāghara, and Kosi—host heavy tourist and pilgrim traffic. The Ganges Canal cuts across the densely populated Doab (two rivers) region from Haridwar to the Yamuna River. The cities of Delhi and Agra, and Mathura and Vrindavan of Mahabharata lore, are on the banks of the Yamuna, which joins the Ganges at Allahabad. This is called Triveni Sangam (three-river confluence) in memory of the ancient Sarasvati River, which disappeared into the earth, probably as the result of seismic events.

The Ganges flows past the cities of Kanpur, Ramnagar, and Varanasi. In the northeast Indian state of Bihar, the tributaries Gomati, Ghāghara, Gandak, Bhagmati, Kosi, and Phalgu (on the banks of which is found the Buddhist holy city of Gaya) join the Ganges, and it flows past the state capital city of Patna.

The city of Kolkata (formerly known as Calcutta) is on the navigable Hugli River, an important channel of the Ganges that branches southward at the Bangladesh border. North of the Faridpur district of Bangladesh, the Ganges joins the lower Brahmaputra River and they become the Padma River, which joins the Meghna River and branches off through the vast Sundarbans (beautiful forest) delta to the Bay of Bengal.

The ancients revered the purity of the Ganges, and the river continues to be worshiped as a provider of life and annual cleanser by flood; it has been estimated that two million people engage in ritual bathing in the Ganges every day. The river's ecosystem—which is home to more than 140 unique fish species and 90 amphibian species and is also the site of five bird sanctuaries—has become threatened over time by high levels of pollution. Among the causes of the river's decline have been invasions, colonial poverty, industrialization, urbanization, agricultural runoff containing fertilizers, and efficient mass transport that brings millions of tourists. Pollution threatens many freshwater species native to the Ganges, such as the Ganges River dolphin, and allows invasive marine species to survive far upstream. Further, soil erosion and diversion of the river's water for irrigation have reduced water levels and inhibited navigation.

The Indian government undertook the Ganga Action Plan (GAP), an effort to reduce pollution in the river, in 1985; among other steps, sewage treatment plants were built, but little progress was made. A second GAP phase was later introduced; it included tough laws requiring industries to build effluent treatment plants, as well as provisions for proactive com-

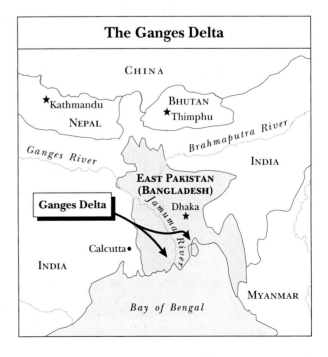

The Ganges Delta

munity education, reforestation, and passive gravity-fed filtering systems.

Narayanan M. Komerath
and Padma P. Komerath

FURTHER READING

Hollick, Julian Crandall. *Ganga: A Journey down the Ganges River.* Washington, D.C.: Island Press, 2007.

Mukherjee, D., M. Chattopadhyay, and S. C. Lahiri. "Water Quality of the River Ganga (the Ganges) and Some of Its Physico-chemical Properties." *Environmentalist* 13, no. 3 (September, 1993): 199-210.

Rao, R. J. "Biological Resources of the Ganga River, India." *Hydrobiologia* 458 (2001): 159-168.

Ray, P. *Ecological Imbalance of the Ganga River System: Its Impact on Aquaculture.* Delhi: Daya, 1998.

Great Lakes International Joint Commission

CATEGORY: Organizations and agencies

IDENTIFICATION: Independent organization established by the United States and Canada to resolve transboundary water disputes between the two nations and to advise on issues related to shared water resources

DATE: Established in 1909

SIGNIFICANCE: The border between the United States and Canada stretches thousands of miles and crosses many major waterways crucial to both nations, including the Great Lakes-St. Lawrence River system, home to one-fifth of all surface freshwater in the world. The International Joint Commission ensures the cooperative and sustainable use of clean, safe water for both nations.

The Great Lakes International Joint Commission (IJC) was founded with the signing of the Boundary Waters Treaty of 1909. This treaty gives the organization jurisdiction over all rivers, lakes, and other waterways that cross the U.S.-Canada border. The IJC has two basic functions. First, in its quasi-judicial role, it is given the authority to approve projects that affect transboundary waters. This includes activities upstream that affect the natural flow of water downstream, although because of sovereignty issues the IJC does not have authority over tributaries that feed these bodies of water. Second, when requested to do so by the Canadian and U.S. governments, the commission investigates and provides recommendations on transboundary water issues.

The IJC is headed by six commissioners, three appointed by each country. These members are expected to act as impartial judges rather than as national representatives. Several boards of experts from the United States and Canada have been assembled to assist the IJC in its investigative and decision-making processes. The body investigates water issues only when requested to do so by the governments and offers only nonbinding resolutions. However, the IJC does hold the power to arbitrate agreements between governments, although it has never been called on to use this authority.

In 1991 Canada and the United States signed the Air Quality Agreement, an executive agreement aimed at addressing issues of transboundary air quality and reducing air pollution. The Air Quality Committee was established within the IJC to report on the progress of the agreement every two years, thus expanding the commission's role, although water issues continue to predominate.

As the largest transboundary body of water and the largest surface freshwater system in the world, the Great Lakes-St. Lawrence River system is of critical importance to the commission. The first step to monitor and control water quality in the system, the Great Lakes Water Quality Agreement, was signed in 1972. Amendments and a new protocol created in 1987 set specific objectives for water quality, and the governments were required to create procedures to meet these targets. The IJC's plans for individual severely degraded areas as well as larger "lakewide management plans" take a holistic ecosystem-based approach in order to reduce human impacts on the system and remediate damage already done. The IJC reviews these plans and the progress made periodically in required reports submitted by both governments.

The commission has had high levels of success in achieving its aims since its establishment, resolving more than one hundred disputes and fostering dialogue both between the governments and with the general public. As part of its mandate, the commission must ensure that all interested parties are given the opportunity to voice their opinions. Public participation in the process and the involvement of multiple levels of governments are thus of paramount importance. The commission holds public meetings every two years to discuss the cleanup of the Great Lakes and regularly arranges other forums for public participation.

Daniel J. Connell

FURTHER READING

Bakker, Karen J. *Eau Canada: The Future of Canada's Water.* Vancouver: University of British Columbia Press, 2007.

Garrido, Alberto, and Ariel Dinar, eds. *Managing Water Resources in a Time of Global Change: Mountains, Valleys, and Flood Plains.* New York: Routledge, 2009.

Thompson, Stephen A. *Water Use, Management, and Planning in the United States.* San Diego, Calif.: Academic Press, 1999.

Groundwater pollution

CATEGORY: Water and water pollution

DEFINITION: Degradation, by chemicals and other substances, of the water found below the surface of the earth

SIGNIFICANCE: Many public and private water supplies rely on wells that tap important groundwater reserves. Pollution of groundwater leads to changes in water quality that can affect groundwater use for a given purpose.

Humans require vast amounts of fresh water for use in homes, livestock operations, agriculture, and industrial processes. Groundwater is an important source of fresh water. The pollution of groundwater by human activity can contaminate water-supply wells, making the water they provide unacceptable for drinking and other purposes. This can lead to a need for new water supplies that may not be readily available or easily accessible. In some instances polluted groundwater interacts with surface water, thus contaminating the surface-water environment as well.

Groundwater constitutes a small but significant portion of the world's overall water supply. Much of the earth's surface is covered by water, but an estimated 97.2 percent of it exists as salt water. Since fresh surface water may account for as little as 0.009 percent of the earth's water, groundwater is a significant source of readily available fresh water. Groundwater occurs in the saturated zone of the earth, which is the area below the surface where pores between particles—void spaces in the soil or rock—are filled with

water. In some places groundwater may be encountered near the surface, but in other areas, such as arid regions, it can be quite deep below the surface. Groundwater flows from areas of high hydrostatic head to areas of low hydrostatic head. Shallow groundwater often mimics topography, flowing downhill toward streams and lakes.

The soil and rock through which groundwater flows consist of particles of varying size, which help determine the classification of the soil or rock and how well water will move through the material. Sand-sized particles are seen in unconsolidated sandy soils or sandstones. Smaller particles may form silty or clayey soils or their bedrock equivalents of siltstones and shales. In the saturated zone, groundwater satu-

---

The Freshwater Crisis

Toxic chemicals are contaminating groundwater on every inhabited continent, endangering the world's most valuable supplies of fresh water, reports a study published in 2000 from the Worldwatch Institute, a Washington, D.C.-based research organization on the environment. This worldwide survey of groundwater quality shows that pesticides, nitrogen fertilizers, industrial chemicals, and heavy metals are contaminating groundwater everywhere, and that the damage is often worst in places where people most need water.

There are at least three essential roles of groundwater: providing drinking water, irrigating farmland, and replenishing rivers, streams, and wetlands. About one-third of the world population relies almost exclusively on groundwater for drinking. Groundwater provides irrigation for some of the world's most productive farmland. Over 50 percent of irrigated croplands in India, and 40 percent in the United States, is watered by groundwater. Groundwater plays a crucial role in replenishing rivers, streams, and wetlands. It provides much of the flow for great rivers such as the Mississippi, the Niger, the Yangtze, and many more.

The range of groundwater contamination is stunning. Groundwater in all twenty-two major industrial zones surveyed by the Indian government in the late 1990's was unfit for drinking. In a 1995 study of four northern Chinese provinces, groundwater was contaminated in more than 50 percent of surveyed locations. One-third of the wells tested in a California region in 1988 contained the pesticide 1,2-dibromo-3-chloropropane (DBCP) at levels ten times higher than the maximum allowed for drinking. The list goes on. There is a compelling urgency to prevent groundwater contamination.

rates the pores and voids between the particles. The size of the pores and the degree to which they are interconnected affect hydraulic conductivity—a measure of the ability of water to move through the rock or soil.

Transmissivity is the measure of the ability of an aquifer to transmit water and is a measure of the hydraulic conductivity multiplied by the saturated thickness of the aquifer. Therefore, a thick aquifer with relatively poor hydraulic conductivity might be able to transmit as much water as a thinner aquifer composed of materials with greater hydraulic conductivity. Groundwater is recharged by rainwater percolating through the soil, snowmelt, and rivers and streams.

THREATS TO GROUNDWATER

Humans produce a wide array of pollutants and combinations of pollutants. The degree and extent to which individual pollutants can affect groundwater quality is dependent on a large number of variables, which can include the amount of contaminant introduced into the environment, the time frame in which it is introduced, its toxicity, its mobility, whether it will readily degrade in the environment, and the chemical and physical characteristics of the soil or rock through which it will pass.

Even something as common as nitrogen can lead to pollution in groundwater. Nitrogen can be mobile in the environment in the form of dissolved nitrates and nitrites. Sources for pollution include septic tanks, leaks from sewage treatment plants and lagoons, and animal wastes. Nitrogen is also an important component of many fertilizers used in agriculture, and such fertilizers may become dissolved by rainwater and percolate down into groundwater. In high enough concentrations, nitrates can make water unacceptable for human consumption. At even higher concentrations, the water can become unacceptable for livestock and other animals.

Gasoline spills and leaks from underground storage tanks are relatively common sources of groundwater pollution. Some of the dissolved-phase components of gasoline are quite mobile in the environment; however, many are also susceptible to biological degradation. Gasoline and other substances less dense than water can float on the surface of groundwater, but seasonal fluctuations in the water table can smear such contaminants in the soil, potentially making them more difficult to remove. Other contaminants, such as chlorinated solvents, can be denser than water and have the capacity to sink into aquifers.

Although metals as a group are generally not considered very mobile and tend to be adsorbed onto soils, some are quite mobile, and contamination by heavy metals can be a relatively common form of groundwater contamination. Although less common, radiological contamination of groundwater can be a concern. Groundwater often moves slowly, but radioactive half-lives can be quite long.

Raymond U. Roberts

FURTHER READING

Appelo, C. A. J., and D. Postma. *Geochemistry, Groundwater, and Pollution.* 2d ed. New York: Balkema, 2005.

Chiras, Daniel D. "Water Pollution: Sustainably Managing a Renewable Resource." In *Environmental Science.* 8th ed. Sudbury, Mass.: Jones and Bartlett, 2010.

Heath, Ralph C. *Basic Groundwater Hydrology.* Reston, Va.: U.S. Geological Survey, 2004.

Sampat, Payal. *Deep Trouble: The Hidden Threat of Groundwater Pollution.* Washington, D.C.: Worldwatch Institute, 2000.

Todd, David Keith, and Larry W. Mays. *Groundwater Hydrology.* 3d ed. Hoboken, N.J.: John Wiley & Sons, 2005.

Younger, Paul L. *Groundwater in the Environment: An Introduction.* Malden, Mass.: Blackwell, 2007.

Gulf War oil burning

CATEGORIES: Disasters; atmosphere and air pollution

THE EVENT: Fires started in Kuwait oil fields by retreating Iraqi soldiers

DATES: January-November, 1991

SIGNIFICANCE: When Iraqi armed forces damaged an oil pipeline and set fire to more than five hundred oil wells, they began what became the worst oil-field disaster in history.

The Persian Gulf is a shallow, northwest-trending body of water that covers an area of about 260,000 square kilometers (100,400 square miles). The Gulf is actually a large bay about 800 kilometers (500 miles) long, 200 kilometers (125 miles) wide, and 90 meters

(300 feet) deep at the deepest point. It is bordered by Iran, Iraq, Kuwait, Saudi Arabia, Bahrain, Qatar, Oman, and the United Arab Emirates. The Shatt-al-Arab, a river formed by the merging of the Tigris and Euphrates rivers, has created a combined river floodplain and delta region at the head of the Persian Gulf that covers more than 3,200 square kilometers (1,235 square miles).

The Persian Gulf is teeming with wildlife. The coastal mangrove swamps and coral reefs provide habitats for birds and fish. Hundreds of species of fish, including mackerel, snapper, and mullet, live in the region and feed on the abundant algae. Wading birds such as shanks and sand plovers feed along the coastal mudflats. Also, valuable crustaceans such as prawn and shrimp are farmed along the Persian Gulf's shores.

The region holds more than one-half of the world's proven reserves of oil and natural gas. The Persian Gulf also provides the world's major shipping lanes for oil tanker traffic. It has been estimated that some 40 million liters (10 million gallons) of oil spills or leaks into Persian Gulf waters each year. The results of these oil releases are usually absorbed by the environment without significant ecological damage. However, in January, 1991, the area was hit by an environmental disaster in the form of the Persian Gulf War.

On August 2, 1990, Iraqi forces invaded the small, oil-rich neighboring nation of Kuwait. On November 29, 1990, the United Nations voted to permit the use of force to expel Iraqi forces from Kuwait. On January 16, 1991, air attacks on Iraqi targets began, followed on February 23 with a ground attack against Iraq by a coalition of forces from twenty-eight countries, including the United States, Saudi Arabia, Egypt, and Great Britain.

Soil and Water Pollution

During the ground war, which lasted only one hundred hours, Iraqi soldiers departing from Kuwait damaged an oil pipeline and set fire to more than five hundred Kuwaiti oil wells. These damaged wells poured hundreds of thousands of liters of oil into the surrounding countryside, forming large lakes up to 1.6 kilometers (1 mile) long and nearly 1 meter (3.28 feet) deep. More than 800 million liters (211 million gallons) of oil issued from the damaged wells each day. The spilled oil threatened to pollute the water supply of Kuwait City and other inhabited areas, and

the contaminated soil and vegetation threatened to harm wildlife. Soil is adversely affected by the oily mist from such spills, as the mist forms a thin film over the topsoil and reduces the amount of oxygen and water that can penetrate the soil profile. This seal reduces the activity of a number of microbes and earthworms that help to keep the soil fertile.

Because currents in the upper Persian Gulf generally move counterclockwise around the bay, a thick oil slick spread northwest to southeast along the western coast from disrupted oil terminals, pipelines, and individual wells in the vicinity of Kuwait City to the lower part of Saudi Arabia; a thin oil film spread from the coastal region to the middle of the upper Persian Gulf. The colossal oil slick threatened the entire ecosystem of the Persian Gulf. It resulted in the deaths of some twenty thousand birds, including flamingos, as the oil soaked their feathers and caused them to drown or die from exposure. The Persian Gulf's populations of sea cows (dugongs), dolphins, and green turtles were at risk, as were the endangered hawksbill turtles that lay eggs on the local islands. Although many scientists believe that most marine life requires only three years to recover from the effects of exposure to crude oil, marine life exposed to refined oil, especially in enclosed areas such as the Persian Gulf, may require ten years or longer to recover.

Air Pollution

A number of the wells that were ignited released poisonous gases into the air that endangered people (including military personnel) and wildlife. The smoke released by the fires contained noxious gases such as deadly carbon monoxide and sulfuric acid. The sky was darkened by clouds of toxic black smoke, causing temperatures to drop 5.5 degrees Celsius (10 degrees Fahrenheit) lower than normal.

The Burgan Oil Refinery complex south of Kuwait City was devastated. Most of the damage occurred within an 800-kilometer (500-mile) range that included most of Iran, Iraq, and Kuwait. Soot and acid rain clouds extended nearly 1,920 kilometers (1,200 miles) away from the sabotaged oil fields. In March, 1991, *The New York Times* reported that the pollution "rained on Turkey and reached the western shore of the Black Sea, touching Bulgaria, Rumania, and the southern Soviet Union, becoming more prevalent over Afghanistan and Pakistan." The newspaper also indicated that the toxic clouds resulted in a significant increase in respiratory diseases among the elderly and the very young. In *Oil Spills* (1993) Jane Walker reports that many cattle and sheep "died in Kuwait either from breathing oil droplets in the air, or from eating oil-covered grass."

CLEANUP

The cleanup operation was undertaken in two phases: extinguishing the burning wells and controlling the oil slick. Several professional firefighting groups were called upon to extinguish the oil-field fires; the process took less than one year. Among the techniques used to combat the fires were cooling the well equipment with water, removing the well debris, cutting off oxygen to the fires by blowing flames out with explosives (usually dynamite), capping well heads with stingers (plugs), and attaching new valve assemblies to shut off the flow of oil.

The main technique used to confine and recover oil from the waters of the Persian Gulf was skimming. Oil-skimming ships scraped the greasy layer off the water's surface, recovering between 20,000 and 30,000 barrels (about 3 to 5 million liters) of oil per day. The Saudi Arabian national oil company, Saudi Aramco, placed about 40 kilometers (25 miles) of floating booms along the periphery of the spill and sent more than twenty oil-recovery craft to the area.

Donald F. Reaser

FURTHER READING

Browning, K. A., et al. "Environmental Effects from Burning Oil Wells in Kuwait." *Nature*, May 30, 1991, 363-367.

Falola, Toyin, and Ann Genova. "Environmental Concerns." In *The Politics of the Global Oil Industry: An Introduction*. Westport, Conn.: Praeger, 2005.

Hawley, T. M. *Against the Fires of Hell: The Environmental Disaster of the Gulf War.* Orlando, Fla.: Harcourt Brace Jovanovich, 1992.

Hobbs, Peter V., and Lawrence F. Radke. "Airborne Studies of the Smoke from the Kuwait Oil Fires." *Science* 256 (March 26, 1993): 987-991.

Horgan, John. "Burning Questions: Scientists Launch Studies of Kuwait's Oil Fires." *Scientific American,* July, 1991, 17-22.

Irrigation

CATEGORY: Agriculture and food

DEFINITION: Watering of land through human-created means

SIGNIFICANCE: Like many other human modifications to natural ecosystems, the use of water for irrigation achieves some remarkable but temporary advantages that are complicated by long-term environmental problems.

The demands of feeding and clothing the rapidly expanding world population require the production of increasing amounts of food and fiber. One important strategy for achieving the necessary levels of production has been the use of irrigation techniques to supply additional water to arid and semiarid regions where few, if any, crops could otherwise be grown.

Approximately 141.6 million hectares (350 million acres) of land worldwide are irrigated. In the United States more than 10 percent of all crops, encompassing approximately 20.2 million hectares (50 million acres), receive water through irrigation techniques; 80 percent of these are west of the Mississippi River. In certain other countries, including India, Israel, North Korea, and South Korea, more than one-half of food production requires irrigation. From 1950 to 1980, the amount of irrigated cropland doubled worldwide; increases since the 1980's have been more modest.

An often-cited example of irrigation success is that of the Imperial Valley of Southern California. The valley, more than 12,900 square kilometers (5,000 square miles) in size, was originally considered to be a desert wasteland. The low annual rainfall resulted in a typical desert, with cacti, lizards, and other arid-adapted plants and animals. In 1940, however, engineers completed the construction of the All-American Canal, which carries water 130 kilometers (80 miles) from the Colorado River to the valley. The project converted the Imperial Valley into a fertile, highly productive area where farmers grow fruits and vegetables all year.

Successful agriculture in Israel also requires irrigation. As a result of continuing settlement of the area throughout the twentieth century, large amounts of food had to be produced. To fulfill this need, a system of canals and pipelines was built to carry water from the northern portion of the Jordan Valley, where the rainfall is heaviest, to the arid south.

METHODS

All types of irrigation are expensive, requiring advanced technologies and large investments of capital. In many cases, irrigation systems convey water from sources hundreds of miles distant. In the United States, such vast engineering feats are largely financed by taxpayers. Typically, water from a river is diverted into a main canal and from there into lateral canals that supply each farm. From the lateral canals, various systems are used to supply water to the crop plants in the field.

Flood irrigation supplies water to fields at the surface level. Using the sheet method, land is prepared so that water flows in a shallow sheet from the higher part of the field to the lower part. This method is especially suitable for hay and pasture crops. Row crops are better supplied by furrow irrigation, in which water is diverted into furrows that run between the rows. Both types of flood irrigation cause erosion and loss of nutrients. However, erosion can be reduced in the latter type through the contouring of the furrows.

Sprinkler irrigation systems, though costly to install and operate, are often used in areas where fields are steeply sloped. Sprinklers may be supplied by stationary underground pipes, or a center pivot system may be used, in which water is sprinkled by a raised horizontal pipe that moves slowly around a pivot point. Aside from its expense, another disadvantage of sprinkler irrigation is loss of water by evaporation. In drip irrigation, in contrast, water is delivered by perforated pipes at or near the soil surface. Because water is delivered directly to the plants, much less water is lost to evaporation than is the case with sprinkler irrigation.

Much of the water utilized in irrigation never reaches the plants. It is estimated that most practices deliver only about 25 percent of the water to the root systems of crop plants. The remaining water is lost to evaporation, supplies weeds, seeps into the ground, or runs off into nearby waterways.

NEGATIVE IMPACTS

As fresh water evaporates from irrigated fields over time, a residue of salt is left behind. The process, called salinization, results in a gradual decline in productivity and can eventually render fields unsuitable for further agricultural use. Correcting saline soils is

A sprinkler irrigation system in use on a hay field. (©Steve Baxter/iStockphoto.com)

not a simple process. In principle, large amounts of water can be used to leach salt away from the soil, but in practice the amount of water required is seldom available, and if it is used, it may waterlog the soil. Also, the leached salt usually pollutes groundwater or streams. One way in which farmers address the problem of salinization is by using genetically selected crops adapted to salinized soils.

As the number of hectares of farmland requiring irrigation increases, so does the demand for water. When water is taken from surface streams and rivers, the normal flow is often severely reduced, changing the ecology downstream and reducing its biodiversity. Also, less water becomes available for other farmers downstream, a situation that often leads to disputes over water rights. In other cases water is pumped from deep wells or aquifers. Drilling wells and pumping water from such sources can be expensive and may lead to additional problems, such as the sinking of land over aquifers. Such land subsidence is a major problem in several parts of the southern and western United States. Subsidence in urban areas can cause huge amounts of damage as water and sewer pipes, highways, and buildings are affected. In coastal areas, depletion of aquifers can cause the intrusion of salt water into wells, rendering them unusable. In the United States, the federal government spends millions of dollars each year to repair damage to irrigation facilities.

Like many other human modifications to natural ecosystems, the use of water for irrigation achieves some remarkable but temporary advantages that are complicated by long-term environmental problems. Assessments of the total financial costs and environmental impacts of irrigation are continuously weighed against gains in production.

Thomas E. Hemmerly

FURTHER READING

Albiac, José, and Ariel Dinar, eds. *The Management of Water Quality and Irrigation Technologies*. Sterling, Va.: Earthscan, 2008.

Graves, William, ed. "Water: The Power, Promise, and Turmoil of North America's Fresh Water" (special issue). *National Geographic*, November, 1993.

Meiners, Roger E., and Bruce Yandle, eds. *Agricultural Policy and the Environment*. Lanham, Md.: Rowman & Littlefield, 2003.

Molden, David, ed. *Water for Food, Water for Life: A Comprehensive Assessment of Water Management in Agriculture*. Sterling, Va.: Earthscan, 2007.

Wescoat, James L., Jr., and Gilbert F. White. *Water for Life: Water Management and Environmental Policy*. New York: Cambridge University Press, 2003.

Kesterson Reservoir

CATEGORY: Animals and endangered species
IDENTIFICATION: Series of holding ponds for drainage from irrigated agricultural lands in California's San Joaquin Valley
SIGNIFICANCE: After the transfer of subsurface drainage water from the San Joaquin Valley into the Kesterson Reservoir led to widespread death and deformity of migratory birds at the Kesterson National Wildlife Refuge, owing to toxic levels of dissolved selenium in the water, the U.S. Geological Survey set up programs to study the ecosystem effects of irrigation drainage water.

Selenium is a naturally occurring trace element that is essential for health in concentrations ranging from 0.05 to 0.3 parts per million (ppm) but becomes increasingly toxic at concentrations exceeding these low dietary levels. Selenium is found in igneous rocks, sedimentary rocks, and fossil fuels. Some soils contain naturally high selenium concentrations, and selenium occurs in the drainage from these soils because its ionic forms are readily soluble.

The Kesterson Reservoir in Merced County, California, was a series of holding ponds, spread over more than 486 hectares (1,200 acres), that collected the surface and subsurface drainage from irrigated agricultural land in the western San Joaquin Valley. Because development had eliminated more than 90 percent of California's wetlands and because of the scarcity and high price of water in California, the U.S. Bureau of Reclamation and the U.S. Fish and Wildlife Service mutually agreed to incorporate the reservoir and its waters as part of the National Wildlife Refuge System in the mid-1970's.

By 1982 virtually all the water entering the Kesterson Reservoir was from subsurface drainage, and in 1983 scientists found that aquatic and migratory birds nesting in the refuge had grossly deformed embryos and high embryo mortality rates. By 1984 dead adult birds were being discovered in the area in unusually high numbers. Agricultural chemicals were initially suspected to be the cause of the deaths and deformities, but tissue analysis of the birds revealed that they had selenium concentrations one hundred times in excess of normal concentrations because of selenium bioaccumulation in the food chain.

In 1986 discharge of drainage water into the Kesterson Reservoir was halted, and the reservoir was allowed to drain naturally. In 1988, to protect migratory waterfowl from nesting in periodically flooded zones of the reservoir, about 60 percent of the lowest-lying parts of the reservoir were filled with enough selenium-free backfill to ensure that the average seasonal groundwater level remained 15 centimeters (6 inches) below the soil surface. These steps were taken because wildlife biologists determined that the potential for selenium contamination of wildlife was much more limited in dryland environments than in wetland environments.

The Kesterson Reservoir has continued to be monitored because studies indicate that selenium concentrations in plants and wildlife in the area will remain elevated for decades. Bioremediation schemes were also investigated, and it was observed that microorganisms, particularly fungi, were able to volatilize up to 50 percent of the selenium in their vicinity within one year.

Mark Coyne

FURTHER READING

Byron, Earl R., et al. "Ecological Risk Assessment Example: Waterfowl and Shorebirds Feeding in Ephemeral Pools at Kesterson Reservoir, California." In *Handbook of Ecotoxicology*, edited by David J. Hoffman et al. 2d ed. Boca Raton, Fla.: CRC Press, 2003.

Fordyce, Fiona. "Selenium Deficiency and Toxicity in the Environment." In *Essentials of Medical Geology: Impacts of the Natural Environment on Public Health*, edited by Olle Selinus et al. Burlington, Mass.: Elsevier Academic Press, 2005.

Klamath River

CATEGORIES: Places; animals and endangered species; resources and resource management

IDENTIFICATION: River that flows from south-central Oregon through northern California to the Pacific Ocean

SIGNIFICANCE: The Klamath River and its tributaries epitomize the conflicting economic, social, and environmental considerations involved in water management in a region of low rainfall and periodic drought. The central question is how best to reconcile the preservation of endangered fish species with local agricultural needs and regional demand for hydroelectric power.

The Klamath River is sometimes dubbed an "upside-down river" because it originates in a shallow, highly eutrophic (overly nutrient-enriched) lake in an area of intensive agricultural development and ends up as a swift and apparently pristine stream. In prehistoric times the marshes surrounding Upper and Lower Klamath lakes supported a great wealth of wildlife and large populations of Native American hunters. Despite the dispersal of tribal lands in the twentieth century, many of their descendants still occupy the area.

Development of the Klamath River basin has been steady since the beginning of white settlement but increased dramatically during the 1950's and 1960's with construction of hydroelectric dams on the river and its tributaries, diversion of increasing amounts of water for irrigation, increases in agricultural runoff, and conversion of wetland wildlife habitat to farmland. During this same period, logging and the manufacture of wood products, once mainstays of the local economy, declined in importance because of unsustainable logging practices on federal lands.

Environmental problems and conflicts surfaced during a drought in the 1990's after the U.S. Bureau of Reclamation, which allocates irrigation water, proposed a water management plan that threatened two endangered species of suckers, fish native to Klamath Lake, with extinction and also threatened a distinct population of coho salmon. Provisions of the Endangered Species Act effectively blocked irrigation, and the region experienced considerable economic damage.

Lake water levels and stream flow are not the only factors that have threatened fish populations in the Klamath River basin. Phosphates from agricultural runoff have caused massive blooms of blue-green algae, depleting oxygen in the water and raising pH levels. Increased alkalinity and higher water temperatures were implicated in a 2002 fungal epidemic that killed off large numbers of salmon. In addition, logging and recreational development have compromised spawning streams, and hydroelectric dams have created serious barriers to salmon migration.

The results of an integrated study showed that any plan that could effectively restore endangered fish populations in the Klamath River would require the removal of several hydroelectric dams. In November, 2008, officials of PacifiCorp, the power company that operates the dams, reached a tentative nonbinding agreement on water rights with representatives of the region's farmers, fishers, Native American tribes, and recreational users; the agreement, which called for the removal of four dams beginning in 2020, assumed more concrete form in February, 2010. In the meantime, dry years spell disaster for farmers in the upper Klamath basin, and it is unclear whether efforts that have been implemented will prevent extinction of threatened fish before 2020.

Legitimate questions have also been raised regarding whether it makes sense, from an overall point of view, to expend scarce environmental dollars to demolish sources of clean, carbon-neutral energy for which any possible replacement also has its acknowledged downsides. Replacing hydroelectric dams with wind farms, for example, would entail huge energy costs for start-up; in addition, critics argue that wind farms are eyesores and that they pose threats to migratory birds.

Martha A. Sherwood

Further Reading

Blake, Tupper Ansel. *Balancing Water: Restoring the Klamath Basin.* Berkeley: University of California Press, 2000.

Committee on Endangered and Threatened Fishes in the Klamath River Basin. *Hydrology, Ecology, and Fishes of the Klamath River Basin.* Washington, D.C.: National Academies Press, 2008.

Most, Stephen. *River of Renewal: Myth and History in the Klamath Basin.* Portland: Oregon Historical Society Press, 2006.

Lake Baikal

CATEGORIES: Places; ecology and ecosystems

IDENTIFICATION: Freshwater lake located in Siberian Russia

SIGNIFICANCE: When industrial water pollution began to threaten the unique nature of Lake Baikal, with its pure waters and distinctive plant and animal life, the Soviet Union experienced its first environmental protests.

Lake Baikal is the oldest and deepest lake on earth. Almost 650 kilometers (400 miles) long, its surface area is approximately the same as that of Lake Superior, but its water volume makes up one-fifth of all fresh water on the earth's surface. The lake itself is more than 1.6 kilometers (1 mile) deep. Below the surface lies a floor of sediment approximately 6.4 kilometers (4 miles) deep; the sediment has drifted down through the lake's waters over some twenty to thirty million years. Lake Baikal lies atop a rift where several tectonic plates meet along a little-studied geological fault. The activity of these plates has apparently widened the rift and deepened the lake over many millennia.

Lake Baikal essentially has a closed ecosystem. Several hundred rivers feed into it, but the watershed consists entirely of the mountain area surrounding the lake, unconnected to other river systems. Baikal has only one outlet, the Angara River, which flows out from its southeast corner, past the old frontier city of Irkutsk, and ultimately to the Arctic Ocean. Because of the lake's isolation, it is the habitat of many species that are found nowhere else on earth. It is a fascinating site for biological study.

Among the lake's intriguing fauna is the silver-furred nerpa, the smallest known seal. Its closest relative, the Arctic seal, lives some 3,200 kilometers (2,000 miles) away. How the nerpa reached Baikal and adapted to fresh water is one of the lake's many mysteries. Nerpas eat an oily fish also found only in Baikal, the golomyanka. This almost transparent fish gives birth to live young, then promptly sinks and dies. Algae, plankton, and similar microscopic creatures form the bottom of the lake's food chain. These serve as prey for a tiny crustacean called epishura, which strains Baikal's waters to a pristine clarity.

The land around Lake Baikal—consisting of taiga, or northern woodlands—shelters a variety of Siberian wildlife. Mountains ring the lake, creating spectacular scenery. Olkhon Island, located near the western shore in the midsection of the crescent-shaped lake, has a dry, almost snowless climate and contains grasslands and sand dunes. The smaller islands are seal nesting grounds. The lake surface freezes to a depth of more than 1 meter (3.28 feet) during the long Siberian winter.

Despite its remote location, the region has not been immune to technological forces. The Trans-Siberian Railroad's builders left clear-cut areas and debris in the southern reaches, a problem repeated with the building of the Baikal-Amur Mainline paral-

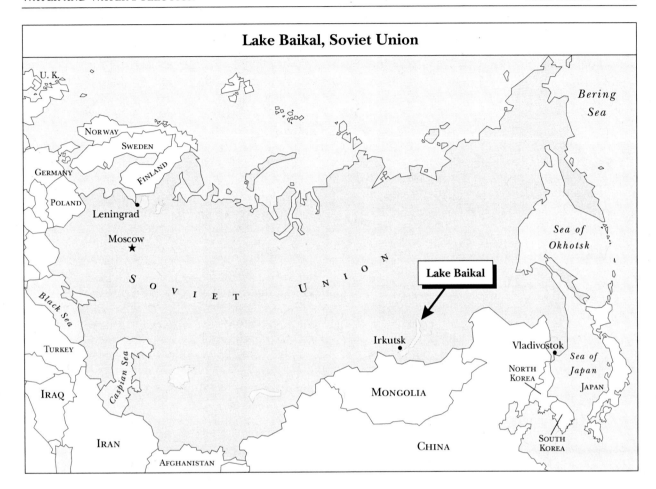

Lake Baikal, Soviet Union

leling the northwest shore decades later. By the early twentieth century, sable in the surrounding forests had been hunted almost to extinction. Sturgeon and sturgeon eggs, valued as luxury food items, were dangerously depleted by the 1950's.

Buryat Mongols, indigenous inhabitants of the region, lived unobtrusively on the land, much as Native Americans lived for thousands of years in the Americas. Russian settlers, arriving either by choice or by involuntary exile, had to make a living in the isolated region. Although fisheries could sustain operations without depleting populations of marine life, they did not always do so. Meanwhile, timbering and farming methods took a major toll in erosion.

ENVIRONMENTAL DAMAGE

The greatest environmental damage to the Lake Baikal region came with the establishment of large-scale industry. During Joseph Stalin's regime as the Soviet leader (1922-1953), the Soviet Union emphasized industrial production over every other goal. Sta-

lin's immediate successors retained this policy. A huge cellulose production plant opened at Baikalsk on the southern shore of the lake in 1966 and began spewing toxic chemicals into the lake water and murky smoke into the air. A pulp plant at Selingiske, located on one of Lake Baikal's major tributaries, and factory wastes and sewage from Ulan-Ude farther upriver created another major pollution area around the Selenga River delta. Hydroelectric dams built near Irkutsk in the 1950's brought more heavy industry and noxious by-products.

The harm wrought by these factories was unquantifiable but quite visible. In many places along the southern shore of the lake, the formerly pure water became unfit to drink. Many square miles of lake area simply died, becoming unable to support aquatic life. Elsewhere, the populations of many native species shrank drastically. In some places newly introduced, hardier species began to replace them, with unpredictable consequences.

EFFORTS TO PROTECT THE LAKE

Distrust of the Baikalsk manufacturing project spawned the first environmental protests in the Soviet Union. Although these did not prevent the plant's opening, a precedent and framework was created for the future. By the time of Mikhail Gorbachev's term as Soviet leader (1985-1991), the lake's pollution was obvious, and the political scene had become less repressive. Gorbachev pledged to convert the Baikalsk plant to nonpolluting activities, but political turmoil and the Soviet Union's breakup intervened, after which Lake Baikal became Russia's responsibility.

The biggest problems for Lake Baikal in the 1990's were those of inaction caused by Russia's political and economic problems. Antipollution laws and plans were adopted, but the money to implement them was scarce, and coordination among local political entities was difficult. Declining industrial activity caused by economic slowdown may have slowed pollution of the lake more effectively than any active measures. The Baikalsk plant was eventually closed down in 2008—not because of environmental concerns, but because it had become unprofitable. Although the owner had sworn it would not reopen, it began operating again in 2010.

In 1996, the United Nations Educational, Scientific, and Cultural Organization (UNESCO) named Lake Baikal a World Heritage Site, and many Russians have embraced the lake as a national treasure deserving of protection. In the early years of the twenty-first century, plans were drawn up to lessen or reverse damage to the lake and region, and Russia began to draw on outside resources, both scientific and business-oriented, for help in this effort. Investors also began to promote the relatively clean industry of tourism at Lake Baikal.

Emily Alward

FURTHER READING

Belt, Don. "Russia's Lake Baikal: The World's Great Lake." *National Geographic,* June, 1992.

Matthiessen, Peter. *Baikal: Sacred Sea of Siberia.* San Francisco: Sierra Club Books, 1992.

Minoura, Koji, ed. *Lake Baikal: A Mirror in Time and Space for Understanding Global Change Processes.* New York: Elsevier, 2000.

Thomson, Peter. *Sacred Sea: A Journey to Lake Baikal.* New York: Oxford University Press, 2007.

Venable, Sondra. *Protecting Lake Baikal: Environmental Policy Making in Russia's Transition.* Saarbrücken, Germany: VDM, 2008.

Lake Erie

CATEGORY: Places

IDENTIFICATION: Large freshwater lake bordering Ontario, Canada, and the U.S. states of Michigan, Ohio, Pennsylvania, and New York

SIGNIFICANCE: In ecological trouble even before European settlement of its region, Lake Erie was badly damaged by human tampering with its ecosystem and the careless introduction of chemical fertilizers and industrial wastes. By the mid-twentieth century, the lake was severely polluted, but sustained efforts to rehabilitate it that began in 1965 gradually brought about a general recovery.

Lake Erie, the shallowest and southernmost of the Great Lakes, was far along in the process of eutrophication, or natural aging, prior to settlement by Europeans. Early settlers accelerated this process by draining coastal wetlands and stripping away vegetation, which increased the amount of sediment carried to the lake. With the advent of widespread agriculture, artificial fertilizers also began to wash into Lake Erie, which contributed to overenrichment of the lake's waters. Sewage and fertilizers, such as phosphorus and nitrogen, caused the rapid growth of surface algae scums, which affected the taste and odor of drinking-water supplies, clogged water intakes, and forced beach closures. More important, decaying algae consumed the water's oxygen, leading to the suffocation of bottom-dwelling organisms. Eventually, desirable fish stocking the lake were stressed by lack of adequate food, and populations declined.

Industries along the lake's main tributaries contributed to the problem by injecting industrial wastes, oil, floating solids, and heavy metals into the water supply. Heavy metals such as lead and mercury, as well as organic chemicals such as polychlorinated biphenyls (PCBs) and dioxin, magnify in concentrations as they pass up the food chain. These bioaccumulation and biomagnification effects may increase levels of toxic materials by one million times in fish such as salmon and trout. Fish consumption advisories were required for some species because of contamination levels. By 1965 Lake Erie had become so polluted that public indignation over its condition led to action by government officials.

Four U.S. states (Michigan, New York, Pennsylvania, and Ohio) and one Canadian province (Ontario)

Lake Erie

CANADA

Lake Superior

Lake Erie

Lake Huron

Lake Michigan

Lake Ontario

WISCONSIN

MICHIGAN

Buffalo

NEW YORK

Milwaukee •

Detroit •

Chicago •

Toledo • Lorain • Cleveland

PENNSYLVANIA

OHIO

ILLINOIS

INDIANA

The Great Lakes Fishery Commission, created in 1955 by Canada and the United States, is concerned with restoring and stocking lake fish. The population of whitefish in the lake has shown signs of recovery. Lake trout and coho salmon are stocked in the lake, and walleye and yellow perch are managed for recreational and commercial fishing. Tests have also revealed that the levels of PCBs in some Lake Erie fish have diminished over time.

In 1985 the Great Lakes Charter was inaugurated to resist the transfer of Great Lakes water to other areas. The charter authorized the development of an information database for surface-water and groundwater resources. In 1986 the Great Lakes Toxic Substances Control Agreement (GLTSCA) was formed to coordinate the actions of the Great Lakes states to reduce toxic substances in the basin. The 1987 protocol to the Great Lakes Water Quality Agreement called for forming specific ecosystem objectives and indicators. This approach has enhanced the evolution of full ecosystem management strategies, which incorporate mathematical modeling.

Ronald J. Raven

share in managing Lake Erie. The International Joint Commission was established by Canada and the United States in 1909 to arbitrate disputes over shared boundary waters. In 1972 the commission established the Great Lakes Water Quality Agreement, which provided for reduction in nitrogen and phosphorus discharge in Lake Erie by improving the municipal sewage treatment systems. The retention of sanitary and storm-sewer overflow for later treatment greatly reduced health problems in the region, and beach closures at Lake Erie became less frequent with improved treatment of sewage.

The International Reference Group on Great Lakes Pollution from Land Use, under the International Joint Commission Authority, prepared reports that provided the groundwork for the ecosystem approach to reducing pollution in Lake Erie promulgated in the 1978 revisions to the Water Quality Agreement. The agreement states that the programs must center on the physical, chemical, and biological relationships among air, land, and water resources. The ecosystem approach mandated by the 1978 agreement means that standards and monitoring methods must take into account the air, land, and water movement of pollutants and their risks to humans and other organisms.

FURTHER READING

Caldwell, Lynton Keith, ed. *Perspectives on Ecosystem Management for the Great Lakes: A Reader.* Albany: State University of New York Press, 1988.

Grady, Wayne. *The Great Lakes: The Natural History of a Changing Region.* Vancouver: Greystone Books, 2007.

McGucken, William. *Lake Erie Rehabilitated: Controlling Cultural Eutrophication, 1960's-1990's.* Akron, Ohio: University of Akron Press, 2000.

Leachates

CATEGORIES: Pollutants and toxins; waste and waste management

DEFINITION: Liquids produced when fluids dissolve the constituent elements in landfill wastes

SIGNIFICANCE: Some of the potentially toxic materials

found in landfills include mercury, lead, cadmium, chromium, arsenic, many organic compounds, and even pathogenic organisms. Because leachates may contain high concentrations of such materials, care is taken in modern landfills to prevent leachates from escaping and contaminating groundwater supplies.

Leachate fluids can vary a great deal depending on the composition of material in the landfill, the age of the leachate, and the speed of the addition and removal of water in the landfill. The flow of water depends on the amount of rainfall, the permeability of the garbage and surrounding rocks (that is, how readily water flows through the material), the kind of liner placed at the base of the waste material, and whether or not a cover has been placed over the landfill to prevent water inflow.

COMPOSITION

Underground water moves slowly and may take years to flow through a landfill. The water thus has a lot of time to dissolve materials such as motor oil, paint, batteries, chlorinated hydrocarbons, pesticides, and other industrial wastes. Many of these materials have long been banned from landfills in the United States, but tens of thousands of old landfills still contain such materials. In fact, many old waste disposal sites were simply depressions in the ground in which almost anything was placed. The U.S. military was one of the worst offenders in creating poor landfills in the past, as military facilities generate more than 500,000 tons of waste per year.

The composition of leachates varies from landfill to landfill and even within a single landfill. The upper concentrations of certain constituents in some leachates can greatly exceed the maximum concentration of those constituents allowed in drinking water. For example, lead concentrations have been found to exceed 5 milligrams per liter in some leachates; drinking water in the United States is required to have less than 0.01 milligram of lead per liter. Zinc concentrations have been found to exceed 1,300 milligrams per liter in some leachates; drinking water is required to have less than 5 milligrams of zinc per liter.

The concentrations of constituents in the leachate in a given landfill may also change over time. For example, large amounts of carbon dioxide are initially produced in the landfill by organisms reacting with biodegradable waste. The carbon dioxide reacts with water to produce acidic waters so that inorganic materials can more readably dissolve. The initial acidic leachate gradually becomes less acid over time as it dissolves the inorganic materials. The total amount of dissolved materials in leachates has been found to be as high as 40,000 milligrams per liter (most drinking water has less than 500 milligrams per liter).

A number of toxic and carcinogenic organic constituents have also been found in landfills, such as dioxin compounds. Dioxins are a group of chlorinated hydrocarbons that are not very soluble in water, but they concentrate in the fatty tissues of animals. They are chemically stable, so they concentrate upward in the food chain. Dioxins are toxic and can cause problems with the immune and reproductive systems; they may also cause some cancers. Other toxic organic constituents that may be present in landfill leachate include certain alcohols, chlorobenzene, acetone, methylene chloride, and toluene.

MANAGEMENT

The goal of leachate management is to prevent leachates from escaping landfills and polluting groundwater supplies. Methods have been developed to achieve this goal and to collect and treat leachates to remove dangerous impurities.

Modern landfills are lined with impermeable and durable materials that prevent leachates from moving into the groundwater. Some of these liners consist of clay minerals that are compacted; others are geomembranes, such as polyethylene sheets. The clay minerals used to line landfills are fine-grained minerals formed naturally during the weathering of coarser-grained minerals. Some of the clay minerals used, such as smectites, may also adsorb many of the metal ions from leachate so the metals do not move with the fluid.

Polyethylene liners are useful in landfills because they are durable and easy to install in addition to being relatively impermeable to most fluids. Such liners can, however, be torn or otherwise damaged by some materials placed into landfills. The most effective system for lining landfills to prevent the movement of leachates out of the landfills and into groundwater combines the two kinds of liners, alternating layers of compacted clay minerals with polyethylene sheets.

Landfills are ideally placed in impermeable sedimentary rocks, such as mudrocks (which also contain abundant clay minerals), that are above the water table rather than in permeable materials such as sand or sandstone. A dry climate also is desirable, but this may not be possible since transportation costs to move material to a landfill may be too high if the landfill is too far from the communities that use it.

Modern landfills also install systems to collect leachate and move it to sites where the worst impurities and contaminants can be removed through chemical and biological treatment. Sometimes leachate may be recycled through a landfill again so that bacteria can further reduce certain impurities. Leachate may also be placed into an oxygen-rich lagoon so that other bacteria may oxidize some of the dissolved materials contained in the leachate. Chemical treatment of leachate can further reduce some kinds of undesirable materials. For example, the precipitation of calcium or sodium hydroxide solids can remove many dissolved metals.

Robert L. Cullers

FURTHER READING

Bagchi, Amalendu. *Design of Landfills and Integrated Solid Waste Management.* 3d ed. Hoboken, N.J.: John Wiley & Sons, 2004.

Bedient, Philip B., Hanadi S. Rifai, and Charles J. Newell. *Ground Water Contamination: Transport and Remediation.* 2d ed. Upper Saddle River, N.J.: Prentice Hall, 1999.

Rogers, Heather. *Gone Tomorrow: The Hidden Life of Garbage.* New York: New Press, 2005.

Tammemagi, Hans. *The Waste Crisis: Landfills, Incinerators, and the Search for a Sustainable Future.* New York: Oxford University Press, 1999.

Westlake, Kenneth. *Landfill Waste Pollution and Control.* Chichester, West Sussex, England: Albion, 1995.

London Convention on the Prevention of Marine Pollution

CATEGORY: Treaties, laws, and court cases

THE CONVENTION: International agreement intended to halt the reckless dumping of wastes in marine waters

DATE: Opened for signature on December 29, 1972

SIGNIFICANCE: While not the largest source of marine pollution, dumping of wastes at sea was the norm for the decades leading up to the Convention on the Prevention of Marine Pollution. With a burgeon-

ing global population and new technology generating greater amounts of more potent waste, the need to limit this practice was and remains crucial.

The Convention on the Prevention of Marine Pollution by Dumping of Wastes and Other Matter, also known as the London Convention, was drafted and opened for signature in 1972 and entered into force in 1975. The aim of the convention is to prevent indiscriminate dumping of wastes at sea that could pose a threat to human health, damage marine life, or interfere with other uses of the sea. The convention applies to all marine waters other than a nation's internal waters; it excludes land-based dumping. By 2010 eighty-six nations had become parties to the convention.

The convention employs a so-called black list/gray list system. The black list specifies a number of dangerous pollutants that the parties to the convention are banned from dumping into marine waters, except in some cases where there are only trace levels of the pollutant or it is "rapidly rendered harmless." Examples of pollutants found on the black list include radioactive waste, persistent plastics, mercury, cadmium, organohalides, and materials for chemical or biological warfare. In contrast, pollutants found on the gray list can be dumped with a permit and under conditions specified by the convention.

Signatory nations are responsible for setting up their own laws to implement the convention's policies, and dumping figures are self-reported. The practice of self-reporting has at times hampered the convention's effectiveness, such as during the 1980's, when the Soviet Union regularly failed to report its dumping of radioactive waste. The convention, however, includes arbitration procedures for those times when parties disagree on reporting. When issuing permits for dumping, member nations are required to record the types and amounts of materials dumped, when and where the dumping takes place, and the condition of the seas of the area where the materials are dumped.

The contracting parties to the convention meet regularly at annual consultative meetings at which issues are raised and addressed and policies are shaped. The meetings are organized by the International Maritime Organization, which acts as the secretariat of the convention. Generally these meetings have widened the scope of the convention, adding new pollutants to the black list and setting tougher standards for permitting. The parties to the convention receive scientific and other expert input in making their decisions from a number of groups. The Scientific Group on Dumping, the convention's principal advisory board, is made up of experts chosen by the contracting parties; the group provides advice on issues related to the implementation of the convention's policies based on the latest scientific information.

In 1996 the London Protocol, a new agreement aimed at modernizing and eventually replacing the convention, was drafted. The protocol takes a much stricter stance on marine dumping, employing both the precautionary principle and the polluter pays principle. Regardless of the absence of conclusive evidence, the protocol regards all pollutants as detrimental to the marine environment. Thus, instead of black and gray lists, this agreement uses a "reverse list" that notes the pollutants permissible for dumping with a permit and bans all others. Also, parties are banned from exporting their waste to noncontracting parties for the purpose of dumping at sea. The London Protocol went into effect in 2006, and by 2010 thirty-seven nations had become parties to the agreement.

Daniel J. Connell

Further Reading

Guruswamy, Lakshman D., with Kevin L. Doran. "Dumping." In *International Environmental Law in a Nutshell.* 3d ed. St. Paul, Minn.: Thomson/West, 2007.

Louka, Elli. "Marine Environment." In *International Environmental Law: Fairness, Effectiveness, and World Order.* New York: Cambridge University Press, 2006.

Los Angeles Aqueduct

CATEGORY: Preservation and wilderness issues

IDENTIFICATION: System of canals, tunnels, and pipes built to divert water from the Owens River to Los Angeles

DATE: Completed on November 5, 1913

SIGNIFICANCE: The Los Angeles Aqueduct was constructed to meet the growing demand for water in the city of Los Angeles, but the diversion of water from the Owens River led to the drying of the Owens River Valley and the subsequent collapse of that region's agricultural industry.

The Los Angeles Aqueduct extends 378 kilometers (235 miles) from the Owens River a few miles north of Independence, California, to San Fernando, California, on the north side of Los Angeles. Begun in 1908 and completed in 1913, it is a complex system of unlined, lined, and lined and covered canals, tunnels, and steel pipes. For seventy-three years the entire flow of the Owens River at the aqueduct intake point, an average of about 984 million liters (260 million gallons) per day, was diverted from the Owens Valley to Los Angeles. Beginning in 1986, a portion of the original flow was restored to the Owens River below the intake point. The aqueduct was extended north to the Mono Lake basin in 1940, and a parallel aqueduct was completed in 1970.

In 1900 the population of Los Angeles was about 200,000 and was rapidly increasing. The city's water supply came from the Los Angeles River and a few wells and local springs. A substantial supply of water was required for the city to continue to grow, and there was no local source. To solve the problem, Fred Eaton, an engineer and former mayor of Los Angeles, conceived the Los Angeles Aqueduct and discussed his idea with William Mulholland, superintendent of the Los Angeles Department of Water. Mulholland spent forty days surveying the proposed aqueduct route and discussed the proposal with the Los Angeles Board of Water Commissioners. All this was done in secret to avoid a burst of land speculation. Eaton had already obtained options to buy most of the private land along the aqueduct route and later agreed to sell the options to Los Angeles at cost.

One obstacle remained. The U.S. Reclamation Service (which was created in 1902 and renamed the Bureau of Reclamation in 1923) was in the process of planning a major irrigation project in the Owens Valley and had withdrawn the public lands in the area from claim. Part of the aqueduct route passed through these public lands. The residents of the valley were enthusiastically in favor of the irrigation project.

Plans for the aqueduct were made public, and a committee from the Los Angeles Chamber of Commerce met with President Theodore Roosevelt. To the disappointment of the Owens Valley residents, President Roosevelt reached the conclusion that the Owens River water would be much more beneficial to Los Angeles than to Owens Valley, and in 1906 the U.S. Congress granted the necessary right-of-way for the aqueduct. To ensure its right to the Owens River water and increase the available supply, the city of Los Angeles be-

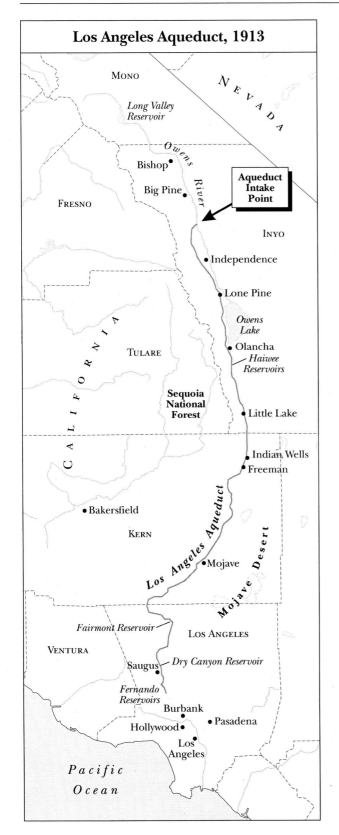

Los Angeles Aqueduct, 1913

gan buying the irrigated ranches and farms above the aqueduct intake in addition to properties below the intake that were now useless for lack of water. It was this maneuver, rather than the building of the aqueduct itself, that angered Owens Valley residents.

The Owens River Valley lies between the Sierra Nevada mountain range to the west and the White Mountains and Inyo range to the east. It is about 16 kilometers (10 miles) wide and 160 kilometers (100 miles) long. In its pristine state, the valley was a desert. The Owens River, flowing south from the Sierra Nevada, supported a fringe of willows and other riverside vegetation; the rest of the valley was thinly covered with cactus, chaparral, and sagebrush. The river ended at Owens Lake, an alkaline lake with no outlet. Because of evaporation over many thousands of years, the lake water was highly mineralized, primarily with sodium bicarbonate, but also with sulfates, chlorides, and other salts. The upper end of the lake was a freshwater marsh, which provided good habitat for waterfowl, as did the river north of the lake. The river, its fringe of vegetation undoubtedly home for many native birds, was on a major migratory pathway for several species of birds. Irrigation ditches serving farms, ranches, and orchards extended as far as 8 kilometers (5 miles) from the river. Carp, an exotic fish imported from Europe, swam in the irrigation ditches.

On completion of the Los Angeles Aqueduct in November, 1913, the lower 85 kilometers (53 miles) of the Owens River channel became dry; partial flow was not restored until 1986. The narrow fringe of riverside vegetation died, the marshes at the head of Owens Lake dried, and, eventually, the lake itself dried. Windstorms crossing the dry lake bed carried irritating alkali dust through the valley and often far beyond. The irrigated farms and ranches almost entirely disappeared, and Los Angeles, which owned most of the valley, allowed it to return to desert. The economy of the valley changed from one based on agriculture to one based on tourism and outdoor recreation. In purely economic terms, the income from tourism and outdoor recreation has vastly exceeded what might have been expected from an expansion of irrigation-based agriculture in the region.

By 1970 Los Angeles was using large quantities of well water to supplement aqueduct flow, lowering groundwater levels and drying local springs. In addition, the water level at Mono Lake was declining, threatening island breeding grounds of California gulls by creating land bridges that coyotes could cross.

If the aqueduct had not been built, the Reclamation Service probably would have constructed massive irrigation systems that might have been much more damaging to the environment of Owens Valley. Indeed, a Sierra Club spokesman once said, "We recognize that Los Angeles is probably the savior of the valley. Our goal is to save the valley as it is now."

Robert E. Carver

FURTHER READING

Deverell, William, and Greg Hise, eds. *Land of Sunshine: An Environmental History of Metropolitan Los Angeles.* Pittsburgh: University of Pittsburgh Press, 2005.

Fradkin, Philip L. *The Seven States of California: A Natural and Human History.* New York: Henry Holt, 1995.

Hundley, Norris, Jr. *The Great Thirst: Californians and Water—A History.* Rev. ed. Berkeley: University of California Press, 2001.

Mulholland, Catherine. *William Mulholland and the Rise of Los Angeles.* Berkeley: University of California Press, 2000.

Nadeau, Remi. *The Water Seekers.* 4th ed. Santa Barbara, Calif.: Crest, 1997.

Wood, Richard Coke. *The Owens Valley and the Los Angeles Controversy: Owens Valley as I Knew It.* Stockton, Calif.: University of the Pacific, 1973.

Mediterranean Blue Plan

CATEGORY: Water and water pollution

IDENTIFICATION: A multinational effort to curb pollution in the Mediterranean Sea

DATE: Initiated in 1980

SIGNIFICANCE: Action plans developed by researchers working with Blue Plan Regional Activity Centers have helped to reduce pollution in the Mediterranean, despite some difficulties posed by the need for international cooperation.

In 1980, under the auspices of the United Nations Environment Programme (UNEP), the nations bordering the Mediterranean Sea signed an agreement setting forth ways in which they would cooperate to reduce pollution of their common sea. The agreement, which soon came to be known as the Blue Plan (or Plan Bleu) for its efforts to clean the Mediterranean's waters, represented the culmination of several years of international efforts. In 1975, for example, UNEP had provided more than $7 million to the Mediterranean Action Plan (MAP), an earlier program designed to help Mediterranean countries fight pollution. Early in 1979, however, UNEP informed signatories to the 1975 agreement that it would cut back future financial support for MAP. UNEP thus called a February, 1979, conference in Geneva, Swit-

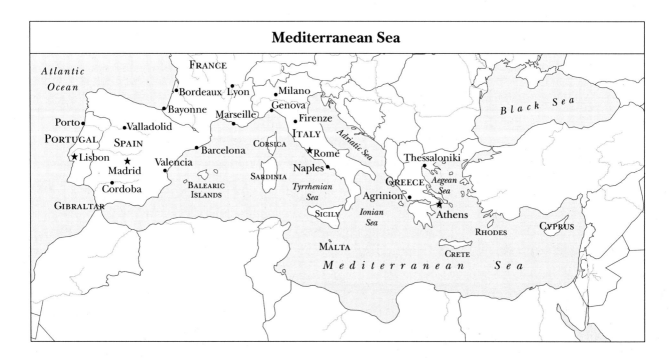

Mediterranean Sea

zerland, to prepare a new approach to budgetary demands for immediate environmental remedies and to map out a strategy for protecting the ecology of the Mediterranean basin. In Geneva, a program was drafted identifying twenty-three environmental protection projects demanding immediate attention. A budget of $6.5 million was established, one-half to come from the participating countries, one-fourth from UNEP, and the remainder from contributions of services and staff time by environmental organizations.

Staffs of international researchers formed Blue Plan Regional Activity Centers, which provide information to signatory governments to help them plan future economic development in such a way as to prevent a repetition of the environmental damages that had been done to the sea and its coastline in earlier decades. The role of UNEP is to facilitate communication among these centers and to sponsor international meetings to share findings and propose solutions on a regular basis. Blue Plan researchers have focused their attention on food production, industry, energy use, tourism, and transport. In the early years of the plan, for example, jointly sponsored research suggested that some ecologically harmful industries, such as mining and metallurgical processing and petrochemical production, were overproducing in Mediterranean areas; in such cases, plan officials suggested ecologically preferable and economically logical adjustments.

The attainment of such goals, however, has sometimes been complicated by political and economic factors. For example, efforts to streamline supply and production of coal and steel on a geographic basis were hindered by long-standing tensions between Turkey and Greece. Similarly, Tunisia and Algeria have resisted energy market cooperation with each other, although Tunisia needs the natural gas and petroleum that neighboring Algeria produces; Tunisia thus has continued to pursue, at substantial economic and ecological cost, its own limited petroleum production. Despite such setbacks, Blue Plan efforts have had some effect, and pollution levels in the Mediterranean have dropped.

Alexander Scott

FURTHER READING

Blondel, Jacques, et al. *The Mediterranean Region: Biological Diversity Through Time and Space.* 2d ed. New York: Oxford University Press, 2010.

Skjærset, Jon Birger. "The Effectiveness of the Mediterranean Action Plan." In *Environmental Regime Effectiveness: Confronting Theory with Evidence*, by Edward L. Miles et al. Cambridge, Mass.: MIT Press, 2002.

Wainwright, John, and John B. Thornes. *Environmental Issues in the Mediterranean: Processes and Perspectives from the Past and Present.* New York: Routledge, 2004.

Mississippi River

CATEGORIES: Places; ecology and ecosystems

IDENTIFICATION: Major inland tributary with headwaters at Lake Itasca in northern Minnesota, running south through ten U.S. states to a delta below New Orleans, Louisiana

SIGNIFICANCE: The second-longest river in the United States, the Mississippi serves as the drainage basin for 40 percent of the country, supplies nearly one-fourth of the country's drinking water, and is the principal route for inland waterborne commerce in the nation. Efforts to control its flow to accommodate commercial interests have created significant environmental problems that have adversely affected ecosystems and human communities along its banks.

The Mississippi River flows irregularly for approximately 3,750 kilometers (2,330 miles) through the midsection of the United States. It is fed by more than one hundred tributaries, including the Missouri and Ohio rivers. The Upper Mississippi, the region between the headwaters in Minnesota and the area in Illinois and Missouri where its two major tributaries join, is fairly narrow and shallow, at many points running between high bluffs. By contrast, the Lower Mississippi, shaped by activity during the Pleistocene glacial advance, is wide and deep. It runs through an alluvial floodplain that, before human intervention, frequently flooded in the spring.

The Mississippi River has been home to thousands of life-forms, including several endangered species; hundreds of species of birds and mammals populate its shorelines. It is the most important bird and waterfowl migration route in North America. Its bottomlands are the largest wetlands area and support the largest hardwood forest in the United States. Since the nineteenth century, however, engineering projects undertaken to benefit commercial enterprises have caused serious degradation of the Mississippi as a site for balanced natural ecosystems. Major damage has occurred principally in two forms: pollution introduced directly from commercial enterprises or indirectly by projects designed to control the flow of the river for commercial or recreational purposes, and flooding exacerbated by efforts to channel the river to maintain optimal shipping lanes.

COMMERCIALIZATION AND ITS IMPACTS

Since the nineteenth century the Mississippi River has served as a major route for commerce traveling from America's heartland to the Gulf of Mexico and from there to locations around the world. Numerous commercial enterprises and ports sprang up along the river during the nineteenth century, and farming became a major activity all along the Mississippi; in the lower regions, farms and plantations in the rich bottomlands took away natural habitats for wildlife,

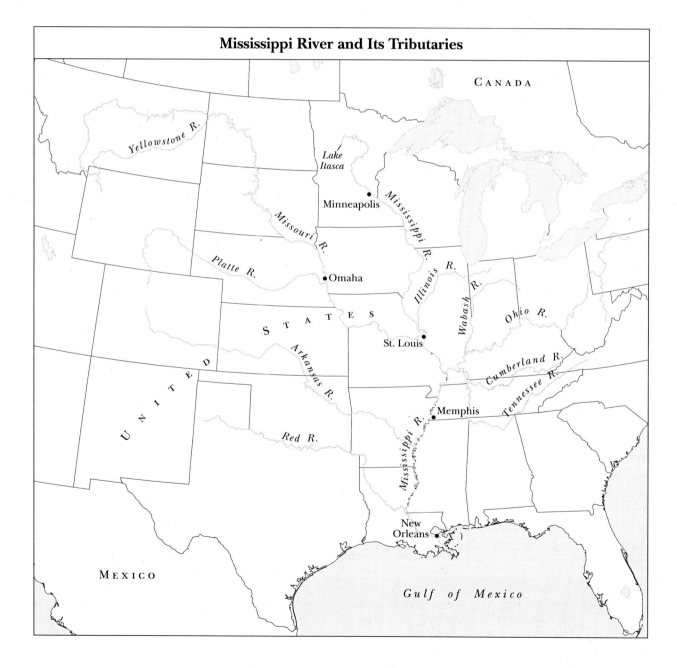

Mississippi River and Its Tributaries

weakened the riverbanks through erosion, and diminished natural cover for the soil.

Charged with managing the nation's waterways, the U.S. Army Corps of Engineers began improving navigability on the Mississippi in 1879. Over the years the Corps has undertaken a number of engineering projects to optimize the river's value for commerce. After a disastrous flood in 1927, the Corps initiated several programs aimed at flood control. A series of twenty-seven locks and dams were constructed to create a continuous nine-foot shipping lane from Minneapolis to St. Louis, Missouri, guaranteeing the easy passage of barge traffic. Large earth-and-concrete levees were constructed to prevent flooding below St. Louis. In addition to flood prevention, the levees were designed to increase the force of the water to maintain a deep channel in the river. Nevertheless, for decades the Corps has been forced to conduct systematic dredging, especially near the delta, where silt buildup makes it difficult for larger ships to travel into and out of the Gulf of Mexico.

These initiatives allowed commercial use of the river to increase dramatically; for example, in 2000 more than 83 million tons of cargo moved down the river. Farm crops make up the majority of this cargo, and farmers' ability to use the river to send goods to ports around the country and the world has kept down the need for overland transport. Another twentieth century development was the construction of paper mills, chemical plants, and oil refineries along the river's banks, which proved an ideal location for companies wishing to ship large quantities of their products.

POLLUTION PROBLEMS

The benefits of commercial use of the Mississippi have been balanced, and perhaps outweighed, by damage done to the river's ecosystems. Numerous species of fish and wildlife disappeared from the upper river as pools and backwaters between dams became silted. The high levees below St. Louis caused wetlands adjacent to the river to dry up, eliminating habitat for numerous species. Cities and towns have often dumped sewage into the river, and chemical runoff from farms, particularly phosphorus and nitrogen, has polluted the waterway from its northernmost reaches down to the Gulf. As far north as Minnesota, chemical plants have dumped toxic waste into the Mississippi, polluting it with a variety of toxins, including furan, trichlorobenzene, dichloro-diphenyl-trichloroethane (DDT), trichloroethane (TCA), and

polychlorinated biphenyls (PCBs). The problem has become exacerbated farther south, especially from Baton Rouge, Louisiana, to the mouth of the river, where chemical plants and oil refineries are concentrated. The cumulative effects of toxic waste disposal, oil spillage, and other forms of refuse dumping have materially degraded the use of the river and its banks for fishing, hunting, and trapping and have led to the creation of a hypoxic (depleted of oxygen) area, known as a dead zone, at the mouth of the river extending into the Gulf of Mexico. This area is one of the largest dead zones in the world.

Until the 1960's, many commercial enterprises used the river as a dumping ground for waste, and little was done to protect the natural environment. Since the 1960's, however, environmental groups such as the Izaak Walton League and Greenpeace, as well as organizations sponsoring recreational use of the river, have been increasingly active in demanding that the federal government take measures to protect the Mississippi's ecosystems. Their efforts have sparked modest programs to reduce pollution and reverse the adverse environmental effects of the levees, locks, and dams. A government-sponsored environmental management plan implemented in 1986 is aimed at restoring wetlands. Monitoring by the government and private groups has resulted in a reduction in point source pollution (that is, pollution caused by specific sources, such as refuse dumped by a specific business or city), but nonpoint source pollution, especially runoff from agricultural regions, has been much harder to control.

FLOODING AND FLOOD CONTROL

Traditionally, spring runoff from as far away as the Rocky Mountains to the west and the Appalachians to the east has caused the Mississippi River to rise above its banks and flood adjacent lands. The natural environment historically benefited from this seasonal event, as flooding created rich alluvial soil and wetland habitats. Efforts to control the flow of the Mississippi changed flood patterns significantly, however, as the river was hemmed in by high levees. Waters rushing downstream now do so more rapidly until, in extreme cases, their power creates levee breaks. Debris from the natural landscape and human structures swept away by the current and pollutants being carried downstream have wreaked havoc in flooded areas, and attendant damages to residential and commercial centers built up along the river have often run into the billions of dollars. In turn, the Army Corps of

Engineers has been called upon to devise more stringent measures to keep the river within manageable boundaries, further reducing the wetlands environments along the banks and concentrating pollutants within the river's main channel. The Corps has also been active in implementing measures to keep the Mississippi from changing its main channel, a phenomenon common before the nineteenth century. Such changes could cause cities and towns along the river to become landlocked, which would materially affect their commerce.

Efforts to control flooding while maximizing the river's commercial potential have also had negative effects downstream, especially around New Orleans. In 1965 the Corps created the Mississippi River Gulf Outlet (MRGO), a direct channel giving commercial ships a shorter route from the city to the Gulf of Mexico. The channel had little impact on reducing ship traffic, but its presence led to considerable erosion of marshes and wetlands south of the city. The impact was most noticeable when Hurricane Katrina hit in 2005. While the levees along the Mississippi were not breached, the surge from the Gulf traveled up the MRGO and over terrain bereft of natural barriers, causing breaches in flood walls of canals leading off the river into urban areas. Waters inundated New Orleans, creating the worst natural disaster in the history of the United States.

Laurence W. Mazzeno

FURTHER READING

Anfinson, John O. *The River We Have Wrought*. Minneapolis: University of Minnesota Press, 2003.

Fischer, Katherine. *Dreaming the Mississippi*. Columbia: University of Missouri Press, 2006.

Fremling, Calvin R. *Immortal River: The Upper Mississippi in Ancient and Modern Times*. Madison: University of Wisconsin Press, 2005.

Hall, B. C., and C. T. Wood. *Big Muddy: Down the Mississippi Through America's Heartland*. New York: Dutton, 1992.

Hilliard, Sam B., ed. *Man and Environment in the Lower Mississippi Valley*. Baton Rouge: Louisiana State University School of Geoscience, 1978.

Meyer, Gary C. "Preservation and Management of the River's Natural Resources." In *Grand Excursions on the Upper Mississippi River: Places, Landscapes, and Regional Identity After 1854*, edited by Curtis C. Roseman and Elizabeth M. Roseman. Iowa City: University of Iowa Press, 2004.

Mono Lake

CATEGORIES: Places; ecology and ecosystems

IDENTIFICATION: Natural saline lake located in east-central California

SIGNIFICANCE: The diversion of stream water from Mono Lake for use by the city of Los Angeles led to lowered water levels and higher-than-normal salinity in the lake, which had serious impacts on the lake's delicate ecosystem.

Mono Lake, which covers about 150 square kilometers (58 square miles), receives most of its water from underground water flow and from streams that drain from the Sierra Nevada to the west. The lake has no outlet, so evaporation is the main natural cause of water loss. Since 1941, the city of Los Angeles has diverted water from the streams that drain into Mono Lake into the Los Angeles Aqueduct to supply the city with water. This loss of stream water into the lake resulted in a drop in the lake's water level of more than 15 meters (49 feet), with a consequent increase in dissolved constituents in the lake.

By the early twenty-first century, Mono Lake's water contained about three times the concentration of dissolved salts found in seawater. The main kinds of dissolved ions (charged particles) found in the lake are sodium, chloride, and carbonate-bicarbonate. Lesser amounts of potassium, magnesium, and sulfate ions are also present. In addition, the waters have a very low hydrogen ion concentration (low acidity) and high hydroxide ion concentration compared with most natural waters. Nitrate, phosphate, and ammonium ion concentrations are also fairly high compared with most natural waters, especially in the lower portions of the lake. These ions help to stimulate the growth of phytoplankton in the lake waters.

The high concentrations of calcium and carbonate-bicarbonate ions in some places in Mono Lake have caused chemical precipitation of tufa towers (composed of calcium carbonate) underwater, often helped by the action of algae. As the lake levels have dropped, the tufa towers have become exposed around the edges of the lake in certain places. The towers provide nesting places for owls, falcons, and small mammals.

PLANTS AND ANIMALS

Mono Lake is too salty for fish and most water birds. In the spring, however, the lake explodes with millions of tons of algae and other small plants. Two larger organisms feed on the algae: brine shrimp and small alkali flies. Brine shrimp are small crustaceans, often red in color and each only a little more than 1 centimeter (0.4 inch) long, with small appendages that they use to move algae into their mouths. They are found in Mono Lake, mostly in the upper, oxygen-rich waters, only from spring to fall; it has been estimated that some seven trillion shrimp may inhabit the lake at their seasonal peak. Alkali flies occur in swarms along the shoreline of the lake. They feed on the algae and lay eggs in algal mats underwater.

A few species of birds have adapted to being able to use Mono Lake at least during some parts of the year, especially when there are large quantities of brine shrimp and alkali flies to eat. The California gull is one such bird; these gulls are abundant in the summer, when they form nests on some of the small islands in the lake. The gulls migrate toward the ocean during the winter. The eared grebe is another bird that lives in the lake in the summer and fall, consuming vast amounts of brine shrimp before flying south in the winter to the Gulf of California. The red-necked phalarope and Wilson's phalarope stop over at Mono Lake, where they consume large quantities of alkali flies, before flying more than 4,800 kilometers (about 3,000 miles) south in the winter to places in South America. The American avocet, a long-legged wading bird, stops at the lake in the spring when flying to the north and in the fall when flying to the south. Many kinds of ducks also stop by the lake, although the waters are too salty for them to spend much time there. Before Los Angeles diverted the freshwater streams draining into Mono Lake, many more kinds and numbers of ducks used to stop at nearby streams and visit the less salty waters in the lake near the streams.

Environmental Problems

The diversion of stream flow from Mono Lake to the Los Angeles Aqueduct that began in the 1940's resulted over time in a large drop in the average volume of water in the lake and thus lowered the lake level. The salinity of the waters eventually doubled in concentration, reducing the production of algae and thus the populations of brine shrimp that fed on the algae. The lake's recreational uses were also affected, as boat docks and beaches were left without water near them as the water level dropped. Up to five-sixths of the average flow of stream water that had originally gone to

Mono Lake was being diverted to Los Angeles, and in years with low rainfall, some streams simply dried up. The fish populations, vegetation, and wetlands that depended on these streams were severely damaged.

Beginning in 1979, environmentalists brought lawsuits intended to force the city of Los Angeles to stop diverting water from Mono Lake. After many court decisions and appeals, in the mid-1990's Los Angeles was required to reduce its diversion of Mono Lake waters so that the original level and salinity of the lake could eventually be restored.

Robert L. Cullers

Further Reading

Carl, David, and Don Banta. *Mono Lake Basin, California.* Mount Pleasant, S.C.: Arcadia, 2008.

Flaherty, Dennis, and Mark A. Schlenz. *Mono Lake: Mirror of Imagination.* Santa Barbara, Calif.: Companion Press, 2007.

Hart, John. *Storm over Mono: The Mono Lake Battle and the California Water Future.* Berkeley: University of California Press, 1996.

Mono Basin Ecosystem Study Committee. *The Mono Basin Ecosystem.* Washington, D.C.: National Academy Press, 1987.

Monongahela River tank collapse

Category: Disasters

The Event: Collapse of an oil storage tank near the Monongahela River in Pennsylvania that resulted in a massive oil spill

Date: January 2, 1988

Significance: When a faulty storage tank released millions of gallons of oil near the Monongahela River, creating the worst inland oil spill in U.S. history to that date, the environmental damage included the deaths of thousands of fish and waterfowl.

In the early evening of January 2, 1988, the rupture of a storage tank at the Ashland Oil terminal in Floreffe, Pennsylvania, 40 kilometers (25 miles) southeast of Pittsburgh, released 3.9 million gallons of diesel oil. The oil spilled over a containment dike and flowed across a road into a ravine, and much of the oil eventually found its way into a storm sewer leading to the Monongahela River.

Because of darkness and freezing weather, the extent of the damage was not fully recognized until the next morning, by which time nearly 750,000 gallons of oil had flowed through the storm sewer into the Monongahela. Nevertheless, response efforts from a number of agencies, including the local volunteer fire department, borough police, and the Mt. Pleasant Hazardous Materials Team, began almost immediately. Within hours, a team from the Pennsylvania Emergency Management Agency (PEMA) was en route.

The first concern of those responding was to stop the flow of fuel, but darkness and cold made the operation difficult. Moreover, a strong odor of gasoline indicated an additional gas leak of unknown origin. The mixture of gasoline and diesel fuel presented a dangerous situation made even more serious by the presence of hazardous chemicals at a nearby chemical plant, and the decision was made to evacuate twelve hundred nearby residents. Emergency crews and firefighters worked throughout the night to contain the oil.

A coordinator from the U.S. Environmental Protection Agency (EPA) arrived the following morning and discovered the condition of the river to be worse than expected, as the oil had dispersed through the water volume rather than remaining on the surface. Water intakes for communities downstream on the Monongahela and the Ohio River were shut off as a preventive measure.

Containment booms placed downstream had little effect, so deflection booms were used to move the oil to collection areas. Because of the cold temperatures, the oil formed heavy globs that could be picked up from the river edges and bottom. Over the next two months, nearly 205,000 gallons of oil, or 29 percent of the total spilled into the river, were recovered.

The damage caused to wildlife in and near the river was difficult to assess, as many species were hibernating or otherwise inactive in the winter weather. Researchers estimated that the spill killed eleven thousand fish and two thousand waterfowl.

Investigations into the cause of the collapse discovered a small flaw in the steel plates at the base of the storage tank. The tank's forty-year-old steel had been weakened by reassembly, and the temperature was low enough to cause a brittle fracture. When the tank was filled, the resulting stress caused a crack near a weld.

Ashland Oil had not secured a written permit before constructing the tank, and the tank had not been properly tested before it was filled. The company was

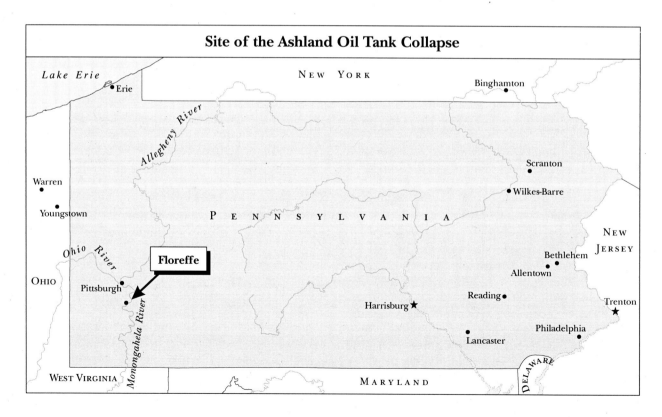

Site of the Ashland Oil Tank Collapse

held liable for all damages, and it paid a federal fine of $2.25 million for violating the Clean Water Act and the Refuse Act; it also paid $11 million in cleanup costs and tens of millions more to other injured parties.

Alexander Scott

FURTHER READING
Fingas, Merv. *The Basics of Oil Spill Cleanup.* 2d ed. Boca Raton, Fla.: CRC Press, 2001.
Lehr, Jay, et al. "Oil Spills and Leaks." In *Handbook of Complex Environmental Remediation Problems.* New York: McGraw-Hill, 2002.

Nile River

CATEGORIES: Places; ecology and ecosystems
IDENTIFICATION: Major river flowing northward from Central Africa into the eastern Mediterranean Sea
SIGNIFICANCE: The Nile River is of inestimable value to the populations of the otherwise dry countries of northeast Africa, but the control of its waters is in dispute and its environmental health is deteriorating.

At 6,820 kilometers (4,238 miles), the Nile is the longest river in the world. It flows through several bioregions and, along with its branches and tributaries, drains one-tenth of the African continent, an area of approximately 3.1 million square kilometers (1.2 million square miles) that is home to some 150 million people.

The branch of the river known as the White Nile rises in Burundi but loses almost half its volume through evaporation and transpiration in the swamps of the Sudd in southern Sudan. Thus the Blue Nile, which is fed by the summer monsoon rains of the Ethiopian highlands and which joins the White Nile at Khartoum, is largely responsible for the annual floods on which the populations downriver depend. The ancient Egyptians dug canals and erected earthworks on the lower reaches of the river in order to irrigate their fields, a practice continued by succeeding generations. During the first half of the nineteenth century, Turkish viceroy Muḥammad ʿAlī Pasha was responsible for creating a more effective series of diversion dams and canals.

While the Nile's floods are predictable, their size is not. Egypt's British occupiers completed a dam at Aswan in 1902 in the hope of controlling excessive flooding and mitigating the effects of drought, but the dam's reservoir submerged the first cataract of the Nile. Four more dams on the Nile and its tributaries in Sudan followed between 1925 and 1966. The need for hydroelectricity led to the construction of a dam at Owen Falls in Uganda in 1954, which caused the submersion of Ripon Falls near Lake Victoria. Environmental trade-offs continued with the completion of the Aswan High Dam in 1970. The dam brought with it a number of undeniable benefits, including flood control, the generation of hydroelectricity, and the provision of a constant supply of water for irrigation. However, a number of grave consequences ensued as well, including the spread of waterborne diseases and the erosion and salinization of the downriver floodplain. In the twenty-first century, rising sea levels caused by global warming threaten to speed the erosion of the Nile Delta.

Fluctuating weather patterns have compounded the river's environmental problems. Greater-than-average precipitation from 1961 through 1964, blamed on the El Niño weather pattern, destroyed riparian communities and filled the reservoir behind the Aswan High Dam to dangerous levels. Subsequent droughts created massive famine in Ethiopia and exacerbated international rivalries throughout the region. In 1978 Egypt and Sudan began work on the Jonglei Canal, which was designed to allow more of the White Nile's waters to bypass the stagnant Sudd, but construction was halted in 1984 by the Second Sudanese Civil War. In 2008 the two countries agreed to begin work on the project again. Other international cooperative ventures include the Nile Basin Initiative, created in 1999 by nine of the ten countries sharing the basin with the aim of safeguarding its waters and sharing them equitably.

As the population of the Nile basin grows, shortages of fresh water threaten to become increasingly common. By some measurements of per-capita requirements, several countries in the southern basin are already water-deficient, and Egypt—where the Nile's waters have grown heavily polluted—and Ethiopia are expected to become water-deficient in 2025.

Grove Koger

FURTHER READING
Collins, Robert O. *The Nile.* New Haven, Conn.: Yale University Press, 2002.

Hamza, W. "The Nile Estuary." In *Estuaries*, edited by Peter J. Wangersky. New York: Springer, 2006.

Park, Chris S. *The Environment: Principles and Applications.* 2d ed. New York: Routledge, 2001.

North American Free Trade Agreement

CATEGORIES: Treaties, laws, and court cases; atmosphere and air pollution

THE TREATY: International agreement providing for the removal of trade barriers and reduction of many important legal and financial restrictions among the United States, Canada, and Mexico

DATE: Signed on December 17, 1992

SIGNIFICANCE: The North American Free Trade Agreement is considered by its supporters to mark new directions in international relations by opening the borders of three very different countries in ways that are intended to enhance not only economic but political and cultural relations as well. Although results have fallen short of original expectations, provisions of the North American Agreement on Environmental Cooperation, a side treaty that went into effect at the same time, are intended to raise awareness of environmental protection issues in all three countries.

The North American Free Trade Agreement (NAFTA), an unparalleled trade accord among the United States, Canada, and Mexico, was signed on December 17, 1992. Once ratified by the legislative bodies of the three nations, the agreement went into effect on January 1, 1994. Although the United States and Canada had established open bilateral trading terms in 1988 (the Canada-United States Free Trade Agreement), NAFTA not only aimed at expanding the earlier agreement, particularly in terms of liberalization of conditions for cross-border private investment, but it also sought to integrate terms of trade and investment between two highly developed national economies and a third emerging, or developing, country. An important aspect of Mexico's role in NAFTA was an expectation that the steps toward liberalization of the Mexican economy begun in 1985 (that is, privatization of traditionally state-run companies and increased emphasis on market-oriented

economic activity) would continue at a regular pace.

A first and major aim of NAFTA was to eliminate tariff-based trade "barriers" that historically had shielded domestically produced goods, whether agricultural or industrial, from competition from lower-priced foreign imported goods. High tariffs automatically raise prices for imports. An equally important goal was to eliminate, as much as possible, individual national laws hampering the free flow of labor and capital across the signatories' borders.

Beyond measurable economic results, the "spirit" of NAFTA aimed at improving political relations among the three signatories, especially between the United States and Mexico. A very high priority, for example, was (and continues to be) the need for political cooperation in the war against commerce in illicit drugs—increasingly a military as well as a political necessity. Decades-old concerns over the movement of illegal Mexican immigrants across the border into the United States stood to be reexamined in light of NAFTA's commitment to free trade not only in goods but also in cross-border labor arrangements. Another area dependent on mid- to long-term cooperation across national borders involves proposed programs, largely through shared technology, for ecological sustainability.

Numerous research reports appeared before NAFTA went into effect and continued to appear as analysts tried to estimate the relative attractions and disadvantages for one or another of the signatories that might result from the application of the agreement. In fact, during the first decade and a half of NAFTA's operation, certain patterns, some expected and welcomed, others quite controversial, began to take form. Parties that had opposed the agreement seemed convinced that their negative position had been justified. One argument, for example, was aimed at cross-border investment patterns. Opponents of NAFTA argued that, as U.S. private investment in Mexico increased, levels of investment in the United States itself would be decreased proportionately. Although statistics from the mid-1990's showed some shift in the value of U.S. capital going to Mexico, the overall weight of the movement—not overwhelmingly great—had to be compared with capital going to other, non-NAFTA countries that continue to attract very high levels of U.S. private investment.

On the positive side, supporters of NAFTA could argue that gradual but continuous growth of the Mexican economy would increase its capacity to import a wide variety of goods from its northern neighbors, especially from the United States. The movement of imports into Mexico would obviously be enhanced by reduced Mexican tariff rates—historically as much as three times the tariff rates of the United States. Estimates of rising levels of U.S. exports to Mexico seemed convincing, rising from about twelve billion dollars in 1986 to more than forty billion dollars in 1993.

Perhaps the strongest arguments against trends facilitated by NAFTA have had to do with potentially controversial effects on labor conditions, particularly on both sides of the Mexico-U.S. border. Critics claim that, as more and more companies opt to move their manufacturing activities to locations in Mexico, where labor costs are considerably lower, U.S. factories are losing orders even to the point of having to close down. Another major concern is symbolized by the Spanish term *maquiladora*, which refers to a factory set up in Mexico with the specific aim of importing (duty-free under NAFTA's terms) machinery and parts needed for assembly of a wide range of goods (ranging from clothing to automobiles) to be exported (again duty-free) for sale on the U.S. market. Many *maquiladoras* have been criticized for exploitative labor practices (substandard wages and working conditions, tenuous job security, and so on) that, according to critics, have been ignored by those profiting north of the border.

Support for goals set by NAFTA's founders during the 1990's continued to be voiced by Mexico's political leadership through the first decade of the new century. In an interview aired on American television in March, 2010, for example, President Felipe Calderón stressed his continued belief that a complementarity exists between Mexico's labor-intensive economy and the capital-intensive economies of its northern neighbors, especially the United States. Whether his words reflected a realistic appraisal or hopeful idealism, he concluded that the two nations "need each other."

This shared need is especially clear in matters touching on environmental protection. Although initially there were expectations that NAFTA would create positive conditions for ecological improvements in all three member states, such hopes gradually fell short of realities. On one hand, optimists predicted that hoped-for increases in per-capita income in Mexico as a result of higher levels of capital investment, accompanied by an expected shift away from traditional pollution-intensive industries south of the U.S. border (such as cement and base metals production), would help reduce heavy levels of pollution in Mexico. On the other hand, pessimists claimed that laxity in Mexico's regulation of pollution might even attract heavy polluters from the more developed NAFTA members to the north. The outcomes predicted by either side have not materialized in statistically provable terms.

Tremendously high levels of pollution in and around Mexico City aside (as this problem is beyond the purview of NAFTA technical observers), Mexico's record in dealing with soil erosion, water pollution, and urban solid waste pollution remains controversial. Although NAFTA has from the outset been "armed" with an institution specifically designated to coordinate environmental protection efforts (the Commission for Environmental Cooperation, or CEC, which was created by the North American Agreement on Environmental Cooperation, a side treaty of NAFTA), only one-third of the CEC budget (about nine million dollars in the late 1990's) goes to Mexico. In fact, although Mexico did emerge from the major slump that hit its economy in the 1980's, by 2010 expenditures for environmental improvements (including vital inspections of pollution-intensive industries) had never reached target levels laid down by the CEC.

Many environmental protection frustrations identified in the first decades of NAFTA's existence remained and even grew in the first decade of the twenty-first century. Severe budgetary problems that originally seemed to be solely a Mexican dilemma, for example, affected both Canada and the United States when near collapse of the world financial system struck in 2008-2009. This development raised fears of necessary reductions in funding for environmental projects.

Byron Cannon

Further Reading

Cameron, Maxwell A., and Brian W. Tomlin. *The Making of NAFTA: How the Deal Was Done.* Ithaca, N.Y.: Cornell University Press, 2000.

Gallagher, Kevin. *Free Trade and the Environment: Mexico, NAFTA, and Beyond.* Stanford, Calif.: Stanford University Press, 2004.

Grinspun, Ricardo, and Yasmine Shamsie, eds. *Whose Canada? Continental Integration, Fortress North America, and the Corporate Agenda.* Montreal: McGill-Queens University Press, 2007.

Hansen, Patricia Isela. "The Interplay Between Trade and the Environment Within the NAFTA Framework." In *Environment, Human Rights, and International Trade*, edited by Francesco Francioni. Portland, Oreg.: Hart, 2001.

Hufbauer, Gary Clyde, and Jeffrey J. Schott. *NAFTA Revisited: Achievements and Challenges.* Washington, D.C.: Institute for International Economics, 2005.

McPhail, Brenda M., ed. *NAFTA Now! The Changing Political Economy of North America.* Lanham, Md.: University Press of America, 1995.

Ocean currents

CATEGORY: Weather and climate

DEFINITION: Continuous surface and deep-level movements of ocean waters in certain directions

SIGNIFICANCE: For environmentalists, the study of ocean currents relates directly to two major concerns: the potential impact of the currents on global climate and weather changes and how the currents can assist in the conservation and sustainable cultivation of food and other marine resources.

Scientists understand a great deal about the significant large-scale movements of all ocean waters, but the specific driving forces are still under investigation. Studies of ocean currents are usually divided between a focus on surface currents, which are largely driven by prevailing winds, and a focus on deep-level currents, which are driven by more complex factors, including saline density, water temperatures, the gravitational pull of the moon, and sea-bottom depths as well as shoreline formations. The impacts of marine life-forms on water circulation, including the movement of microscopic plankton species, are also part of the study of ocean currents.

SURFACE OCEAN CURRENTS

Ocean currents in the upper 400 meters (roughly 1,300 feet) of the ocean depths are largely driven by wind currents, which represents the movement of roughly 10 percent of the ocean water in total. Surface currents and winds have been studied and measured for centuries. While precise modern models are quite complex, in general scientists refer to prevailing winds, which blow from west toward the east in the latitudes between 30 and 60 degrees, and trade winds, which blow from east to the west closer to the equator (below 30 degrees latitude). These winds create the classic sailing routes, such as the routes between the eastern United States and Europe, where sailing more north assists in a heading toward Europe and sailing more south (toward the equator) assists in a heading toward the eastern United States seaboard.

The study of ocean currents and flows, however, reveals that this general picture is made far more complex by the existence of related currents called meanders, rings, eddies, and gyres. These are relatively smaller patterns of flow within the larger general current pattern. For example, an oceanic gyre or ring is created when winds and limitations of shorelines create circular movement of currents (the circles can be smaller, rings, or involve entire sections of an ocean surface between major continents, such as the South Pacific Gyre, the Indian Ocean Gyre, and the North Atlantic Gyre).

These smaller-scale currents are important for sea life as well as for navigation. Circular rings and eddies, rather like air weather patterns of cyclones or tornadoes, can draw materials from the bottom of the ocean and mix layers of currents that provide nourishment for the development of microscopic life, starting an important food chain that supports various levels of higher sea life. Many of these rings thus sustain areas historically known for specific species of sea life. Consequently, disruptions in these patterns have potential implications for cultivation of these traditional stocks.

It has become increasingly important for scientists to understand long-term cycles of shifting weather and ocean current patterns. Prevailing winds and currents have been noted to run in regular patterns for thirty to fifty years and then shift for an equal amount of time before returning again to the previous conditions. This has important implications for commercial fisheries, for example, because oceanographers must account not only for the human-made (anthropogenic) dangers of overfishing but also for the apparently natural shifts in current patterns that have impacts on the availability of certain species. These patterns have been found to have positive effects on some species and negative effects on others.

VERTICAL CURRENTS

In contrast to wind-driven surface currents, which have been known for centuries, below-surface currents were not believed to be significant until relatively recently. In the twentieth and twenty-first centuries, however, deep-ocean currents have received considerable attention. In addition to the horizontal movements in ocean waters are the vertical movements usually referred to as thermohaline circulation. The term "thermohaline" comes from the Greek words for heat and salt, the two major influences on deepwater currents in addition to gravitational pull from the moon and the impacts of coastline formations. Thermohaline circulation is sometimes popularly referred to as the oceanic conveyer belt. The slow movement of these currents can extend into the hundreds of years.

Put simply, dense, and thus heavier, waters are created in the extreme cold conditions of the polar seas. These waters sink, following currents away from the poles and pushing up warmer waters to interact with the cooler atmospheric temperatures. Deep ocean currents affect 75 percent of ocean waters, which have a temperature from 0 to 5 degrees Celsius (32 to 41 degrees Fahrenheit). Deepwater circulation involves the vast majority of ocean waters as opposed to the surface, horizontal movements driven by prevailing winds.

ENVIRONMENTAL IMPACTS

One of the most important implications of the vertical currents of the world's oceans concerns the amount of carbon dioxide in the earth's atmosphere. Colder water absorbs carbon dioxide, whereas warmer water releases it. Another important factor in carbon dioxide distribution is the process known as the biological pump, which moves carbon from the ocean surface to the seafloor. While the presence of carbon dioxide is part of the reason the earth is habitable (the greenhouse effect is one reason the earth is warm enough for human occupation), there is concern that human activity has created abnormal levels of carbon dioxide. The rate at which carbon dioxide is being added to the atmosphere has not been exceeded in the past 420,000 years, and the increase since the mid-nineteenth century has been greater than any observed during the past 20,000 years. Two-thirds of this increase comes from the burning of fossil fuels; the last one-third can be accounted for by deforestation. If global temperatures continue to rise beyond the ability of the ocean currents and the biological pump to mitigate the effects, it is possible that ocean levels will rise enough to inundate low-lying coastlines around the world.

Scientists have also speculated about whether anthropogenic impacts on the atmosphere could actually interfere with the thermohaline circulation. Such interference could potentially have catastrophic impacts on both weather patterns and marine life in and near landmasses around the world. Many European nations, for example, have historically had relatively mild climates in part because of the warming impact of ocean currents on weather patterns. Sudden shifts in these currents could thus result in rapid changes in historic weather patterns. Oceanographic scientists do not all agree, however, regarding the likelihood of such

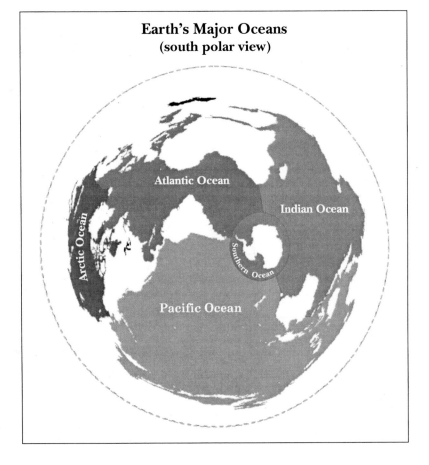

Earth's Major Oceans
(south polar view)

Atlantic Ocean

Indian Ocean

Arctic Ocean

Southern Ocean

Pacific Ocean

catastrophic changes. An ongoing debate among scientists concerns the ability to measure long-term cyclical change versus anthropogenic change.

In addition, questions remain concerning impacts on the oceans and the energy sources that drive currents. Nigel Calder, for example, has pointed out that whereas it was once presumed that salinity levels and temperature are primary producers of currents, as recently as 1998 two American oceanographers suggested instead that winds and especially the moon's gravitational pull have a much more significant impact on ocean currents, and particularly on the circulation of ocean waters and their interactions with the land borders. Calder concludes, "If the tidal story is correct, the value of 20th-century computer models of the ocean circulation, based as they were on heat-salt effects, is seriously in question."

Oceanographers are increasingly taking greater numbers of variables into consideration in their analyses of ocean currents and the impacts of weather patterns. Ocean water reacts with sunlight, with various temperatures of air, and with temperature differences between layers of the open sea, and the ways in which changes in ocean currents and temperatures actually take place are not entirely understood. Most scientists agree, however, on the importance of learning more about the potential for change in ocean currents in the short and the long term.

Daniel L. Smith-Christopher

FURTHER READING

Calder, Nigel. "Ocean Currents." In *Magic Universe: The Oxford Guide to Modern Science.* New York: Oxford University Press, 2003.

Longhurst, Alan. *Ecological Geography of the Sea.* 2d ed. Boston: Elsevier, 2007.

Mann, K. H., and J. R. N. Lazier. *Dynamics of Marine Ecosystems: Biological-Physical Interactions in the Oceans.* 3d ed. Malden, Mass.: Blackwell, 2006.

Park, Chris C. "Oceans and Coasts." In *The Environment: Principles and Applications.* 2d ed. New York: Routledge, 2001.

Ocean dumping

CATEGORY: Waste and waste management
DEFINITION: Disposal of waste products in the world's oceans

SIGNIFICANCE: The disposal of sewage, dredging spoil, garbage, chemicals, and other waste into the ocean disrupts individual ecosystems and kills fish and marine life. Although many marine pollution treaties and laws have been written to regulate dumping, such treaties and legislation have proven difficult to enforce.

The ocean is the final stop for much of the garbage generated on land. Sewage processing centers release treated wastewater into the ocean. Waste management officials at overflowing landfills have looked to the ocean as an alternative to burying rubbish and debris. Oil tankers have rinsed and flushed holding compartments in the open ocean. Fishing vessels dump scrap parts and unwanted or spoiled fish into the water. For decades, these sources of pollution were thought to have little effect on the world's oceans because they are so large. Whether in large or small amounts, however, marine dumping upsets the balance of ocean ecosystems, altering the environments to which fish, plants, and other marine organisms are accustomed. Some survive the changes, but others do not.

Industrial facilities have found the ocean useful for the disposal of waste products as well. Some companies have sealed waste chemicals into metal containers and dumped them "harmlessly" onto the ocean floor. There, the life cycles of crabs, ground fish, and other marine-floor creatures have been disrupted by these alien containers. Over time some of these containers have begun to leak, sometimes releasing radioactive waste or chemicals harmful to the environment.

Most of the garbage dumped directly into the oceans has come from ships and boats (although trash continues to make its way from the land into oceans via storm drains, winds, and beach littering). The number of fishing boats, naval vessels, cruise ships, cargo ships, and recreational boats taking to the sea daily is estimated to be in the millions. Many of the larger vessels are like floating towns. With thousands of people on board, these ships can quickly accumulate large amounts of sewage, garbage, and other waste, and space for storing it is often limited. Some ships, such as fishing and naval vessels, remain on the open ocean for weeks or months at a time; it is therefore not surprising that many of these vessels solve their garbage problems by dumping waste overboard. Although the disposal of sewage and wastewater in this way is illegal, many seafaring vessels ignore such laws because they are difficult to enforce.

ANTIDUMPING TREATIES

The environmental threat posed by ocean dumping was apparent by the early 1970's and led to the international Convention on the Prevention of Marine Pollution by Dumping of Wastes and Other Matter, also known as the London Convention, in 1972. One of the earliest global treaties for protection of the marine environment, it entered into force in 1975. The London Convention bans the dumping of certain hazardous materials and requires permits for the dumping of other materials. The 1996 London Protocol, which entered into force in 2006, revises the 1972 treaty to prohibit all dumping except for the following: dredged material; sewage sludge; fish wastes; vessels and platforms; bulky items made up primarily of iron, steel, and concrete; inert inorganic geological material such as mining waste; organic material of natural origin; and carbon dioxide captured from the atmosphere and introduced into the ocean as part of a carbon sequestration system. By 2010 eighty-six nations were parties to the 1972 convention and thirty-seven were parties to the 1996 protocol.

Of the types of garbage that have been dumped, plastics are among the most dangerous to marine creatures. Plastic does not degrade readily and can persist in the ocean for decades, if not centuries. Medical equipment, such as needle syringes and wrappers, is often made of plastic and has been known to wash up on beaches months after being dumped into the deep ocean. Marine birds and mammals often mistake plastic bags and pellets for food. Though an animal feels full after eating plastic, the material offers no nutritional value, and the animal dies. Sea turtles and whales have died after eating plastic bags that became entangled in their intestines. Marine birds and seals have starved to death after their beaks or snouts have become stuck in plastic rings such as those used to join beverage six-packs. Plastic that has broken down into smaller particles may not kill marine life outright, but it presents a dietary source of toxins that becomes increasingly concentrated farther up the food chain. During the late 1980's it was estimated that 7.3 billion kilograms (16 billion pounds) of plastic was being dumped into the ocean annually.

In December, 1988, an annex to the International Convention for the Prevention of Pollution from Ships (known as MARPOL, for "marine pollution") banned the dumping of plastics anywhere in the ocean. Referred to as Annex V of the MARPOL treaty, it also set severe restrictions on other garbage discharges within coastal zones and special areas affected by heavy maritime traffic or low water exchange; required ships to have garbage management plans and to maintain written records of all garbage disposal and incineration operations; and required governments to provide garbage reception facilities at ports. By 2010 the MARPOL treaty had been signed by 150 countries, and Annex V had been signed by 140 countries.

THE FATE OF FLOATING DEBRIS

In 1997 oceanographer Charles Moore of the Algalita Marine Research Foundation reported finding a massive area of floating marine trash between California and Hawaii. Dubbed the Great Pacific Garbage Patch, it has proved to be only one of several such areas where wind and ocean currents have trapped and concentrated anthropogenic (human-caused) debris. Although visions of a huge island of floating trash have captured the public imagination, the Pacific Garbage Patch is not actually visible in aerial photographs or satellite images. Rather, it is (as the Ocean Conservancy has described the area) a "chunky soup" of small, broken-down plastic particles intermixed with larger, recognizable objects such as rain boots, food containers, and toothbrushes. Samples have revealed that, in some spots within the Pacific Garbage Patch, plastic is six more times abundant than plankton by weight.

While marine trash can remain caught up in ocean gyres (massive rotating current systems) far from human habitation, other currents carry much of the debris back to shore. A number of conservation groups annually clean this litter from beaches in public-participation events, and many record the amounts and types of materials recovered. The Ocean Conservancy reports that on a single fall day in 2009, volunteers around the globe collected more than ten million individual pieces of trash weighing a total of 3.4 million kilograms (7.4 million pounds) from the world's beaches. By number, the most abundant items recovered that year were cigarettes and cigarette filters, plastic bags, and food wrappers and containers. "Legal and illegal dumping of domestic and industrial garbage, construction materials, and large household appliances" accounted for more than 198,000 of the items found, including cars and car parts, tires, and 55-gallon drums.

Lisa A. Wroble
Updated by Karen N. Kähler

FURTHER READING

Clark, R. B. *Marine Pollution*. 5th ed. New York: Oxford University Press, 2001.

Gorman, Martha. *Environmental Hazards: Marine Pollution*. Santa Barbara, Calif.: ABC-CLIO, 1993.

Hamblin, Jacob Darwin. *Poison in the Well: Radioactive Waste in the Oceans at the Dawn of the Nuclear Age*. New Brunswick, N.J.: Rutgers University Press, 2008.

International Maritime Organization. *Guidelines on the Convention on the Prevention of Marine Pollution by Dumping of Wastes and Other Matter, 1972*. London: Author, 2006.

Laws, Edward A. *Aquatic Pollution: An Introductory Text*. 3d ed. New York: John Wiley & Sons, 2000.

Ocean Conservancy. *Trash Travels: From Our Hands to the Sea, Around the Globe, and Through Time*. Washington, D.C.: Author, 2010.

Ringius, Lasse. *Radioactive Waste Disposal at Sea: Public Ideas, Transnational Policy Entrepreneurs, and Environmental Regimes*. Cambridge, Mass.: MIT Press, 2001.

United Nations Environment Programme. *Marine Litter: A Global Challenge*. Nairobi: Author, 2009.

Ocean pollution

CATEGORY: Water and water pollution

DEFINITION: Introduction by direct or indirect human action of harmful materials into the marine environment

SIGNIFICANCE: Ocean pollution can harm marine organisms, alter or destroy marine habitats, negatively affect human health, and impede or halt fishing operations. Land-based sources account for approximately 80 percent of the pollutants that enter the marine environment; the remainder come from maritime operations and dumping.

Five major types of pollutants can be found in the oceans. The first type, degradable waste, makes up the greatest volume of discharge and is composed of organic material that will eventually be reduced to stable inorganic compounds such as carbon dioxide, water, and ammonia through bacterial attack. Included in this category are urban wastes, agriculture wastes, food-processing wastes, brewing and distilling wastes, paper pulp mill wastes, chemical industry wastes, and oil spillage.

The second type of pollutant is fertilizer, which has an effect similar to that of organic wastes. Nitrates and phosphorus compounds are carried from agricultural lands by runoff from irrigation and rainfall into rivers and from there into the oceans. Once in the sea, they enhance phytoplankton production, sometimes to the extent that the accumulation of dead plants on the seabed produces anoxic (oxygen-deprived) conditions.

A third kind of pollutant, dissipating waste, is composed mainly of industrial wastes that lose their damaging properties after they enter the sea. Their effects are therefore confined to the immediate area of the discharge. Some examples are heat, acids, alkalis, and cyanide.

A fourth type of pollutant is particulates. These are small particles that may clog the feeding and respiratory structures of marine animals. They can also reduce plant photosynthesis by reducing light penetration; when settled on the ocean bottom, they may smother animals and change the nature of the seabed. Some examples are dredging spoil, powdered ash from coal-fired power stations, china clay waste, colliery (coal-works) waste, and clay from gravel extraction. Larger objects such as containers and plastic sheeting have impacts similar to those of particulates.

The last type of pollutant is conservative waste. Such waste is not subject to bacterial attack and is not dissipated, but it can react with plants and animals. Examples of conservative waste include heavy metals, such as mercury, lead, copper, and zinc; halogenated hydrocarbons, such as polychlorinated biphenyls (PCBs) and dioxins; and radioactive materials.

POLLUTION INPUTS FROM LAND

Pollutants can reach oceans in many ways. According to the United Nations Environment Programme (UNEP), land-based activities are responsible for as much as 80 percent of the pollutant load in coastal waters and deep oceans. Rivers that have been polluted by land runoff are the largest source of harmful substances. River water enters the sea carrying a staggering load of pollutants accumulated along the river's entire length. In agricultural areas, nutrients from fertilizers and livestock wastes, as well as silt from eroding fields, are common pollutants in runoff. Herbicides and pesticides that drain from fields introduce carcinogens and other harmful chemical components into receiving waters. In urban areas, runoff carries an array of pollutants. Typical among these are wastes deposited by motor vehicles, including gasoline, oil, grease, and heavy metals; sediment from construction sites; herbicides and pesticides from lawns and gardens; road salts; viruses and bacteria from inefficient septic systems; and spilled chemicals from industrial sites.

Another type of pollutant input from the land is direct outfall from pipes that empty into oceans. This pollution comes from urban and industrial wastes that are deposited directly into coastal waters. During the nineteenth century, rivers such as the Thames and the Tees in England, the Clyde in Scotland, and the Hudson in New York state became incredibly polluted by this type of input. With increasing pressure to preserve inland sources of drinking water, newer industries that need large quantities of water have sought out coastal locations, which has resulted in increased levels of ocean pollution. Urban areas on the coast also present the problem of municipal wastes and sewage. In many coastal population centers, these wastes are treated. However, roughly 40 percent of the world's population lives on the coast, often in fertile and productive estuarine and delta areas. This makes it almost impossible to process all wastes before they enter the sea. According to a 2006 UNEP report on the state of the marine environment, in many developing countries more than 80 percent of sewage that enters coastal zones is untreated.

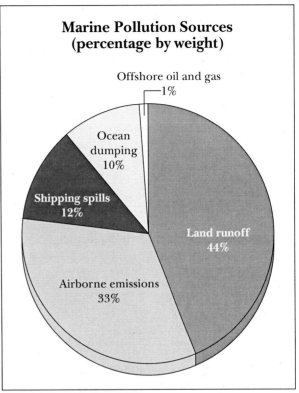

Source: Data taken from United Nations Environment Programme, *The State of the Marine Environment.* Oxford, England: Blackwell Scientific Publications, 1991.

POLLUTION INPUTS AT SEA

On the open water, ships can pollute the ocean in many ways. They often carry toxic substances such as oil, liquefied natural gas, pesticides, and industrial chemicals. Shipwrecks can lead to the release of these chemicals and result in serious damage. Examples include the *Torrey Canyon* (1967), *Amoco Cadiz* (1978), *Exxon Valdez* (1989), and *Sea Empress* (1996) oil spills, which fouled coastlines and caused the deaths of many seabirds and marine animals. Noxious or dangerous materials are frequently carried on deck as a safety precaution and can be lost overboard during storms. During routine operations, ships discharge oily ballast water, bilgewater, and cargo tank washings (not always legally). They also discard much of their garbage overboard. Marine dumping of any form of plastic, however, has been illegal since 1988.

Another offshore pollutant input comes from activities such as dumping dredging spoil and sewage sludge. Dredging spoil is the waste sediment generated by dredging operations, which may be conducted to keep shipping channels and entrances to ports open, as an underwater mining method, or as a

means for removing polluted bottom sediments. While dredged material is sometimes disposed of on land, especially if it is highly toxic and in need of treatment, it is often barged out to sea to be dumped. Dredging spoil from harbors contains large quantities of heavy metals and other contaminants that are transferred to dumping grounds. Even clean spoil, however, can have a negative impact on marine life: Dumping it makes the water column more turbid (cloudy), which can fatally clog the gills of fish and shellfish. Sewage from the treatment of land-based sewage has been dumped at sea in large quantities. This sludge is contaminated with heavy metals, oils and greases, and other substances. Additional offshore industrial activities that can pollute the ocean include oil exploration and extraction, sand and gravel extraction, and mineral extraction. Other harmful wastes that are dumped at sea include ashes from power stations and colliery waste. Until the practice was banned in 1993, containers of low-level radioactive waste were disposed of at deep ocean sites. Conventional munitions, incendiary devices, and chemical weapons were also routinely dumped at sea until the early 1970's.

The last type of input comes from the air. While this type of input is complex and challenging to quantify, scientists believe that it represents a large and significant contribution to pollution. Atmospheric contaminants may exist as gases or aerosols. They are deposited by gas exchange at the sea surface, fall out as particles (dry deposition), or are scavenged from much of the air column by precipitation within clouds (wet deposition). A nontoxic atmospheric gas of increasing concern is carbon dioxide (CO_2). The world's oceans absorb about one-fourth of the CO_2 that human activity adds to the atmosphere annually. The dissolution of CO_2 in seawater, which forms carbonic acid, is creating increasingly acidic oceans. This change in pH is impeding the ability of some marine organisms to form shells and skeletal structures.

IMPACTS

Nutrients from sewage, treated or untreated, are increasing the rate of plant growth in coastal waters, a phenomenon known as cultural eutrophication. Sewage and agricultural runoff are high in nitrogen and phosphorus, which encourage ocean plants to grow. This results in unsightly algal scum on beaches. When the extra algae die and sink to the bottom, the resulting bacterial decomposition uses available dissolved oxygen, causing deoxygenation on the bottom waters. In extreme cases, this can kill fish. Some algal blooms contain toxic substances. Fish and shellfish that eat these algae become unfit for human consumption.

Water-soluble compounds from crude oil and refined products include a variety of compounds toxic to a large number of marine plants and animals. Chemicals released during oil spills from tankers or from offshore drilling operations are toxic to a wide range of plankton, which is at special risk because it lives near the water's surface. Salt marshes and mangrove swamps trap oil from oil spills. When the plants are in bloom, the blossoms become coated with oil and thereafter rarely produce seeds. A 2002 report from World Wildlife Fund Canada estimated that, in the waters of Atlantic Canada alone, roughly 300,000 seabirds die from operational discharges of oil at sea every winter.

Antifouling paints and other coatings that discourage the growth of barnacles and other marine organisms on ships and marine structures can be highly toxic to the ocean environment. Antifouling agents leach from surfaces to which they are applied and persist in the water. Tributylin (TBT), an effective antifouling substance introduced during the 1960's, was subsequently found to cause deformations in oysters and sex changes in whelks. A complete global prohibition on the use of TBT and related compounds for ship antifouling went into effect at the beginning of 2008.

Conservative pollutants are not affected by bacteria; when consumed by animals, they cannot be excreted and thus remain in the body. This process is called bioaccumulation. Animals that eat polluted plants and animals receive an enriched diet of those conservative materials, which they also are unable to excrete. The pollutants can accumulate in their bodies over time, eventually reaching concentrations high enough to cause illness or death. This process, called biomagnification, particularly affects the ocean predators. Bioaccumulation and biomagnification can render seafood unsafe for human consumption.

Discarded plastic items can cause harm to the larger animals of the sea. They can trap mammals, diving birds, or turtles, causing them to drown. Fishing gear lost overboard can continue to drift, snaring fish and entangling seabirds. Marine animals routinely mistake plastic items for food, ingest them, and die. Oceanographers have discovered extensive "garbage patches" far from land where ocean currents have trapped huge masses of plastic particles and intact or semi-intact plastic items. It is not known what effect the increasingly small particles of plastic will have on marine life and human health as they become an inescapable part of the food web.

EFFORTS TO REPAIR THE DAMAGE

In late 1988 a global ban went into effect prohibiting the marine dumping of plastics. However, illegal dumping, uncontrolled runoff, beach littering, and (in the case of lightweight plastic shopping bags) even wind continue to carry plastics into oceans, where they can persist for decades, if not centuries.

A number of international agreements have tackled other aspects of ocean pollution. The Convention on the Prevention of Marine Pollution by Dumping of Wastes and Other Matter, also known as the London Convention, entered into force in 1975; an update, the London Protocol, entered into force in 2006. This treaty regulates ocean dumping. The United Nations Convention on the Law of the Sea, adopted in 1982, addresses economic and environmental issues on the open sea. It was a replacement for related agreements in 1958 and 1960 that were inadequate to handle modern marine pollution problems and other concerns. Agenda 21, approved by governments that attended the Earth Summit held in Rio de Janeiro in 1992, called for all coastal countries to develop integrated coastal zone management plans by the year 2000. Coastal areas remain a high priority because they are most affected by pollution sources on land. Other global efforts to curb ocean pollution include the 1973 International Convention for the Prevention of Pollution from Ships and the 1978 Protocol that modified it. Known as MARPOL 73/78, the treaty and its several annexes address various marine pollution sources and the means for controlling or eliminating them.

Some countries have begun to control pollution in their estuaries and bays, and fish and shellfish have returned to formerly polluted areas. Maritime ship-based activities have considerably less impact on the ocean than in the past, mainly because of the introduction of international treaties limiting the discharge of wastes at sea. In addition, schools, aquariums, nonprofit groups, and governments all work on an ongoing basis to educate the public about the need to prevent ocean pollution.

> *David F. MacInnes, Jr.*
> *Updated by Karen N. Kähler*

FURTHER READING

Allsopp, Michelle, et al. *State of the World's Oceans.* New York: Springer, 2009.

Clark, R. B. *Marine Pollution.* 5th ed. New York: Oxford University Press, 2001.

Field, John G., Gotthilf Hempel, and Colin P. Summerhayes, eds. *Oceans 2020: Science, Trends, and the Challenge of Sustainability.* Washington, D.C.: Island Press, 2002.

Gorman, Martha. *Environmental Hazards: Marine Pollution.* Santa Barbara, Calif.: ABC-CLIO, 1993.

Hofer, Tobias N., ed. *Marine Pollution: New Research.* New York: Nova Science, 2008.

Laws, Edward A. *Aquatic Pollution: An Introductory Text.* 3d ed. New York: John Wiley & Sons, 2000.

Ocean Conservancy. *Trash Travels: From Our Hands to the Sea, Around the Globe, and Through Time.* Washington, D.C.: Author, 2010.

United Nations Environment Programme. *Marine Litter: A Global Challenge.* Nairobi: Author, 2009.

Oil spills

CATEGORY: Water and water pollution

DEFINITION: Accidental or intentional discharges of raw or refined petroleum products on land or at sea

SIGNIFICANCE: Oil spills pose both short- and long-term environmental threats, including injuries and deaths among fish, birds, and other wildlife; damage to shoreline recreational areas; and pollution of water supplies.

Oil spills commonly occur in both terrestrial and marine settings. Terrestrial spills affect land areas, including drainage courses and bodies of surface water impounded in lakes and ponds. Subsurface waters (groundwater) are also at risk from leakage of polluted water downward through the vadose zone (zone of aeration) to the water table (zone of saturation). Some crude oil is lost during exploratory drilling, workover operations, and tank storage. Mud pits utilized during rotary drilling usually contain oil recovered from the well during testing or oil derived from an oil-based mud employed in the drilling process. Oil and brine released from wells are sometimes stored in unlined ponds, and these fluids can soak into the ground and kill beneficial microbes in the soil and plant life in the immediate area. Subsurface water can also be contaminated if the oil or brine migrates downward to the groundwater table. Runoff from these areas can enter streams and ponded bodies of water and kill fish and other aquatic animals as well as reduce the natural vegetation.

Terrestrial oil spills also occur during the loading, transportation, and offloading of petroleum from tank trucks and railroad tank cars. Petroleum pipelines, both buried and aboveground, are highly vulnerable to rupture from welding defects, corrosion, earthquakes, and shifting soils. Fire is a constant danger associated with such spills. During the mid-1980's a ruptured pipeline near São Paulo, Brazil, caused the deaths of more than five hundred people and resulted in the destruction by fire of twenty-five hundred homes in the town of Vila Socco. During the 1991 Persian Gulf War, large areas of Kuwait were devastated when Iraqi soldiers damaged oil pipelines and refineries and set fire to hundreds of oil wells. Pools of oil formed near the wells and infiltrated the porous and permeable soil and rock, thereby endangering the water supply of Kuwait City and other areas.

The disposal of petroleum products (diesel fuel, gasoline, kerosene, jet fuel, and used motor oil) is a significant problem worldwide. Some of these products contain carcinogens such as benzene, toluene, and xylene, which require special handling. Many millions of gallons of used oil products are disposed of on land every year, and it has been estimated that more than 6.6 million tons, or about 45 million barrels, of petroleum and petroleum products enter the oceans per year. Of this total, 44 percent is land-derived. These inputs include coastal city contributions from refineries, wastewater outlets, and other sources (13 percent); urban runoff, including storm drains (5 percent); and river runoff (26 percent).

MARINE SPILLS

The waters of oceans and restricted seas can be polluted by oil in several ways. Oil sources include natural seeps along the ocean floor, stream runoff from the land, wastewater drainage outlets from industrial complexes, offshore drilling accidents, deliberate purging of ballast or cargo areas of ships, and accidents involving oil supertankers. The petroleum input into the marine environment from ocean-derived factors has been estimated at about 56 percent. This calculation includes transportation losses during loading and unloading (30 percent), oil spills (5 percent), offshore production losses (1 percent), atmospheric pollution (10 percent), and offshore oil seeps (10 percent).

Supertanker accidents that result in oil spills are major events; causes include shipboard explosions, collisions with other vessels, and grounding on barriers (mostly rocks or coral reefs) because of navigation error, mechanical failure, or inclement weather. Although such oil spills are often quite dramatic, and the damage they do to the environment receives extensive news media coverage, only about 5 percent of the total input of petroleum into the oceans results from oil spills.

Oil slicks are especially problematic in semienclosed bodies of water, such as the Baltic and Mediterranean seas. Because tides are minor in these seas, any oil spilled is not easily eliminated. These places are among the world's most polluted bodies of water.

When an oil spill occurs in the open ocean, the oil floats on the surface of the water because of a density contrast between the two substances. Water has a specific gravity from 1 to 1.2, while oil is lighter, with a specific gravity from 0.7 to 1.0. The lighter components of the spilled petroleum immediately begin to evaporate; also, oil-degrading bacteria in the water begin to feed on the organic deposit and multiply. Warmer water and ambient air temperatures increase the rates of bacterial growth and evaporation. The major part of petroleum dumped into the open ocean evaporates or is reduced by bacteria. With time, the oil turns into an inert, tarlike substance that becomes extremely hard; some such residues have been found with barnacles attached to them.

In areas where the spilled oil is washed ashore and subjected to intense wave action, a gooey emulsion sometimes forms. This foamy mass, which has been described as resembling chocolate mousse, coats every-

Time Line of Supertanker Disasters

YEAR	VESSEL NAME	LOCATION	BARRELS OF OIL LOST
1967	Torrey Canyon	Land's End, England	870,000
1976	Argo Merchant	Nantucket, Massachusetts	180,952
1978	Amoco Cadiz	Portsall, France	1,500,000
1983	Castillo de Bellver	Cape Town, South Africa	2,023,810
1989	Exxon Valdez	Prince William Sound, Alaska	261,905
1990	American Trader	Southern California	6,249
1990	Berge Broker	North Atlantic Ocean	95,238
1990	Mega Borg	Gulf of Mexico	75,476
1992	Aegean Sea	Spain	14,821
1993	Braer	Shetland Islands, Scotland	619,048
1996	Sea Empress	Southwest Wales	380,952
1999	New Carissa	Oregon	9,524
1999	Erika	Bay of Biscay, France	83,333
2000	Westchester	Mississippi River, below New Orleans	15,750
2002	Prestige	Spain	1,860
2003	Tasman Spirit	Karachi, Pakistan	3,835
2004	M/V Selendang Ayu	Aleutian Islands, Alaska	9,360
2006	M/T Solar 1	Guimaras Island, Philippines	14,720
2007	Hebei Spirit	South Korea	77,775

thing along the beach, including sand-sized particles, large boulders, aquatic animals and plants, pleasure boats, and human-made shore facilities. The polluted waters can devastate resort beaches, oyster and shrimp beds, fish hatcheries, and prime fishing grounds.

The potential damage resulting from a large oil spill in the ocean includes the loss of substantial numbers of commercial and rough fish, waterfowl, aquatic mammals, shellfish, algae, and plankton. Oil contamination reduces the amount of oxygen in the water column, and this can cause the deaths of large numbers of fish in polluted areas. Millions of fish died as a result of the 1989 *Exxon Valdez* disaster in Alaskan waters, and the Alaskan fishing industry, which is extremely important to the state's economy, was seriously threatened. Although this event is generally considered a major disaster, David McConnell reported in the *Journal of Geological Education* (1999) that, compared with other spills worldwide, the *Exxon Valdez* spill ranked only fifty-third in size.

When seabirds come into contact with spilled oil to the extent that their feathers are soaked, they lose the ability to fly and float, as well as their natural body insulation. Many such birds starve to death, die from exposure, or drown. The *Exxon Valdez* disaster resulted in the deaths of more than 200,000 seabirds. During the Persian Gulf War, more than 20,000 birds perished from oil-related causes. Oil spills also cause the deaths of aquatic mammals, which die from the loss of their food supply, exposure to cold, or poisoning when they ingest the toxic oil. Volunteer workers have saved many birds and mammals at animal centers set up after large spills; workers wash the animals with solvents to remove oil and often hold them until their normal body resilience returns.

Shellfish in bays and marshes can perish in oil-polluted waters from asphyxiation or toxicity. Some effects of oil pollution remain for years. Shellfish in a salt marsh in Massachusetts were quarantined for more than five years after heating oil was spilled nearby in 1969, and traces of petroleum persisted for decades.

CLEANUP PROCEDURES

Oil spills in the open ocean have been reduced or eliminated using several techniques. Igniting the slick, if attempted shortly after a spill, can be effective; however, if the volatile components of the oil have evaporated, it is difficult to start and maintain such fires. In 1967, when the damaged supertanker *Torrey Canyon* began to founder and break up off the coast of England, Great Britain's air force dropped bombs in an effort to ignite the oil that remained in the vessel.

Another technique used to reduce oil slicks is the application of chemicals such as detergents in an attempt to disperse the oil droplets. This procedure is not viable if the temperature of the water is too low for the chemicals to be effective. Floating booms are sometimes used to confine oil streamers or protect inlet areas. These barriers are useful if the waves are not too high. Skimmers may be used to collect floating oil during the early stages of a spill. Plant material (threshed hay, peat moss, or wood shavings) or pulverized rock (chalk or claystone) is sometimes spread over slicks to absorb the oil. Plant material can then be removed and burned or buried; applied rock particles absorb the oil, clump together, and sink to the ocean floor. In many parts of the oceans, oil-eating microbes (mostly bacteria) utilize petroleum as a nutrient. If these microbes are not present or exist only in small numbers in the area, engineered microbes can be introduced. Under ideal temperature and ocean chemistry conditions, the bacteria will rapidly multiply and consume the oil slick. This technique is known as bioremediation.

In nearshore areas, beach sand and boulders can be steamed clean or washed with water or solvents. Pools of oil can be vacuumed into tank trucks and hauled away from the site. The recovered oil can sometimes be processed into useful products. Plant material can also be applied to crude oil along the shoreline. After the 1969 Santa Barbara oil spill, the beaches along the California coast were coated by approximately ten thousand barrels of gooey oil. Numerous volunteers helped spread fresh hay along the beachfront and later recovered the oil-soaked plant material.

Donald F. Reaser

FURTHER READING

Davidson, Jon P., Walter E. Reed, and Paul M. Davis. *Exploring Earth: An Introduction to Physical Geology.* 2d ed. Upper Saddle River, NJ: Prentice Hall, 2002.

Fingas, Merv. *The Basics of Oil Spill Cleanup.* 2d ed. Boca Raton, Fla.: CRC Press, 2001.

Kemp, David D. "Threats to the Availability and Quality of Water." In *Exploring Environmental Issues: An Integrated Approach.* New York: Routledge, 2004.

Lehr, Jay, et al. "Oil Spills and Leaks." In *Handbook of Complex Environmental Remediation Problems.* New York: McGraw-Hill, 2002.

Montgomery, Carla W. *Environmental Geology*. 9th ed. New York: McGraw-Hill, 2010.

National Research Council. *Oil in the Sea III: Inputs, Fates, and Effects*. Washington, D.C.: National Academies Press, 2003.

_____. *Oil Spill Dispersants: Efficacy and Effects*. Washington, D.C.: National Academies Press, 2005.

Ott, Riki. *Not One Drop: Betrayal and Courage in the Wake of the Exxon Valdez Oil Spill*. White River Junction, Vt.: Chelsea Green, 2008.

Walker, Jane. *Oil Spills*. New York: Gloucester Press, 1993.

Pacific Islands

CATEGORIES: Places; resources and resource management

IDENTIFICATION: The several thousand islands of Melanesia, Micronesia, and Polynesia scattered throughout the tropical Pacific

SIGNIFICANCE: The environmental challenges in the Pacific Islands region are diverse. They include depletion of nearshore fisheries, pollution of limited freshwater resources, soil degradation, reduction of biodiversity, and waste management problems. These environmental challenges are complicated by such factors as the islands' limited natural resources and their geographic isolation, as well as by the lack of monetary resources to address the problems.

The Pacific Islands region comprises nearly thirty thousand islands scattered over 30 million square kilometers (11.6 million square miles). Approximately one thousand of the islands are inhabited. The region is divided into the three island groups of Melanesia, Micronesia, and Polynesia, which reflect the cultures and ethnic features of the indigenous inhabitants of the islands. The main countries and territories in the region are American Samoa, Cook Islands, Federated States of Micronesia, Fiji Islands, French Polynesia, Guam, Kiribati, Marshall Islands, Nauru, New Caledonia, Niue, Northern Mariana Islands, Palau, Papua New Guinea, Pitcairn Islands, Samoa, Solomon Islands, Tokelau, Tonga, Tuvalu, Vanuatu, and Wallis and Futuna Islands.

The Pacific Islands are also divided into low islands and high islands. The low islands consist mainly of coral reefs and atolls, most of which are only a few meters above sea level; these include the Marshall, Phoenix (Kiribati), Tuamotu (French Polynesia), and Tuvalu groups. The high islands are hilly and some mountainous; these include New Britain, New Caledonia, Papua New Guinea, Fiji, the Marianas, Samoa, the Solomon Islands, and Vanuatu. The total population of the Pacific Islands region in 2008 was about 9.5 million. Population is growing by approximately 2 percent annually and is expected to exceed 15 million by 2030 if this rate continues. The islands with the fastest-growing populations, owing to high birthrates, are the Solomon Islands (2.7 percent) and Vanuatu (2.6 percent). Those islands with decreasing populations, owing to emigration, are Niue (−2.4 percent) and the Northern Mariana Islands (−1.7 percent).

The environmental challenges of the Pacific Islands region are diverse and sundry. They include depletion of nearshore fisheries, pollution of fresh water, soil degradation, urbanization, reduction of biodiversity, damage to nearshore nursery habitats, waste management problems (involving solid, nuclear, and chemical wastes), and stressed natural resources related to tourism. The most serious environmental challenges facing the small island developing states are complicated by traditional approaches to land management, limited natural resources, small and fragile ecosystems, geographic isolation, and poverty (thus a lack of adequate capacity for response). The Pacific Islands region can be divided into three zones, each with its distinguishing environmental problems: the low island states, the small and midsize high islands, and the larger high islands of the western Pacific. All countries in the region share some environmental challenges, however.

LOW ISLAND STATES

The small, low-lying coral islands of the Pacific region (Cook Islands, Kiribati, Tuvalu, Federated States of Micronesia, the Marshall Islands, Niue, Nauru) have extremely limited resources and are economically deprived; thus their capacity to respond to environmental problems is limited. The most serious environmental issues facing most of these countries are the pollution of limited groundwater with sewage and salt, problems with solid waste disposal, lack of land available for agriculture, and rapid population growth. For example, more than 65,000 Marshall Islanders live on 180 square kilometers (69 square miles) of

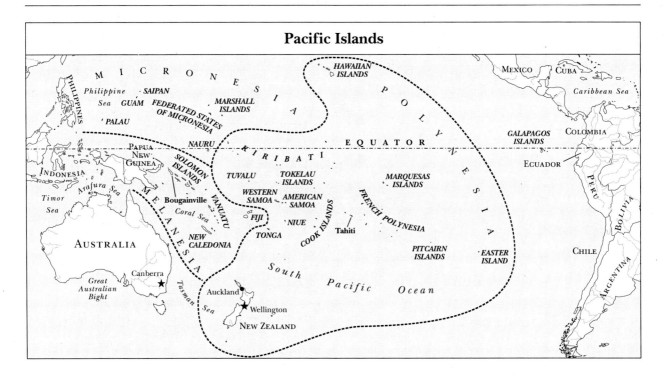

Pacific Islands

atoll land, which provides each person only 0.3 hectare (0.7 acre) of land. On the other hand, each person has economic sovereignty over 40 square kilometers (15 square miles) of ocean. The population of the Marshall Islands is expected to double by 2025.

The low island states constitute one of the most vulnerable places on earth should sea level accelerate due to global warming. The island group of Tuvalu is often used as an example of this projected problem. However, since instrumentation was installed in 1993 to monitor sea level on Tuvalu's main island, Funafuti, no discernible changes have been seen. Some inundation is evident on the island, but it is the result of erosion, sand mining, and construction projects causing an inflow of seawater. Other factors are also involved, such as excessive use of fresh water for irrigation, a consequence of which is seawater encroachment into vegetable growing pits. Part of the problem is related also to the fact that about one-fourth of the island has been paved over with roads and airport runways. This reduces the infiltration of rainwater into the freshwater layer. When this increased runoff is combined with a high tide, flooding along the coast gives the appearance that the sea level is rising. Perception of trends can also be affected, as increasing population on the islands means people are living on flood-prone land that was previously avoided.

Coral is capable of growing along with sea-level rise, and the atolls are not static. The islands grow as they are replenished by coral that breaks off the reefs and is thrown ashore by storms. In this way atolls are self-maintaining, provided humans do not intervene, such as by digging coral for use in construction work and building flush toilets that discharge effluent into the sea and affect coral growth.

SMALL AND MIDSIZE HIGH ISLANDS

The people of the small and midsize high islands of the Pacific (Tonga, Samoa, French Polynesia, Palau, Federated States of Micronesia, Guam, American Samoa, and Northern Mariana Islands) are mainly agrarian. The islands have small or no commercial forests and no commercial mineral deposits. The main environmental issues faced by these islands are shortage of land, loss of the surviving native forests (with associated loss in biodiversity), invasion of exotic animal and plant species, decline of coastal fisheries, coral reef degradation, problems with solid waste disposal, and contamination of groundwater and coastal areas by agricultural chemicals and sewage.

Some of these islands are more fortunate than others; Tonga and Samoa, for example, have nearly self-sufficient food supplies and receive high levels of remittances from expatriate island communities living abroad. French Polynesia is a French territory, and Guam, the Northern Mariana Islands, and American Samoa are U.S. territories; all of these nations have high standards of living based on subsidies.

LARGER HIGH ISLANDS OF THE WESTERN PACIFIC

The larger high islands of the western Pacific (Papua New Guinea, Solomon Islands, New Caledonia, Vanuatu, and Fiji Islands) have relatively large human populations and are comparatively rich in mineral and forestry resources. Environmental pressures on these islands are linked for the most part to rapid population growth and to complications associated with traditional approaches to land management that have led to land degradation. Other common problems arise from unsustainable deforestation, the depletion of nearshore fisheries, the pollution of rivers and lakes caused by mining and agricultural practices, and the invasion of exotic species.

REGIONALLY SHARED ENVIRONMENTAL PROBLEMS

Coastal and marine problems are among the most common kinds of environmental issues in the Pacific Islands region. The main concerns are coastal erosion; depletion and pollution of mangrove forests, sea grasses, and coral reefs; depletion of shallow-water and coastal marine life; and unsustainable management of offshore fishery resources, including destruction by drift-net fishing, commercial bycatch of seabirds and marine mammals, and whaling.

Certain natural hazards are also common among the islands of the Pacific. The region lies on the western perimeter of the Pacific Rim of Fire, an area of severe seismic activity extending from the Northern Mariana Islands in the north to Vanuatu in the south. Earthquakes, volcanic activity, and tsunamis are persistent major threats, and tropical cyclones, floods, and drought are not infrequent. These extremes have serious environmental consequences when combined with unsustainable land-use practices.

Another problem common to many islands in the region, especially atolls, is the pollution of the limited supplies of fresh water available. With increasing population, accompanied by increasing construction, agriculture, and tourism, islands' water supplies have become contaminated owing to agricultural runoff and inadequate sewage management systems. Tourists place additional stress on local ecosystems and place big demands on water supplies and on waste disposal systems.

Declining biodiversity has been seen on many islands in the region. Many unique species of plants and animals evolved in isolation in the Pacific Islands region, and the specialized habitats to which they adapted are vulnerable to destruction by deforestation, land clearance, fire, agricultural chemicals, and nonnative organisms introduced by visitors to the islands.

The extraction, processing, and transport of mineral resources have caused localized environmental damage on some islands. The major mining centers are found in Papua New Guinea, New Caledonia, and Fiji, where regulations intended to minimize damage from mine tailings, processing fumes, and siltation of streams have had varying degrees of success. Mining for construction material is widespread throughout the Pacific Islands region and is a problem that increases in step with population growth. Small islands suffer the most. The removal of sand (for concrete) from beaches causes coastal erosion, and the dredging of coral reefs and lagoon sands, along with the use of corals for building material, often causes irreversible damage.

C. R. de Freitas

FURTHER READING

Banks, Glenn. "Mining and the Environment in Melanesia: Contemporary Debates Reviewed. " *Contemporary Pacific* 14, no.1 (2002): 39-67.

Lal, Brij V., and Kate Fortune, eds. *The Pacific Islands: An Encyclopedia.* Honolulu: University of Hawaii Press, 2000.

Nunn, Patrick D. Climate, Environment, and Society in the Pacific During the Last Millennium. Oxford, England: Elsevier, 2007.

Rapoport, Moshe. *The Pacific Islands: Environment and Society.* Hong Kong: Bess Press, 1999.

PEMEX oil well leak

CATEGORY: Disasters

THE EVENT: Blowout in an oil drilling well in the Gulf of Mexico that resulted in the spilling of some three million barrels of oil into the sea

DATE: June 3, 1979

SIGNIFICANCE: The oil pollution that resulted from the PEMEX oil well blowout and the nine-month-long spillage of oil that followed destroyed Mexico's shrimping industry and threatened other marine life as well as the tourist industry of coastal areas in the Gulf of Mexico.

On June 3, 1979, an offshore oil operation in the Gulf of Mexico drilled into a high-pressure gas pocket, causing a blowout that ignited the oil well. The accident produced a massive oil slick nearly 65,000 square kilometers (25,000 square miles) in area. According to a July, 1979, issue of the *Christian Science Monitor,* at the time it was considered not only "the world's worst oil spill from an oil well, but also the worst spill ever." The runaway well, Ixtoc I, belonged to Petróleos Mexicanos (PEMEX), the Mexican state-owned oil company. The exploratory well was being drilled in the Gulf of Campeche off the Yucatán Peninsula, a low-lying limestone tableland that separates the Caribbean Sea from the Gulf of Mexico.

Natural gas escaping from the well ignited and destroyed the $22 million drilling rig. The crude oil that issued from the damaged well polluted waters in the region and ruined much of Mexico's shrimping industry. The toxic effects of the crude oil also threatened the population of Atlantic sea turtles that nest along the Mexican coast, as the young of this endangered species normally swim out to seaweed beds after they hatch.

The oil slick further posed a threat to certain regions along the Texas coast, including the Padre Island National Seashore area and resort beaches such as Galveston, Texas. As a preventive measure, floating booms and other types of barriers were placed as shields for bays and estuaries along the south Texas coast by the Department of Texas Water Resources. The south Texas beaches escaped extensive damage; only isolated patches of diluted oil reached the Texas coastline. Some Texas beaches were littered with nontoxic, pancakelike hydrocarbon globs that resembled chocolate mousse.

Immediately after the blowout, PEMEX began drilling relief wells, named Ixtoc I-A and I-B, in an attempt to intersect the runaway well and divert the escaping oil. Later, the famous oil-field troubleshooter Paul "Red" Adair and his crew were called in to cap the well. They succeeded in temporarily shutting the well down in late June, but it burst out again shortly thereafter. Over the next several months steel balls, lead balls, and gelatin were pumped down the well in repeated attempts to check or stop the oil flow. Although most of the balls that were first pumped in were expelled, a later injection of 108,000 balls reportedly reduced the flow of oil from 20,000 to 10,000 barrels per day on October 12. Meanwhile, several different organizations, including Oil Mop Incorporated and Shell Oil, were using a variety of equipment in attempts to skim oil from the ocean surface at or near the well site.

Ixtoc I-A and I-B ultimately injected drilling mud, water, and cement into the reservoir rock and base of the well, which cut off flow. The well was finally blocked with three cement plugs on March 22, 1980.

The Ixtoc I and other wells drilled in the Gulf of Campeche are evidence of the presence of large quantities of oil in this offshore region. However, the disastrous blowout of Ixtoc I led to questions about PEMEX's credibility as a company, as well as about Mexico's entire oil policy.

Donald F. Reaser

FURTHER READING

Fingas, Merv. *The Basics of Oil Spill Cleanup.* 2d ed. Boca Raton, Fla.: CRC Press, 2001.

Ornitz, Barbara E., and Michael A. Champ. *Oil Spills First Principles: Prevention and Best Response.* New York: Elsevier, 2002.

Polluter pays principle

CATEGORIES: Treaties, laws, and court cases; atmosphere and air pollution

DEFINITION: Legal rule that the costs of pollution prevention and remediation should be borne by the entity that profits from the process that causes the pollution

SIGNIFICANCE: The polluter pays principle is designed to impose penalties on parties responsible for producing pollution that damages the natural environment and hence society as a whole. Hence the principle is intended to deter activities that pollute the environment.

The polluter pays principle assigns responsibility for the negative impacts arising from polluting activities to the individuals, companies, and other groups that perform those activities. These negative impacts are designated "social negative externalities." The principle is grounded in both the 1992 Rio Declaration, which came out of the United Nations Conference on Environment and Development (also known as the Earth Summit) and states that national governments should "promote the internationalization of environmental costs and the use of economic instruments," and the International Union for Conservation of Nature's Draft International Covenant of Environment and Development, which states that "parties shall apply the principle that the costs of preventing, controlling, and reducing potential or actual harm to the environment are to be borne by the originator."

The Swedish government may have been the first to apply the polluter pays principle, also known as the principle of extended polluter responsibility, in the 1970's. By moving the responsibility for addressing pollution away from taxpayers and governments to the companies and individuals causing the pollution, the principle makes the costs of waste disposal and pollution remediation part of the cost of the process that produces the pollution. Thus companies and individuals have incentive to reduce the amounts of waste and pollution they produce and to increase their efforts to reuse and recycle materials.

The polluter pays principle is applied differently in different situations. Application of the principle tends to be closely related to market-based incentives to regulate consumption or production activity. These policies are broken down between taxes and tradable permit schemes.

Rain gardens

CATEGORY: Urban environments

DEFINITION: Garden areas designed to capture, slow, and filter rainwater runoff

SIGNIFICANCE: Rain gardens provide a number of environmental benefits, including the filtering and neutralization of water pollutants, the reduction of stormwater flooding, and the creation of small islands of natural habitat in the midst of urban areas.

The basic idea behind rain gardens is the replication, on a small scale, of the natural conditions that existed before urbanization. In forests and on farmland, rainwater soaks into the soil and percolates slowly through it. Water that is not recycled by immediate evaporation or used by plants eventually works its way through the soil to end up replenishing underground aquifers. The average suburban lawn is rela-

tively impervious to water infiltration by this process, because the grass has shallow roots and many soils, especially clay, are not porous enough to drain well. A well-sited rain garden planted with native shrubs, perennials, and other hardy plants will allow at least 30 percent more water from rainstorms or snowmelt to seep into the ground than a lawn does.

Although the basic idea is surprisingly simple, rain gardens as a way to counter environmental damage were not widely recognized as a workable concept until the early 1990's. Larry Coffman, the environmental official in charge of creating a plan for handling stormwater in Prince George's County, Maryland, coined the term. The use of rain gardens in some large-scale projects, such as one in Maplewood, Minnesota, in 1996, helped to popularize the practice. Maplewood officials, led by landscape architect Joan I. Nassauer, sponsored the building of rainwater-gathering garden strips along the edges of suburban streets.

Most rain-garden projects in the United States have been small in scale, created by individual home owners or by communities around schools and parks with drainage problems, rather than large initiatives by developers or municipalities. The rain garden's acceptance as a tool to combat water pollution has been rapid, however, and relatively conflict-free. European countries, with their traditions of centralized planning, have been more innovative in using rain gardens than have North American nations.

ENVIRONMENTAL BENEFITS

As cities grow, their land area becomes almost entirely covered with the hard surfaces of buildings, streets, and sidewalk pavements. In order to move rainwater quickly out of the way, most modern cities have built gutters and storm sewers that ultimately drain rainfall into rivers and lakes. In the journey from the city, the water picks up many toxic substances from the urban landscape through which it flows. Oil products, organic wastes, pesticides, and other residues of industrial processes are all carried along in storm runoff. The U.S. Environmental Protection Agency estimates that 70 percent of all water pollution is the result of rainwater runoff. Such water is seldom even treated before it is discharged into lakes and rivers, and any attempts at treatment are likely to be prohibitively expensive.

When stormwater runoff is received by rain gardens, most of the pollutants are filtered out. The soil is enriched by the movement of nitrogen, phosphorus, and other compounds through the plants' root systems and soil processes. As an added benefit, rain gardens' comparatively slow absorption rate helps reduce downstream erosion from the rapid runoff that can come with heavy storms. The existence of garden spaces in urban areas also helps in a small way to combat the heat island effect, which results when heat is absorbed by and then radiates off of the unrelieved hard surfaces of buildings and pavements.

So long as those who create rain gardens follow a few basic rules—such as not putting a rain garden so close to a house that its foundations are undermined by excess water—there is virtually no downside to this conservation concept. Rain gardens bring a touch of nature to urban and suburban residents while helping to purify water resources.

PRACTICAL CONSIDERATIONS

Rain gardens do not necessarily look different from purely ornamental gardens, but the creation of rain gardens requires special attention to location and soil preparation. Because water should flow into a rain garden from impermeable surfaces such as roofs and driveways as well as from lawn areas subject to flooding, the rain garden needs to be somewhat lower than the surrounding ground. Occasionally a natural depression can be used, but normally some digging—to a depth of about 20 to 25 centimeters (8 or 10 inches)—is necessary. The digging also enables the replacement of the original soil with "rain-garden soil," an optimal mix for root establishment and permeability. A mixture of half sand and 20 to 30 percent each of topsoil and compost is usually suggested.

A downspout with a drainpipe or shallow troughs usually need to be installed so that water is directed from roof or driveway to the rain garden. At the upper or higher end of the garden, a border of grass can keep water from entering the garden too fast on stormy days. A berm or even a low wall can keep it from overflowing at the downslope border. With all this, the object is not to create a pond or small swamp. An effective rain garden will drain rain within forty-eight hours after a heavy rainfall.

Effective rain gardens contain a variety of plants that can thrive under both wet and dry conditions. Enough perennials and ornamental foliage fit this description that rain gardens have the potential to be pleasing landscape design elements. Once they are well established, rain gardens often become places where birds and other wildlife shelter, providing additional touches of nature in the city.

Emily Alward

FURTHER READING

Dunnett, Nigel, and Andy Clayden. *Rain Gardens: Managing Water Sustainably in the Garden and Designed Landscape*. Portland, Oreg.: Timber Press, 2007.
Kinkade-Levario, Heather. *Design for Water: Rainwater Harvesting, Stormwater Catchment, and Alternate Water Re-Use*. Gabriola Island, B.C.: New Society, 2007.
Woelfle-Erskine, Cleo, Laura Allen, and July Oskar Cole, eds. *Dam Nation: Dispatches from the Water Underground*. New York: Soft Skull Press, 2007.

Rainwater harvesting

CATEGORY: Resources and resource management
DEFINITION: The collection and storage of rainwater to meet freshwater needs
SIGNIFICANCE: The increasing urbanization throughout the planet requires an ever-increasing supply of water. Rainwater is a free resource that can be collected through a variety of relatively inexpensive methods, and rainwater harvesting can provide water for drinking, irrigation, and the refilling of aquifers.

Because many natural water sources around the world have been depleted or even completely exhausted, rainwater harvesting is becoming increasingly important to the well-being of some populations. Rainwater can be collected from roofs or from areas at ground level. Rainwater collected from roofs is often fit for drinking without any processing, but collected rainwater usually must undergo some processing before it is suitable for human or animal consumption. Harvested rainwater is often suitable for irrigation, flushing toilets, and laundering clothes without processing, however. Harvested rainwater can serve to supplement available water sources; in some areas, collected rainwater is the only readily available source of water. For example, small islands with high annual rainfall may be sustained totally by rainwater harvesting. In urban areas, rainwater harvesting can supplement city water supplies and reduce the likelihood of flooding.

METHODS

Rainwater harvested from roofs can be channeled into storage tanks through systems of gutters and pipes. The gutters must have an incline so that water does not stand in them and must be strong enough to handle peak flow. Pollutants that may be found in rooftop water include pesticides, dust particles, animal and bird feces, minerals, and dissolved gases such as carbon dioxide, sulfur dioxide, and nitrous oxide. The level of pollutants is commonly highest in water from the first rainfall after a dry spell; such water must therefore be discarded or put through some form of decontaminating treatment, such as boiling or chemical treatment.

Ground collection of rainwater involves a number of techniques that can improve the runoff capacity of a land area: clearing or altering vegetation, increasing the land slope, and decreasing soil permeability (penetration) through compaction or the application of chemicals (or both). Ground collection methodologies provide opportunities to collect water from larger surface areas than rooftop collection allows. The placement of a subsurface dike can obstruct the natural flow of groundwater through an aquifer (underground water channel), raising the groundwater level as well as increasing the amount of water stored in the aquifer (this process is known as groundwater recharge).

Harvested water is commonly collected in tanks; these tanks must be covered to prevent evaporative loss, algae growth, and mosquito breeding. The damming of small creeks and streams, including those that contain water only during heavy rains, is an inexpensive method of storing water during dry spells. Sometimes, however, large portions of water stored in this way are lost through infiltration into the ground. Usually this water is unfit for human consumption; thus it is often solely used for irrigation.

WORLDWIDE PRACTICES AND REGULATIONS

Rooftop rainfall harvesting is widespread in China and Brazil, where the water is consumed by humans and animals; it is also used for crop irrigation and replenishment of groundwater stores. In India, where urbanization is growing at a rapid rate, rooftop harvesting is also widespread; in this nation it represents an essential component of the water supply. In island nations such as Bermuda and the U.S. Virgin Islands, rainwater harvesting is commonly practiced. In rural portions of New Zealand, the only source of water for all household activities is the rooftop collection of rainwater. In the United Kingdom, it is a common practice to collect rainwater for irrigating gardens.

In some parts of the world, no statutes are in place to regulate rainwater harvesting or the allowable uses of the water harvested. In the United States, regulations vary among state and local governments. California, for example, has no state laws related to rainwater harvesting, but some local governments in the state have created regulations. San Francisco, for instance, allows the use of rainwater only for toilet flushing and irrigation. California's neighbor to the north, Oregon, which receives high levels of rainfall annually, has established statutes regulating rainwater harvesting, and the city of Portland specifically permits the use of rainwater for human consumption. For a long time Colorado had laws prohibiting rainwater harvesting; the argument for these statutes was that harvesting could infringe on the water rights of those living downstream. The laws were changed after a 2007 study found that in an average year, almost all of the precipitation that fell in the southern suburbs of Colorado never reached a stream; it either evaporated or was absorbed by plants.

Robin L. Wulffson

FURTHER READING

Banks, Suzy, with Richard Heinichen. *Rainwater Collection for the Mechanically Challenged.* 2d ed. Dripping Springs, Tex.: Tank Town, 2006.

Davis, Allen P. *Stormwater Management for Smart Growth.* New York: Springer, 2005.

Dunnett, Nigel, and Andy Clayden. *Rain Gardens: Managing Water Sustainably in the Garden and Designed Landscape.* Portland, Oreg.: Timber Press, 2007.

Gould, John, and Erik Nissen-Petersen. *Rainwater Catchment Systems for Domestic Supply: Design, Construction, and Implementation.* London: Intermediate Technology Publications, 1999.

Kinkade-Levario, Heather. *Design for Water: Rainwater Harvesting, Stormwater Catchment, and Alternate Water Re-Use.* Gabriola Island, B.C.: New Society, 2007.

Lancaster, Brad. *Rainwater Harvesting for Drylands and Beyond.* 2 vols. Tucson, Ariz.: Rainsource Press, 2006-2007.

Rhine River

CATEGORY: Places

IDENTIFICATION: European river arising in Switzerland and flowing generally north to the North Sea

SIGNIFICANCE: Long one of the most polluted rivers in Europe, the Rhine received increased attention in 1986 when a major chemical spill resulted in the destruction of millions of fish and other wildlife. Through the Rhine Action Programme, overseen by the International Commission for the Protection of the Rhine, major environmental improvements have taken place in the Rhine basin.

The Rhine River originates in Switzerland and flows northward through Liechtenstein, Austria, France, Germany, and the Netherlands. Italy, Luxembourg, and Belgium have territory in the Rhine basin. The Rhine is the major river of Western Europe, and with the Danube it forms the most important waterway in the region, cutting across the continent from the North Sea to the Black Sea. The Rhine is one of the most important geographic features of the European continent, both historically and economically. It has dozens of tributaries, and scores of important cities are located along its route.

In the nineteenth and twentieth centuries pollution of the Rhine not only killed plant and animal species dependent on the river but also presented a health hazard to the people who lived along the shore. The river's water was not completely potable, and it caused damage to the infrastructure of the countries and cities through which it flowed. Cooperative efforts to clean the Rhine go back to the nineteenth century. In 1946 the governments of the countries along the river formed the International Commission for the Protection of the Rhine (ICPR).

During the 1980's the Rhine remained one of the most polluted rivers in Europe. In the fall of 1986, as the result of a fire at a chemical storage facility in Basel, Switzerland, the river turned red when agricultural pesticides containing mercury poured into it. The deadly poisons moved northward along the course of the river and killed millions of fish and other wildlife. The public outcry over this incident forced the governments of the riparian countries to form the Rhine Action Programme (RAP) in 1987.

One lofty stated goal of the RAP was to bring salmon back to the Rhine by the year 2000; salmon had disappeared from the river in the 1930's. The RAP's more immediate goals were to cut in half the discharge of dangerous pollutants into the river, to raise safety standards, to take measures to allow fish to swim upstream and spawn in the Rhine's tributaries, and to restore shoreline ecosystems to bring back natural fauna and flora. The RAP program was not incorporated into European Council law, but the ICPR executed and supervised the RAP mission. The member states agreed to enact legislation concerning the discharge of wastes into the river, to require permits for factory emissions, to build purification and measurement stations, and to tax both individuals and factories for environmental protection. They also agreed to cooperate on cleaning the river and conserving and restoring its natural surroundings.

In a 2009 report the ICPR stated that almost all native species had returned to the Rhine. Salmon, the key species, had made a partial return to the river, but more needed to be done. A new target date of 2015 was set to improve the habitat for salmon by improving access for the fish into the river tributaries. The largest improvement was the elimination of direct dumping of chemicals and pollutants into the river by factories in the member states. The governments have also cooperated in protecting and treating the river water and the basin's groundwater to make it safe for consumption.

Frederick B. Chary

FURTHER READING

Hernan, Robert Emmet. "Rhine River, Switzerland, 1986." In *This Borrowed Earth: Lessons from the Fifteen Worst Environmental Disasters Around the World.* New York: Palgrave Macmillan, 2010.

Mellor, Roy E. H. *The Rhine: A Study in the Geography of Water Transport.* Aberdeen, Scotland: University of Aberdeen, 1983.

Pomeranz, Kenneth. "The Rhine as a World River." In *The Environment and World History,* edited by Edmund Burke III and Kenneth Pomeranz. Berkeley: University of California Press, 2009.

Riparian rights

CATEGORY: Water and water pollution

DEFINITION: Benefits associated with the use of water for owners of land bordering on or adjacent to bodies of water

SIGNIFICANCE: Concerns regarding environmental issues and water scarcity have led to some modifications of the traditional doctrine of riparian rights as it is applied in the eastern United States.

The roots of the U.S. system of riparian rights for water usage can be traced back to English common law. Riparian rights and other water laws attempt to reconcile the various demands of users and potential users with the size of the supply of clean water. Increasing demands for water use, coupled with the relative scarcity of adequate water resources and the growing recognition of the importance of habitat protection, have resulted in changing and evolving systems of water law and regulation in the United States.

Two basic water law systems exist for dealing with water-use conflicts in the United States. The eastern states, historically viewed as having adequate water resources, predominantly follow the doctrine of riparian rights. Under this doctrine, water-use rights are based on landownership and require equal sharing among users in times of shortage. Riparian rights typically include the right to hunt and fish and the right to use water for irrigation. The western states, historically seen as lacking abundant water resources, have adopted a system based on the doctrine of prior appropriation, which establishes priorities among competitive users. Under this doctrine, earlier settlers have greater rights to water use. The western water law system developed as a means of encouraging economic development by allowing water rights to be separated from landownership. The right to consume water accessible from one's land is the primary difference between riparian rights and appropriative rights.

Riparian rights treat water resources as a common property, which permits individual users to use the resource freely while spreading the cost of additional resource use to all owners of the resource. As Garrett Hardin warned, overuse of common property resources can result in a "tragedy of the commons." Increasing demands for water, as well as demands that water be used more efficiently and responsibly, have created tensions within the existing schemes of water rights and management. Erratic precipitation and rising per capita water use have led to a number of water emergencies. Likewise, many states now recognize the importance of letting river waters remain untapped to protect fish and wildlife, as well as to preserve aesthetic and recreational values.

Environmental concerns and issues of water scar-

city have led to significant modifications of water law systems. The only restriction on water use under the traditional riparian system is a prohibition against "unreasonable harm" to another riparian user. The absence of an efficient, systemwide mechanism to determine what constitute unreasonable uses and to manage water resources successfully has led eastern states to reconsider how water should be allocated among competing uses, and most eastern states have instituted administrative permit systems to regulate riparian rights. Under such a system, a single agency manages issues of water quality and allocation. The agency is also charged with defining and maintaining some minimum water quality and flow. Such modifications to riparian right systems attempt to protect private values and further public interests. As the evolution of riparian rights suggests, successful methods of allocating water must balance a watershed's consumptive water resources needs with its ecological needs.

Michael D. Kaplowitz

FURTHER READING

Andrews, Richard N. L. *Managing the Environment, Managing Ourselves: A History of American Environmental Policy.* 2d ed. New Haven, Conn.: Yale University Press, 2006.

Ferrey, Steven. "Rights to Use Water." In *Environmental Law: Examples and Explanations.* 5th ed. New York: Aspen, 2010.

Vandas, Stephen J., Thomas C. Winter, and William A. Battaglin. *Water and the Environment.* Alexandria, Va.: American Geological Institute, 2002.

Rocky Flats, Colorado, nuclear plant releases

CATEGORY: Nuclear power and radiation

THE EVENTS: Short- and long-term releases from the Rocky Flats nuclear plant in central Colorado that caused low-level radioactive contamination of off-site reservoirs and land areas

DATES: Notable incidents in 1957, 1969, and 1973; other long-term releases during operational years 1952-1989

SIGNIFICANCE: One of thirteen nuclear weapons production facilities operating in the United States during the Cold War, Rocky Flats was the site of a number of radioactive and toxic releases during its four-decade operational history. Releases from Rocky Flats had the potential to be a major public health hazard because of the facility's proximity to a large population center.

The Rocky Flats nuclear plant site stands 26 kilometers (16 miles) northwest of downtown Denver. From 1952 to 1989 the plant's primary mission was to produce nuclear weapon trigger assemblies. This required the machining of plutonium, uranium, beryllium, and other metals. Plutonium was also recovered from obsolete weapons and recycled at the plant. Radioactive americium 241, a decay product of plutonium, was separated and recovered in this process.

Over the four decades of the plant's operation, emergencies threatened the surrounding population and environment. On September 11, 1957, and May 11, 1969, for example, plutonium stored inside glove boxes at the plant spontaneously combusted, allowing plutonium dust and smoke to escape to the outside environment through the ventilation systems.

During the late 1950's and the 1960's more than five thousand drums of waste oil accumulated on-site that had become contaminated with plutonium and the solvent carbon tetrachloride during machining operations. In 1967 and 1968 the barrels—many of them corroded and leaking—were removed, leaving the soil on which they had stood exposed to the elements. Subsequent windstorms blew the contaminated soil east and southeast of the plant. In 1969 the former storage area was asphalted over to contain the remaining contamination.

In 1973 the radioactive isotope tritium entered the plant's waste stream during scrap plutonium processing. It was discharged in wastewater to an on-site holding pond. From there, it entered Walnut Creek, which carried the radioactive contaminant to Great Western Reservoir, a source of drinking water for the Colorado community of Broomfield. Fortunately, radionuclide concentrations were not detected above levels believed to present a health concern.

Some plant workers went public with their concerns that proper safety guidelines were being disregarded. One infamous example involved a substance known as pondcrete. Until the mid-1980's the plant discharged hazardous chemical wastes mixed with low-level radioactive wastes to solar ponds to reduce the volume of the wastes through evaporation. Beginning in 1985, as the evaporation ponds were being phased out, sludge was dredged from them, mixed with Portland cement, and placed in large plastic-lined cardboard boxes. The pondcrete was supposed to form solid blocks that could be shipped elsewhere for burial, but much of the radioactive, toxic mixture remained mushy. The blocks were stacked in a parking lot and left exposed to the weather for three years, and the decomposing pondcrete was washed into the soil by rain and snowmelt.

Requests from the public for specific information on hazards at the plant were frequently denied by officials, who claimed that such records were classified. A series of investigations finally resulted in a 1989 raid by Federal Bureau of Investigation (FBI) agents and Environmental Protection Agency (EPA) staff, who seized plant records. Evidence of the mishandling of hazardous materials at the plant resulted in an $18.5 million fine for Rockwell International, the company that managed the plant for the U.S. Department of Energy (DOE), and termination of its contract. That same year, Rocky Flats was placed on the National Priorities List (NPL), making it a Superfund cleanup site.

The next management company, EG&G, was also accused of safety violations, despite its expenditure of $50 million on repairs. In 1993, Secretary of Energy James Watkins announced the end of nuclear production at Rocky Flats.

Studies of tissue and urine samples from people living near the plant found that they had received radiation doses much lower than those normally caused by natural background radiation. As part of the cleanup and remediation processes, a new water supply for Broomfield was constructed, along with catch basins and diversion ditches to control contaminated runoff. Radioactive and hazardous chemical wastes, as well as decontaminated construction materials from demolished industrial facilities, were transported off-site to licensed repositories. Still-useful nuclear materials were shipped to other DOE facilities. On-site landfills were covered to meet final closure criteria, and groundwater treatment systems were installed as part of the cleanup.

In late 2005 cleanup of chemical and radiological contamination within the 1,619-hectare (4,000-acre) buffer zone surrounding the former plant site was declared complete. The EPA deleted this portion of the Rocky Flats site from the NPL in 2007 and handed the land over to the U.S. Fish and Wildlife Service for use as a national wildlife refuge. The 529-hectare (1,308-acre) central area, formerly the location of the industrial facilities, remained on the NPL as an active Superfund site under DOE control for monitoring and maintenance purposes.

Charles W. Rogers
Updated by Karen N. Kähler

FURTHER READING

Ackland, Len. *Making a Real Killing: Rocky Flats and the Nuclear West*. Albuquerque: University of New Mexico Press, 2002.

Layzer, Judith A. "Government Secrets at Rocky Flats." In *The Environmental Case: Translating Values into Policy*. 2d ed. Washington, D.C.: CQ Press, 2006.

Rood, Arthur S., and John E. Till. *Estimated Exposure and Lifetime Cancer Incidence Risk from Routine Plutonium Releases at the Rocky Flats Plant: Independent Analysis of Exposure, Dose, and Health Risk to Off-Site Individuals*. Neeses, S.C.: Radiological Assessments Corporation, 1999.

U.S. Department of Energy. *Second Five-Year Review Report for the Rocky Flats Site, Jefferson and Boulder Counties, Colorado*. Grand Junction, Colo.: Author, 2007.

Runoff, agricultural

CATEGORY: Water and water pollution

DEFINITION: Water that flows into rivers, lakes, and other bodies of water from agricultural land and operations

SIGNIFICANCE: Runoff from land used for agriculture, which often contains the residues of chemical and organic fertilizers and pesticides, is one of the major sources of water pollution around the world.

The water that flows into streams from farmland after rain or snowmelt carries the residue of the herbicides, fungicides, insecticides, and fertilizers that farmers have used on the land. Many of the wastes produced by cattle, hogs, sheep, and poultry that are raised on feedlots flow into nearby streams. The water that returns to nearby rivers and lakes after it is used to irrigate farmland may be polluted by salt, agricultural pesticides, and toxic chemicals. These organic materials and chemicals that are carried with soil eroding from farmland and transported by water runoff degrade the quality of streams, rivers, lakes, and oceans.

Agricultural runoff enters rivers and lakes from farmland spread over large areas. Since such runoff is a nonpoint source of water pollution, it is more difficult to control than discharges from factories and sewage treatment plants. The chemicals in agricultural runoff have contaminated surface water in many areas of the United States. Rivers pick up sediments and dissolved salts from agricultural runoff as they flow to the oceans. Salt concentration in the Colorado River, for example, increases from about 40 parts per million to 800 parts per million as the river flows down from its headwaters to Mexico.

Nutrients such as potassium, phosphates, and nitrogen compounds from organic wastes and fertilizers are carried by agricultural runoff into rivers and lakes. In the process known as eutrophication, excessive nutrients in bodies of water stimulate the growth of plants such as pond weeds and duck weeds, plantlike organisms called algae, fish and other animals, and bacteria. As more of these organisms grow, more also die and decay. The decay process uses up the oxygen in the water, depriving the fish and other aquatic organisms of their natural supply of oxygen. Some types of game fish, such as salmon, trout, and whitefish, cannot live in water with reduced oxygen. Fish that need less oxygen, such as carp and catfish, will replace them. If all the oxygen in a body of water were to be used up, most forms of life in the water would die. Eutrophication that results from human activities, such as agriculture, is known as cultural eutrophication. In the late 1950's Lake Erie, 26,000 square kilometers (10,000 square miles) in area, was reported to be eutrophic. Thanks to stringent pollution-control measures, however, the lake has improved steadily since that time.

MITIGATING ENVIRONMENTAL IMPACTS

The 1987 amendments to the Clean Water Act represent the first comprehensive attempt by the U.S. government to control pollution caused by agricultural activities. In 1991 the U.S. Geological Survey began to implement the full-scale National Water-Quality Assessment (NAWQA) program. The long-term purposes of NAWQA are to describe the status and trends in the quality of the nation's water resources and to provide a scientific understanding of the factors affecting the quality of these resources. In October, 1997, an initiative intended to build on the environmental successes of the Clean Water Act was announced. It focused on runoff from farms and ranches, city streets, and other diffuse sources. The plan called for state and federal environmental agencies to conduct watershed assessments every two years.

Irrigation is necessary for survival in many developing countries. Governments struggle to build advanced agricultural systems, and developments in agriculture have improved food production around the world. However, the growing reliance on fertilizers and other agricultural chemicals has contributed to the pollution of rivers and lakes. Therefore, interest has shifted to farming with reduced use of chemicals. Scientists have turned their attention to developing organic ways to grow food that require less fertilizer and fewer pesticides, and many farmers rotate their crops from year to year to reduce the need for chemical fertilizers. Instead of spraying their crops with harmful pesticides, some farmers combat damaging insects by releasing other insects or bacteria that prey upon the pests. Scientists have also developed genetically engineered plants that are resistant to certain pests. Other strategies for minimizing pollution caused by agricultural runoff include maintaining buffer zones between irrigated cropland and sites where wastes are disposed, restricting application of manure to areas away from waterways, avoiding application of manure on land subject to erosion, reusing water used to flush manure from paved surfaces for irrigation, constructing ditches and waterways above and around open feedlots to divert runoff, constructing lined water-retention facilities to contain rainfall and runoff, applying solid manure at a rate that optimizes the use of the nitrogen it contains for a given crop, and allowing excess wastewater to evaporate by applying it evenly to land.

Watersheds are areas of land that drain to streams or other bodies of water. Most nonpoint pollution-control projects focus their activities around watersheds because watersheds integrate the effects that land use, climate, hydrology, drainage, and vegetation have on water quality. In the United States, the National Monitoring Program was initiated in 1991 to evaluate the effects of improved land management in reducing water pollution in selected watersheds. Federal agencies involved in this program include the Environmental Protection Agency (EPA), the Department of Agriculture, the U.S. Geological Survey, and the U.S. Army Corps of Engineers. A composite index was constructed and published to show which watersheds had the greatest potential for possible degradation of water quality from combinations of pesticides, nitrogen, and sediment runoff. The EPA sets criteria on water quality to help states set their own site-specific standards to control nutrient pollution and thus reduce nutrient loading to rivers and lakes.

G. Padmanabhan

FURTHER READING

Copeland, Claudia. *The Clean Water Initiative.* Washington, D.C.: Congressional Research Service, Library of Congress, 1998.

Hill, Marquita K. "Water Pollution." In *Understanding Environmental Pollution.* 3d ed. New York: Cambridge University Press, 2010.

Hunt, Constance Elizabeth. *Thirsty Planet: Strategies for Sustainable Water Management.* New York: Zed Books, 2004.

Sullivan, Patrick J., Franklin J. Agardy, and James J. J. Clark. "Water Pollution." In *The Environmental Science of Drinking Water.* Burlington, Mass.: Elsevier Butterworth-Heinemann, 2005.

Runoff, urban

CATEGORY: Water and water pollution

DEFINITION: Water that flows into streams, rivers, and other bodies of water from lawn irrigation, rainfall, and snowmelt in cities and other developed areas

SIGNIFICANCE: In urban areas, runoff can contribute to environmental problems such as flooding and water pollution.

When rain falls on natural landscapes, much of it is caught by vegetation or soaks into the ground. A coniferous forest, for example, can intercept as much as 50 percent of the rain that falls on it annually. The rain that reaches the ground percolates into the soil and makes its way into the groundwater or travels slowly through the soil to reach the nearest stream hours, days, or even months later.

In developed areas, rainwater falls on impervious surfaces—roofs, roads, and other nonporous materials—where it is prevented from soaking into the ground. The runoff, often referred to as stormwater, then flows across those surfaces in large quantities, collecting and transporting pollutants, until it reaches a storm sewer, stream, or natural area. This large amount of water flowing into streams almost immedi-

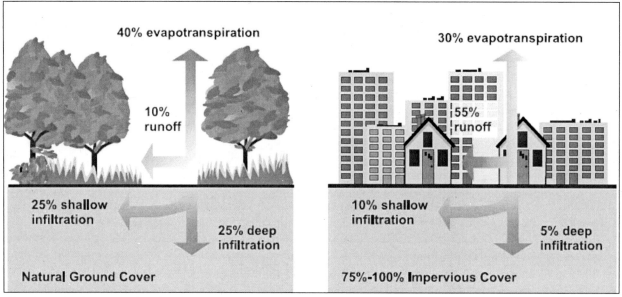

The relationship between surface runoff and the natural or impervious state of land cover. (U.S. Environmental Protection Agency [EPA])

ately after a storm can cause local flooding. Research has shown that the number of small floods increases up to ten times when a watershed reaches 20 percent urbanization. Conversely, since less water is allowed to enter the soil and groundwater, stream flows are greatly reduced in the dry season. This rapid fluctuation of water levels causes stream erosion and siltation and destroys habitat for fish and other aquatic life.

The pollution carried by urban runoff is a form of nonpoint source pollution—pollution that is not easily traced to a particular point, such as the end of a pipe, but instead comes from all over the environment. Automobiles, combined with impervious surfaces, are responsible for a large part of the pollution in urban runoff. In addition to motor oil that is improperly dumped down storm drains, oil and other automotive fluids leak onto parking lots and roads and are picked up by runoff. Heavy metals, such as zinc and copper, accumulate from the dust of tire and brake wear and can be major pollutants in urban streams. Lawns can be relatively impervious as well, and heavy storms or excessive watering can wash pesticides, herbicides, and fertilizers into streams, disrupting the already damaged aquatic environment. Airborne pollutants that fall on impervious surfaces, substances dumped on roads or in storm drains, bird and pet wastes, and street litter also contribute to the toxic mix of stormwater runoff.

An additional runoff problem is caused by the ero-

sion of disturbed soil in areas of active building and development. Sediment that is washed into streams, either through storm drains or directly, can cover gravel that is critical to aquatic insects and fish and can fill stream channels, contributing to downstream flooding.

STORMWATER MANAGEMENT

The first attempts at urban stormwater management consisted of the construction of gutters and the digging of ditches to convey excess water quickly to the nearest natural waterway. In 1869 famed landscape architect Frederick Law Olmsted was the first to design a system of underground pipes to convey muddy, horse-manure-laden runoff from the streets of the new community of Riverside, Illinois, to the nearby Des Plains River. Many cities soon thereafter developed systems that combined storm sewers with sanitary sewers, but as communities grew and the amount of land covered by impervious surfaces increased, these systems often became overloaded and then overflowed, sending stormwater and raw sewage into rivers and streams. These cities later had to work to separate the storm and sanitary sewer systems, with engineering emphasis placed on storing or detaining runoff during storms and then releasing it to the streams later to reduce flooding.

Large-scale stormwater management relies on swales, ponds, and wetlands. Runoff from a town or development can be routed through a swale, a depression in the landscape that directs the runoff to another place or holds it long enough for it to evaporate or soak into the soil. Vegetation in the swale slows the water and also filters out some of the pollutants. A pond or wetland also detains the water and allows some of the pollutants to settle or be filtered by the plants. Some wetland organisms can actually break down oils and other pollutants into harmless elements.

In 1988 the reauthorization of the Clean Water Act required municipalities in the United States to do more to control nonpoint source pollution, most of which reaches waterways through stormwater. The listing of various species of fish as endangered or threatened under the Endangered Species Act also forced some cities to improve fish habitats by limiting pollution and sedimentation in local streams.

Because nonpoint source pollution, and urban runoff itself, accumulates drop by drop from many small sources, the small actions of many people throughout a watershed can help to solve the problem. In many cities, residents are encouraged to disconnect their roof drains, where appropriate, and divert stormwater to their own landscapes. In addition, rain barrels and cisterns can detain stormwater to be used for landscape watering and other purposes. Naturescaping, or gardening with native plants that are naturally adapted to the local climate and resistant to native pests, requires fewer chemical applications and less supplementary watering. The careful use and disposal of landscape and household chemicals and automotive fluids can also reduce pollutants in stormwater. In these ways, residents of a watershed can become part of the solution to the problem of urban flooding and local stream pollution.

Joseph W. Hinton

FURTHER READING

American Society of Civil Engineers. *Urban Runoff Quality Management*. Reston, Va.: Author, 1998.

Debo, Thomas N., and Andrew J. Reese. *Municipal Stormwater Management*. 2d ed. Boca Raton, Fla.: Lewis, 2003.

Hill, Marquita K. "Water Pollution." In *Understanding Environmental Pollution*. 3d ed. New York: Cambridge University Press, 2010.

Hunt, Constance Elizabeth. *Thirsty Planet: Strategies for Sustainable Water Management*. New York: Zed Books, 2004.

Sullivan, Patrick J., Franklin J. Agardy, and James J. J. Clark. "Water Pollution." In *The Environmental Science of Drinking Water*. Burlington, Mass.: Elsevier Butterworth-Heinemann, 2005.

Sacramento River pesticide spill

CATEGORY: Disasters

THE EVENT: Train derailment near Dunsmuir, California, that spilled thousands of gallons of the pesticide metam sodium into the Sacramento River

DATE: July 14, 1991

SIGNIFICANCE: The Sacramento River pesticide spill resulted in the deaths of more than one million fish and thousands of birds and other animals that shared the river habitat. Although the chemical contamination was short-lived, the ecological consequences were long lasting.

On the night of July 14, 1991, a Southern Pacific train derailed at the Cantara Loop north of Dunsmuir, California, causing a chemical tank car to rupture and spill 19,000 gallons of the pesticide metam sodium into the upper Sacramento River. This event, known as the Sacramento River spill or the Cantara spill, was the largest inland ecological disaster that had taken place in California up to that date. As the metam sodium rapidly mixed with the river's water, it released highly toxic compounds, virtually sterilizing what had been one of the premier trout streams in California. The green contaminant plume eventually flowed 58 kilometers (36 miles) downstream into California's largest reservoir, Lake Shasta, where a string of air pipes placed at the bottom of the lake aerated the chemical. The aeration project accelerated the breakdown of the metam sodium, reducing toxic components to undetectable levels by July 29, 1991.

Studies were launched to identify and quantify the spill's damage to natural resources. Exposure to the pesticide had killed all the aquatic life in the Sacramento River between the Cantara Loop and Lake Shasta. More than one million fish died, including more than 300,000 trout. Millions of insects, snails, and clams perished, along with thousands of crayfish and salamanders. Hundreds of thousands of trees, particularly willows, alders, and cottonwoods, eventually died as a result of the pollution of the water, and many more were severely injured. The vegetative damage caused a corresponding dramatic loss of many wildlife species that depended on the river's vegetation for food and shelter. Birds, bats, otters, and mink either starved or were forced to relocate to other areas because their food sources were no longer available. In addition to the devastating effects on wildlife and plant life, the spill produced many reported negative effects on human health. It also halted recreational activities for miles along the river, resulting in substantial economic losses for the residents of the Dunsmuir area.

Although virtually no trace of the metam sodium remained in the river about one month after the spill, it became clear that full recovery remained years away. In 1992 the U.S. Department of Fish and Game planted more than three thousand trees to accelerate the recovery of severely injured vegetation along the river. Some plants, such as elephant ears and torrent sedge, recovered after two growing seasons. During 1994 the trout population reached about one-half of what it was prior to the spill, and trout angling was again allowed on the river. However, strict regulations were established that would allow protection for the recovering wild trout fishery.

By late 1995 ospreys, dippers, sandpipers, and mergansers were all making good progress toward recovery. By 1996 many aquatic and insect populations were nearing numbers that existed prior to the spill; some species, however, particularly clams, snails, crayfish, and salamanders, were struggling to make a comeback. To accelerate recovery, which continued into the twenty-first century, state and federal trustee agencies spent several million dollars to fund specific projects, including research, recovery monitoring, habitat acquisition and restoration, resource protection, and public education.

Alvin K. Benson

FURTHER READING

Elmer-Dewitt, Philip. "Death of a River: An Ecological Catastrophe in California Points to the Need for New Rules on the Transport of Toxic Compounds." *Time,* July 29, 1991, 24.

Friis, Robert H. "Pesticides and Other Organic Chemicals." In *Essentials of Environmental Health.* Sudbury, Mass.: Jones and Bartlett, 2007.

Hill, Marquita K. "Water Pollution." In *Understanding Environmental Pollution.* 3d ed. New York: Cambridge University Press, 2010.

Safe Drinking Water Act

CATEGORY: Treaties, laws, and court cases
THE LAW: U.S. federal law concerning standards for safe public drinking water
DATE: Enacted on December 16, 1974
SIGNIFICANCE: The Safe Drinking Water Act was the first law passed in the United States to set standards regarding acceptable levels of certain pollutants in the more than 170,000 public drinking-water supplies across the nation.

Under the Safe Drinking Water Act of 1974, the U.S. Environmental Protection Agency (EPA) is required to set standards regarding the maximum amounts of certain materials allowed in public drinking water; these include harmful inorganic and organic substances, radioactive substances, microorganisms, and suspended materials. The act requires the individual U.S. states to enforce the EPA's standards, and it requires each public drinking-water supplier to monitor the quality of its water sent to home users. Initially the EPA included twenty-five materials on its list of contaminants, but over time it has added many others.

DRINKING-WATER CONTAMINANTS

The EPA sets maximum levels of contaminants in public drinking water for microorganisms (such as viruses, coliform bacteria, *Giardia,* and *Cryptosporidium*), disinfection by-products (such as bromate and chlorite), disinfectants (such as chloramines and chlorine), inorganic chemicals (such as arsenic, asbestos, chromium, cyanide, fluoride, lead, mercury, and nitrate), organic chemicals (such as atrazine, benzene, dichlorobenzene, and dioxin), and radionuclides. In addition to setting the maximum allowable amount of each contaminant (the maximum contaminant level, or MCL) in drinking water (usually in milligrams of contaminant per liter of water), the EPA states the ideal goal level of the contaminant (usually also in milligrams per liter). The EPA also provides information on the typical sources of the contaminants listed and their possible harmful health effects on humans.

Nitrate, for example, is a common pollutant in natural waters that may come from sewage, animal waste, fertilizer runoff, or the erosion of natural deposits. Nitrate levels thus can become high in groundwater near feedlots for cattle or in areas where large amounts of fertilizers are used, such as agricultural areas. Nitrogen compounds formed from nitrate may bond with hemoglobin in the blood of humans so that less oxygen can be transported through the body by hemoglobin. Humans, especially babies, can become seriously ill from drinking nitrate-polluted waters. The EPA sets the MCL for nitrate (measured as nitrogen) in public drinking water at 10 milligrams per liter.

Harmful microorganisms in water often come from human and animal fecal material. They can produce diarrhea, vomiting, and cramps. Harmful organic materials found in water supplies often come from chemical plants, herbicides, sewage, or insecticides. These can have a variety of negative health impacts, including increased risk of cancer, liver and kidney damage, anemia, reproductive problems, and nervous system problems. Harmful radioactive materials, such as uranium or radium, may enter water supplies from natural materials or as the result of improper disposal of radioactive wastes. Humans and animals exposed to such materials may have increased risk of cancer.

MUNICIPAL WATER SYSTEM PROBLEMS

Individual U.S. states have often failed in their enforcement of the EPA drinking-water standards. In 1985, for example, more than eighteen hundred cases were reported in which water in public supplies contained contaminants at levels higher than the maximum allowed. The most common problems involved levels of microorganisms, nitrate, and fluoride that exceeded EPA-required levels.

Because of such problems, amendments to the Safe Drinking Water Act were passed by Congress in 1986. This legislation gave the EPA deadlines by which it was to set and enforce reasonable standards for more than eighty potentially dangerous contaminants in public water systems. In setting the MCLs, the EPA was required to take into consideration not only the danger of the contaminants but also the costs of meeting these standards in public waters. Also included in this law was a ban on the use of lead solder and pipes in public water systems. In addition, the 1986 amendments required the EPA to monitor materials injected under the ground, such as oil field brines, to ensure that the injected materials do not contaminate groundwater supplies.

Robert L. Cullers

FURTHER READING

Cech, Thomas V. "Water Quality." In *Principles of Water Resources: History, Development, Management, and Policy.* 3d ed. New York: John Wiley & Sons, 2010.

Dorsheimer, Wesley T. "Removing Nitrate from Groundwater." *Water Engineering and Management* 144, no.12 (1997): 20-24.

Gray, N. F. *Drinking Water Quality: Problems and Solutions.* 2d ed. New York: Cambridge University Press, 2008.

Ketcham-Colwill, J. "Safe Drinking Water Law Toughened." *Environment* 28, no. 7 (1986): 42-43.

Royte, Elizabeth. *Bottlemania: Big Business, Local Springs, and the Battle over America's Drinking Water.* New York: Bloomsbury, 2009.

Santa Barbara oil spill

CATEGORY: Disasters

THE EVENT: Blowout in a drilling well in the Santa Barbara Channel off the California coast that resulted in a massive oil spill

DATE: January, 1969

SIGNIFICANCE: The oil that spilled off the coast of the resort city of Santa Barbara threatened marine life and coated beaches, endangering the area's tourism industry. As a result of the spill, the public demanded more stringent regulations on oil companies drilling in offshore areas.

Santa Barbara is an old Spanish mission town situated between the Pacific Ocean and the Santa Ynez Mountains in Southern California. Residents of the city have long been familiar with the effects of minor oil pollution at places along the coast; oil has been escaping from natural fractures in the ocean floor for thousands of years. Hundreds of years ago, Native Americans reportedly caulked their canoes with oil-based substances found near the Santa Barbara shoreline.

In January, 1969, Santa Barbara and other nearby communities along the Pacific coast were confronted by a devastating oil slick. The source of the oil was a blowout at Union Oil Company's drilling platform A, which was less than 13 kilometers (8 miles) offshore in the Santa Barbara Channel. Gas-charged oil escaped from below the metal well casing (a pipe set in the well bore) before the blowout preventers could be closed.

According to observers, ocean water east of the platform "boiled" violently for several hours after the preventers were closed.

Some reports suggested that the oil leaked to the surface along an unmapped fault. In a period of ten days, more than 11,000 tons of free oil reached the surface of the water and rapidly spread over an area of 200 square kilometers (80 square miles). An estimated 10,000 barrels of crude oil eventually reached the shoreline, where it coated gravel-sized beach rocks and rapidly infiltrated the sand. The light-colored Goleta Cliffs a short distance north of Santa Barbara were marked by a black band of gooey oil.

The spreading oil slick threatened marine life in the area, including porpoises, seals, whales, birds, and fish. Numerous oil-soaked birds perished, but many were saved by volunteers who removed the oil with a solvent. U.S. Navy personnel expressed concern that the oil would harm porpoises near the naval base at Point Mugu, California.

Remediation commenced immediately; methods included skimming the oil off the water's surface, burning the oil, applying chemical dispersants, and steam cleaning and vacuuming of beach areas. The most effective technique was the distribution of straw and other plant material along the beaches to absorb the oil. Many residents of Santa Barbara, including student volunteers from the city's campus of the University of California, worked many hours spreading and collecting the oil-soaked plant material, which was then taken away to be burned or buried.

As a result of the spill, Union Oil Company and three partners (Gulf, Mobil, and Texaco)—as well as the U.S. Department of the Interior—were sued for damages by the state of California and several coastal communities. The amounts of the claims ranged from $500 million to approximately $1.3 billion. The accident and the ensuing pollution also had major political repercussions. Public pressure resulted in a temporary halt on drilling in the channel, and more stringent regulations were imposed on oil companies drilling in offshore areas.

Donald F. Reaser

FURTHER READING

Fingas, Merv. *The Basics of Oil Spill Cleanup.* 2d ed. Boca Raton, Fla.: CRC Press, 2001.
Fitzgerald, Edward A. *The Seaweed Rebellion: Federal-State Conflicts over Offshore Energy Development.* Lanham, Md.: Lexington Books, 2001.

Sea Empress oil spill

CATEGORY: Disasters
THE EVENT: Grounding of an oil tanker off the coast of Wales, resulting in the release of thousands of tons of crude oil into the sea
DATE: February 15, 1996
SIGNIFICANCE: The *Sea Empress* grounding resulted in the third-largest tanker spill in United Kingdom waters, causing adverse effects to a number of wildlife species and considerable difficulties for the fishing industry within the region.

On February 15, 1996, the *Sea Empress* oil tanker ran aground on a wave-exposed, current-scoured section of coastline near Milford Haven in southwest Wales. Over the next six days, the vessel released more than 75,000 tons of North Seas light crude oil and about 400 tons of heavy fuel oil. Still leaking oil, the *Sea Empress* was recovered and towed to Milford Haven on February 21.

Weather and wave conditions that prevailed at the time of the spill facilitated the spread of oil slicks well beyond the immediate area of the grounding. Heavy oil slicks drifted into Milford Haven and also flowed north and south along the open Pembrokeshore coast. During the first weeks after the incident, oil was observed across a wide area of the Bristol Channel. More distant shores that were affected included those around Lundy Island and the southeast coast of Ireland.

Initially, the three main concerns were to establish the size of the area affected by oil, plan cleanup measures, and determine how badly various populations of shellfish, finfish, and other wildlife had been contaminated. Shortly after the spill, a fishing exclusion order was applied to the affected region, banning the catching of any fish within a designated area. Some of the spilled oil was mechanically sucked up at sea. Between February 17 and 25, large amounts of chemical dispersants were used to break up the oil into small droplets in order to reduce the risk to the coastline and to birds at sea. Mechanical methods were employed to clean beaches for the most part, but some dispersants were used to remove weathered oil from rocks next to selected beaches. The main recreational beaches were cleaned up by mid-April, allowing visitors to again enjoy them.

As local finfish were found to have little to no contamination, the ban on catching salmon and sea trout was lifted in May, 1996. The shellfish, however, were more heavily contaminated and recovered more slowly. Between 1996 and 1998, research was conducted to assess the impacts of the oil spill and the recovery of a range of key commercial fish species, particularly those that are important for food chains. By June, 1996, more than 6,900 oiled birds of at least twenty-eight species had been recovered dead or alive, and more than 3,000 birds had been cleaned and released.

Approximately one-third of the spilled oil evaporated from the sea surface, but because of a combination of natural and chemical dispersion, approximately 50 percent of the spill volume dispersed into the water column. The ultimate fate of this dispersed oil was unclear for some time, but water samples analyzed in 1997 showed low levels of total hydrocarbons. The impacts of the spill on the marine life in the area lasted for some years, but by 2001 the various populations appeared to have recovered.

Alvin K. Benson

FURTHER READING

Clark, R. B. *Marine Pollution.* 5th ed. New York: Oxford University Press, 2001.

Fingas, Merv. *The Basics of Oil Spill Cleanup.* 2d ed. Boca Raton, Fla.: CRC Press, 2001.

Speight, Martin, and Peter Henderson. "Threats to Marine Ecosystems: The Effects of Man." In *Marine Ecology: Concepts and Applications.* Hoboken, N.J.: John Wiley & Sons, 2010.

Sea-level changes

CATEGORY: Weather and climate

DEFINITION: Long-term rises and falls in mean sea level resulting from natural or human-caused alterations in climate or from deformations of the land

SIGNIFICANCE: Because a significant percentage of the human population lives near the oceans and most of them in large cities, even a modest rise in sea level could wreak great economic damage and displace hundreds of millions of people. It would also change sensitive coastal ecosystems, such as coral reefs and mangrove swamps.

The world's oceans and seas constantly rise and fall over short periods because of tides, currents, winds, air pressure, seasonal heating, and weather phenomena, such as El Niño and La Niña events. Moreover, because cold water is denser than warm water, the sea levels in polar oceans are generally lower than sea levels in tropical oceans. Nevertheless, scientists use data gathered by tidal gauges and satellites to determine an overall mean sea level (MSL), purely a statistical value. In some areas available tidal gauge data extend back more than one hundred years. These data and more recent data sets show that the MSL has been rising since the mid-nineteenth century after about six thousand years of relative stability. The twentieth century saw an average rise of 1-2 millimeters (0.04-0.08 inch) per year, with an increase to 3 millimeters (0.12 inch) per year at the end of the century. If that rate accelerates because of human-caused global warming, as many scientists have concluded will happen, sea levels could become high enough to imperil coastal cities, agriculture, ecosystems, and fisheries during the twenty-first century.

LONG-TERM CHANGE

Scientists distinguish two types of long-term change in sea level. The first, secular (or isostatic) change, comes from local movement of the land and seabed: land rebounding after the ice sheets of the last ice age melted (glacial isostatic adjustment), land subsiding as groundwater is removed, the deposit of sediments, and the effects of volcanoes, earthquakes, and tectonic plate movement. The second type, eustatic change, involves the volume of water in the oceans. The volume varies based on water temperature and on how much of the world's water supply is landbound in lakes, aquifers, and ice (glaciers, ice caps, and ice sheets).

About half of the rise in sea level during the twentieth century came from warming water (thermal expansion). Water added to the oceans from melting glaciers and ice caps contributed most of the rest, a small amount coming from the ice sheets covering Greenland and Antarctica. These changes arise from temperature change caused by several factors influencing the amount of heat energy in the atmosphere, land surface, and water, principally orbital cycles varying the earth's distance from and attitude toward the sun and the concentration of greenhouse gases. For example, when global cooling locked greater volumes of water in land ice during the depths of the last

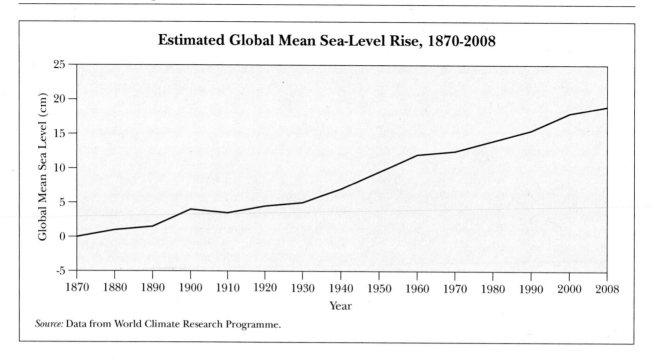

Estimated Global Mean Sea-Level Rise, 1870-2008

Source: Data from World Climate Research Programme.

ice age, twenty thousand years ago, the MSL was about 120 meters (394 feet) lower than that of the early twenty-first century. During the warm epoch of the Pliocene, about three million years ago, levels were 20 to 25 meters (66 to 82 feet) higher.

FUTURE CHANGE

If all the icebound water on the earth melted and ran into the oceans, the MSL would increase an estimated 64-70 meters (210-230 feet) above the contribution of thermal expansion. This is not likely to happen. Thermal expansion and melting will continue, however, accelerated by an anticipated increase in global temperatures of 3 degrees Celsius (5.4 degrees Fahrenheit) because of greenhouse gas emissions.

Projections about sea-level changes in the near future are controversial, but a majority of climate scientists agree that the MSL will rise faster in the twenty-first century than it did during the twentieth century. In 2007, the Intergovernmental Panel on Climate Change estimated that the rise will be somewhere between 18 and 59 centimeters (7 and 23 inches) by 2100. However, that projection did not include possible contributions from the Antarctic and Greenland ice sheets, because scientists did not have sufficient understanding of the ice sheets' dynamics. Subsequent studies found increasing instability in parts of these ice sheets, and in 2009 the Scientific Committee on Antarctic Research forecast accelerated melting in

Greenland and the Antarctic; the committee estimated that the MSL could rise as much as 1.4 meters (4.6 feet) by the end of the twenty-first century. Such a rise could bring serious disruptions to both agriculture and cities in coastal areas, principally because low-lying lan will be much more vulnerable to storm surges and to salinization of groundwater and wetlands. In 2000, some 600 million people were living along the coasts of the world, the majority in large cities.

Sea levels will continue to rise past 2100 because of further recovery from the last ice age, long-period climate variability, and accumulation of greenhouse gases. Scientists calculate that the MSL will come to equilibrium at about 50 meters (164 feet) higher than the MSL of the early twenty-first century in a few thousand years.

Roger Smith

FURTHER READING

Archer, David. *The Long Thaw: How Humans Are Changing the Next 100,000 Years of Earth's Climate.* Princeton, N.J.: Princeton University Press, 2009.

Langwith, Jacqueline, ed. *Water.* Farmington Hills, Mich.: Greenhaven Press, 2010.

McGranahan, Gordon, Deborah Balk, and Bridget Anderson. "The Rising Tide: Assessing the Risks of Climate Change and Human Settlements in Low Elevation Coastal Zones." *Environment and Urbanization* 19, no. 1 (2007): 17-37.

Pilkey, Orrin H., and Rob Young. *The Rising Sea*. Washington, D.C.: Island Press, 2009.

Pugh, David. *Changing Sea Levels: Effects of Tides, Weather, and Climate*. New York: Cambridge University Press, 2004.

Seabed disposal

CATEGORY: Waste and waste management

DEFINITION: Dumping of waste materials into the open sea or burial of such materials in the ocean floor

SIGNIFICANCE: The seabed disposal of debris, containers of toxic or radioactive waste, discarded chemicals, heavy metals, and other harmful wastes can jeopardize marine life by disrupting the balance of delicate ocean ecosystems.

Oceans cover more than 75 percent of the earth's surface. People have long believed that the vast ocean waters can dilute, redistribute, and render harmless any garbage, sewage, or other debris dumped into them. As landfill space becomes increasingly scarce, many have looked to the oceans and their tremendous beds as alternative sites for waste disposal. However, marine biologists and other scientists have learned that the oceans can be harmed by waste disposal. Like the land, which is a network of many different ecosystems, the oceans are made up of many ecosystems serving a variety of marine life. Many marine creatures and their habitats exist in a delicate ecological balance; any change in water quality, temperature, or food source is harmful.

In an effort to protect marine creatures and the balance of ocean ecosystems, many countries have worked together to stop ocean pollution and open-ocean dumping. The International Convention for the Prevention of Pollution from Ships (known as MARPOL, for "marine pollution") outlaws the dumping of plastic items anywhere in the oceans. It also regulates how far from shore ships must be in order to dump other kinds of debris legally. Much of this debris eventually settles on the seabed.

Also scattered across the seabed are containers of hazardous waste, chemicals, and radioactive waste. At one time scientists believed that the ocean floor would be a safe place for the disposal of sealed containers of these wastes; they argued that the materials would not come into contact with marine life at such depths and that the extremely cold temperatures of the deep ocean would keep the wastes safely contained. Dump sites for radioactive waste are located in the far northern parts of the Atlantic Ocean and in the Arctic Ocean. After World War II, several thousand tons of German chemical weapons, undetonated bombs, and other equipment were dumped in the waters off the coasts of Germany, Denmark, Norway, Sweden, and Poland. In 1972 the international Convention on the Prevention of Marine Pollution by Dumping of Wastes and Other Matter (known as the London Convention) banned ocean dumping of high-level radioactive wastes. In 1994 this ban was expanded to cover low-level radioactive wastes. Despite this agreement, Russia continued to dump large amounts of radioactive waste into the Barents and Kara seas.

Research has shown that the dumping of sealed containers of chemicals into the ocean, even in deep waters, poses threats to the environment. For example, several sites for ocean dumping of industrial wastes were established in the middle of fishing grounds off the coast of New England and used for twenty years. Although toxic and radioactive wastes are no longer dumped in these areas, years later they are still marked as hazardous because of the incredible staying power of the chemicals dumped. Unlike organic matter, chemicals do not break down quickly over time. Despite warnings, some people still harvest fish, shrimp, and shellfish from these areas. In a joint effort among several state and federal agencies, seafood from these areas and the surrounding waters was collected and tested for dangerous levels of hazardous or toxic chemicals. Tests performed by the U.S. Food and Drug Administration (FDA) showed only trace contaminants in the seafood—none of the samples tested had levels high enough to pose threats. When the anchor was pulled aboard a boat at one location, however, its tip had traces of waste that was high enough in radioactivity to set off the sensors worn by the study participants.

A video survey was taken of one site, known as the Foul Area, 29 kilometers (18 miles) off the coast of Boston, Massachusetts. The 3.2-kilometer (2-mile) expanse is officially named the Massachusetts Bay Industrial Waste Site. From 1953 to 1976 it served as a dumping ground for toxic and radioactive materials. The survey, taken in 1991, found almost one hundred objects scattered across the ocean floor at eighteen separate sites. Of these objects, sixty-four were identified as cement containers, and more than one-half of them had broken open over time.

Some scientists now advocate subseabed burial as an alternative to seabed dumping. Proposed mostly for high-level radioactive materials, subseabed disposal is argued to be safer than core-drilled burial on land. Proponents argue that the deep seabed is one of the most geologically stable places on the earth. They also argue that the sticky mud and clays found in the mid- and deep-ocean basins cause radioactive particles to cling to or bind with them, keeping them from migrating throughout the ocean waters. The results of tests conducted between 1974 and 1986 by an international team of scientists support these arguments. Opponents note that if any of the materials disposed of deep in the seabed should need to be retrieved, this process would be extremely difficult and costly. They also question the types of containers to be used and how the wastes can be safely transported to the seabed. While proponents were making progress in addressing these concerns, research funding was cut off in 1986 and the focus of decisions regarding disposal of radioactive wastes returned to land-based solutions. Although the London Convention has prohibited the dumping of radioactive waste at sea since 1994, subseabed disposal remains ambiguous, as do its effects on the ocean environment.

Lisa A. Wroble

FURTHER READING

Gorman, Martha. *Environmental Hazards: Marine Pollution.* Santa Barbara, Calif.: ABC-CLIO, 1993.

Hamblin, Jacob Darwin. *Poison in the Well: Radioactive Waste in the Oceans at the Dawn of the Nuclear Age.* New Brunswick, N.J.: Rutgers University Press, 2008.

Koslow, Tony. *The Silent Deep: The Discovery, Ecology, and Conservation of the Deep Sea.* Chicago: University of Chicago Press, 2007.

Laws, Edward A. *Aquatic Pollution: An Introductory Text.* 3d ed. New York: John Wiley & Sons, 2000.

Ringius, Lasse. *Radioactive Waste Disposal at Sea: Public Ideas, Transnational Policy Entrepreneurs, and Environmental Regimes.* Cambridge, Mass.: MIT Press, 2001.

Sindermann, Carl J. *Ocean Pollution: Effects on Living Resources and Humans.* Boca Raton, Fla.: CRC Press, 1996.

Sedimentation

CATEGORY: Water and water pollution

DEFINITION: Deposition of particulate matter by wind, water, chemical precipitation, gravity, or ice

SIGNIFICANCE: Sedimentation, whether the result of natural forces or human influences on nature, can have both negative environmental effects, such as the degradation of water quality, and positive effects, such as beach rejuvenation and growth.

Particulate matter accumulates as sediment through transport and subsequent deposition of materials. Transport mechanisms include wind, running water, gravity, and glaciers. Materials that have been dissolved and transported in solution may be deposited as sediment through chemical precipitation. Sedimentation is an ongoing process, and, in a natural system, a delicate balance exists between positive and negative effects.

Sedimentation takes place in low-energy environments. Particle transport distance is a function of particle shape, size, and mass, and the available energy for transport. High-energy transport mechanisms will transport larger particles than low-energy mechanisms, and less energy is required to transport small particles the same distance as larger particles. Sedimentation can result in a degradation of the quality of land or water, or a loss of use of these resources. Degradation can be measured in terms of the identifiable adverse affects on aquatic organisms, wildlife, and humans.

Sedimentation can have negative environmental effects as a result of natural processes or as a result of processes induced by humans. Negative effects from natural processes can result from landslides, mudslides, the migration of dunes in developed areas, and the in-filling of lagoons or lakes that might otherwise provide recreational or commercial opportunities. Natural degradation of water quality results from sedimentation in areas such as north-central Oklahoma, where large accumulations of salt have precipitated from saline groundwater to form the Great Salt Plains along the Salt Fork of the Arkansas River, thereby affecting the chemistry of the Arkansas River.

The discharge of dredged or fill material, industrial wastes, or other materials into a natural system can affect the chemical, physical, and biological integrity of the system. Industrial wastewaters are a major source of chemicals that may include highly stable organic compounds that are capable of accumulating in high concentrations through sedimentary processes. Both the sedimentation rate and the individual compound's rate of solubility in water will affect the concentration of accumulated materials.

Adult freshwater organisms are generally tolerant of the normal extremes of suspended solids, but the introduction of excess materials and resulting sedimentation will kill eggs, larvae, and insect fauna while altering the characteristics of the aquatic bottom environment. Studies have also shown that high concentrations of suspended solids can interfere with the filter mechanisms of aquatic organisms and the ability of sight feeders to locate prey.

The positive effects of sedimentation can be seen in many natural processes. Beach rejuvenation and growth take place as the ocean's waves and currents deposit materials in quiet-water environments. Similar land growth takes place in the quiet-water environments of lakes and rivers. In many instances, this process has resulted in substantial land growth that has allowed development of commercial or recreational facilities. River floodplains are frequently rejuvenated with nutrients needed for agricultural land use through sedimentation. Salt harvested from brine ponds relies on the natural process of chemical precipitation and sedimentation. Sedimentary processes have also been responsible for creating accumulations of materials such as gold and platinum in river placer deposits.

Kyle L. Kayler

FURTHER READING

Chiras, Daniel D. "Water Pollution: Sustainably Managing a Renewable Resource." In *Environmental Science.* 8th ed. Sudbury, Mass.: Jones and Bartlett, 2010.

Taylor, Kevin G. "Sediments and Sedimentation." In *An Introduction to Physical Geography and the Environment,* edited by Joseph Holden. 2d ed. Harlow, England: Pearson Education, 2008.

Sludge treatment and disposal

CATEGORY: Waste and waste management

DEFINITION: Processing and disposal of the residue that is left after water is removed from sewage and industrial waste

SIGNIFICANCE: The proper treatment and disposal of

sewage sludge is a critical element in environmental planning because improper disposal or inadequate treatment can result in the contamination of groundwater and of drinking-water supplies.

Most wastewater, whether from industrial discharge, storm drains, or sewage systems, goes through a process that separates the solids from the water. This process takes place in up to three stages: primary, secondary, and tertiary treatment. Although it is desirable for wastewater to undergo tertiary treatment before it is discharged into lakes or oceans, in the United States secondary treatment meets the minimum requirement for such sewage. Tertiary treatment involves polishing, or further treating, the liquid—or effluent—that is removed from wastewater during the dewatering process.

Primary treatment involves collecting the wastewater in a sedimentation lagoon or clarifier. The water is allowed to settle so that the solids and liquids separate. The sediment that is left after the liquid is pumped out is called sludge. Sludge usually contains about 95 percent water. It is filtered to remove more water in a process known as dewatering.

The open-lagoon method filters sludge through sand beds, allowing it to air dry. This may take several months. To accelerate the process and reduce offensive conditions, most treatment facilities use clarifying tanks; in such a tank, rotating mechanical rakes move the settled solids to the center of the tank, where they are drawn off. This sludge is further dewatered before it is disposed of in a landfill or through incineration. Sometimes lime or other chemicals are added to increase the amount of solids that settle on the tank's bottom.

Secondary treatment involves using bacteria to break down the organic contaminants in the sludge. Oxygen must be supplied to the sludge so that the microorganisms present can do their work; this is accomplished through the use of aerated lagoons, digesting tanks, trickling filters, or oxidation ponds. The methods differ in the ways in which they supply oxygen.

Aerated lagoons and oxidation ponds both use large, shallow, open pits, where air and sunlight encourage bacteria and algae to grow. These organisms work together to break down the organic matter: The bacteria consume the organic matter, and the algae "feeds" on the sun and provides further oxygen, allowing the bacteria to thrive. Sometimes oxygen is supplied mechanically, enabling relatively small ponds to process larger amounts of sludge than they could otherwise process. Sludge deposits are removed from the ponds on a regular basis through dredging.

Trickling filters can take different forms: Some are large tanks filled with stones, whereas others are large plastic tanks. Settled sewage is sprayed on top of the stones or on the top and walls of the plastic tank. Water from the sediment trickles to the bottom of the tank, where it is collected, removed, and treated. Bacteria attack and metabolize the sediment that clings to the rocks or the tank walls. Sealed digesting tanks use anaerobic bacteria, which work best without oxygen, to break down the organic matter in sludge.

The most common method of sludge treatment is the activated sludge process, which is an aerobic (with oxygen) biological system. Microbes that rely on air are used to help metabolize, or break down, organic waste. During the first stage of this treatment, sludge is mixed with settled sewage in an aeration tank. Large amounts of microorganisms are collected in the aeration tank and mixed with the semisolid slurry. Oxygen is added so that the microorganisms will feed on the organic matter in the wastewater. The organisms consume tiny particles of waste, and large particles are broken down. After about twelve hours, the slurry in the aeration tank is pumped to a sedimentation tank. The sediment settles, and the organisms are returned to the aeration tank where they consume more organic matter. Any remaining liquid is treated to remove nitrogen and phosphorus, which may cause excessive growth of plants or algae, before it is discharged into lakes or the ocean.

About 30 percent of the sludge is pumped back to the aeration tank to repeat the process. Recirculating the sludge and mixing it with fresh sewage sediment in the aeration tank is a key part of the activated sludge treatment process. Remaining sludge is dewatered using centrifuges, which spin the sludge to draw out water. Filter presses use belts or plates to squeeze out excess water. They create drier sludge cake.

The method used to dewater sludge depends on the disposal method. The more water that is removed from sludge, the less volume of sludge cake remains. Sludge cake needs to be very dry if it is to be incinerated. If the sludge cake is to be used as fertilizer, added to composting facilities, or disposed of in landfills, the water content can be higher. Chemicals are sometimes added to the sludge to encourage particles to clump together, which speeds the removal of water.

Separation of sludge from wastewater does not prevent toxins or other pollutants from remaining in the sludge, which means that toxins can enter landfills or crops. Bioremediation remedies this problem; in this process, microorganisms known to consume inorganic particles, oil, and other toxins are added to the sludge. Some agencies responsible for waste treatment in the United States, including the Palm Beach County Solid Waste Authority in Florida, have had great success using bioremedial treatment. Following bioremediation, sludge and solid waste can be composted into usable soil conditioners.

Lisa A. Wroble

FURTHER READING

Hill, Marquita K. "Water Pollution." In *Understanding Environmental Pollution.* 3d ed. New York: Cambridge University Press, 2010.

Lester, J., and D. Edge. "Sewage and Sewage Sludge Treatment." In *Pollution: Causes, Effects, and Control,* edited by Roy M. Harrison. 4th ed. Cambridge, England: Royal Society of Chemistry, 2001.

Miller, G. Tyler, Jr., and Scott Spoolman. "Water Pollution." In *Living in the Environment: Principles, Connections, and Solutions.* 16th ed. Belmont, Calif.: Brooks/Cole, 2009.

Qasim, Syed A. *Wastewater Treatment Plants: Planning, Design, and Operation.* 2d ed. Lancaster, Pa.: Technomic, 1999.

Roseland, Mark. "Water and Sewage." In *Toward Sustainable Communities: Resources for Citizens and Their Governments.* Rev. ed. Gabriola Island, B.C.: New Society, 2005.

Snyder, James D. "Off-the-Shelf Bugs Hungrily Gobble Our Nastiest Pollutants." *Smithsonian,* April, 1993, 67-70, 72, 74, 76.

Soil salinization

CATEGORY: Agriculture and food
DEFINITION: Process in which water-soluble salts build up in soil within the root zone of plants
SIGNIFICANCE: The salinization of soil on agricultural lands can result in poor plant growth and reduced crop yields, and attempts to reduce salinity through increased irrigation can lead to contamination of water supplies.

In the process of soil salinization, water-soluble salts build up in the part of the soil known as the root zone, where the soil comes into contact with the roots of plants, blocking the movement of water and nutrients into plant tissues. Soil salinization rarely occurs naturally. Rainwater is virtually free of dissolved solids, but surface waters and groundwater contain significant quantities of dissolved solids, ultimately produced by the weathering of rocks. Evaporation of water at the land surface results in an increase in dissolved solids in soil that may adversely affect the ability of plant roots to absorb water and nutrients.

In arid regions, evaporation of soil water potentially exceeds rainfall. Shallow wetting of the soil followed by surface evaporation lifts the available dissolved solids to near the surface of the soil. The near-surface soil therefore becomes richer in soluble salts. In natural arid areas, soluble salts in the subsurface are limited in quantity because rock weathering is an extremely slow process, and degrees of soil salinization detrimental to plants are uncommon.

The irrigation of arid-climate soils with surface water or groundwater provides a constant new supply of soluble salt. As the irrigation water evaporates and moves through plants to the atmosphere, the dissolved solid content of the soil water increases. Eventually, the increase in soil salt will inhibit or stop plant growth. It is therefore necessary to apply much more water to fields in arid climates than the amount required for plant growth, so that the water flushes salts away from the plant root zone. If the excess water drains easily to the groundwater zone, however, the groundwater becomes enriched in dissolved solids, which may be detrimental.

If the groundwater table is near the surface, or if impermeable soil zones are close to the surface, overirrigation will not alleviate the problem of soil salinization. Alleviation of this condition requires the installation of subsurface drains to carry the excess soil water and salts to a surface outlet. The problem with this method is that disposing of the salty drain water is difficult. If the drain water is released into surface streams, it degrades the quality of the stream water, adversely affecting downstream users. If the water is discharged into evaporation ponds, it has the potential to seep into the groundwater zone or produce a dangerously contaminated body of surface water, as occurred at the Kesterson National Wildlife Refuge in California, where concentrations of the trace element selenium rose to levels that interfered with the reproduction of resident birds.

Robert E. Carver

FURTHER READING

Blanco, Humberto, and Rattan Lal. *Principles of Soil Conservation and Management*. New York: Springer, 2008.

Vengosh, A. "Salinization and Saline Environments." In *Environmental Geochemistry*, edited by Barbara Sherwood Lollar. Oxford: Elsevier, 2005.

Stormwater management

CATEGORY: Water and water pollution

DEFINITION: Methods of containing and channeling water from precipitation that flows over land or impenetrable surfaces and does not percolate into the ground

SIGNIFICANCE: When stormwater is uncontrolled, water resources may be wasted and destructive flooding may occur; in addition, pollution carried by stormwater can contaminate bodies of water and endanger human and animal health. Stormwater management systems are designed to minimize the environmentally destructive potential of precipitation runoff.

Stormwater management, which has its roots in ancient Greek and Roman cultures, has evolved into the vast systems now present in all developed and many developing nations. The management of stormwater has become increasingly important over time with human development, as the impervious surfaces of buildings, roads, parking lots, and so on do not allow rainwater and snowmelt to penetrate into the ground, resulting in much more runoff than occurs on undeveloped land. All developed and many developing nations have laws in place that set standards for stormwater management.

POLLUTION AND UNCONTROLLED RUNOFF

Stormwater management is necessary to address the problem of water pollution caused by runoff. Polluted stormwater runoff from impervious surfaces such as roads and roofs, as well as from agricultural fields, is a major source of water pollution around the world. Water flowing over human-built surfaces picks up pollutants such as gasoline, oil, trash, and heavy metals (mercury, lead, cobalt, copper, and zinc). Water flowing over lawns and farm fields collects nitrates and phosphates from the fertilizers used on these surfaces.

In the United States, the pollution of waterways became a nationally recognized issue in June, 1969, when the Cuyahoga River, flowing through Cleveland, Ohio, on its way to Lake Erie actually caught fire because it was so polluted. At that time, Lake Erie had become a victim of eutrophication, a process in which an increase in chemical nutrients alters plant growth in an ecosystem. Algae became the dominant plant species in the lake and absorbed all the oxygen in the water, killing most of the native fish and other aquatic species. For decades, far more nutrients entered the lake than it could handle; the main culprit was phosphorus, a component of fertilizers and detergents. Heavy metals and pesticides also contributed to the pollution. Fish that managed to survive in the lake were unfit for human consumption.

Another problem addressed by stormwater management is uncontrolled runoff, which not only results in the waste of a valuable resource but also can cause extensive damage. When the amount of water generated by rain or snowmelt exceeds the capacity of waterways, flooding occurs. Floods are among the most frequent of all forms of natural disasters, and they are also among the most costly in terms of human and animal deaths, destruction of structures and habitats, and soil erosion.

Conditions that result in flooding include heavy or steady rains that last hours or days; such rains can exceed the capacity of the ground to absorb the water, and after the ground is saturated the excess flows to lower areas. In areas where forest or brush fires have recently taken place, denuding the landscape of plants that absorb groundwater and stabilize the soil, subsequent rainfall can result in flooding, often accompanied by mudslides.

METHODS OF MANAGEMENT

Methods of stormwater management address the problems of pollution and uncontrolled runoff. Bodies of water become contaminated by both point source pollution and nonpoint source pollution. Point source pollution occurs when pollutants enter a waterway through a specific entry point, such as a drainage pipe discharging into a river. This type of pollution is much more controllable than nonpoint

source pollution, which originates from a variety of diffuse sources that are difficult to identify; pollution from stormwater is a form of nonpoint source pollution.

An example of pollution control involving stormwater management can be seen in the situation that was present in Lake Erie and the other Great Lakes during the 1960's. Recognition of the levels of pollution in the lakes led to the Great Lakes Water Quality Agreement (GLWQA), signed by the United States and Canada in 1972, and the U.S. federal Clean Water Act, also enacted in 1972. The GLWQA stressed the reduction of the amounts of phosphorus (then an ingredient in many laundry detergents) entering Lake Erie and Lake Ontario through stormwater runoff, and in 1977 maximum allowable levels of phosphorus were set by an amendment to the agreement. (Phosphorus was subsequently banned from detergents in both the United States and Canada.) By 2010 the phosphorus level in Lake Erie was found to be below the maximum allowed by the GLWQA, and the eutrophication of the lake had also abated. Despite these improvements, Lake Erie still has a number of problems, including contaminated sediments.

Ideally, stormwater runoff should be not only channeled to prevent damage but also collected for future use or decontamination. Stormwater collection methods range from rooftop cisterns used to collect and store rainwater for household uses to systems that channel stormwater to reservoirs that can supply water to large populations. Retention basins can both control runoff and allow treatment of the contained water. Stormwater is usually channeled to a retention basin from storm drains. Water entering the basin is restricted from flowing outward unless a major storm event occurs. These basins are often landscaped with varieties of plants that improve the water by removing excess nutrients and other pollutants. Another concept for runoff control is the swale or bioswale, which is a wide and shallow ditch designed to maximize the time water spends within it. Plants in the swale absorb and break down pollutants.

Even small stormwater runoff control systems can be effective. One example is the rain garden, which is a planted area designed to collect runoff from nearby impervious surfaces such as parking lots, driveways, roofs, and walkways. The hardy local plants used in the rain garden help the soil to absorb the runoff and any pollutants it contains.

REGULATIONS

All developed nations and some developing nations have well-established stormwater management policies. In the United States, the Environmental Protection Agency (EPA) oversees stormwater management under the provisions of the Clean Water Act. The EPA's National Pollutant Discharge Elimination System (NPDES) regulates stormwater discharges from municipal storm sewer systems, construction activities, and industrial activities. In addition to implementing NPDES requirements, many state and local governments in the United States have passed their own laws concerning stormwater management.

The treaty that created the European Union established environmental policy as one of the functions of that body. The aims of this policy are to protect and improve the quality of the environment, to protect the health of the population, to promote the careful and rational use of natural resources, and to promote measures at the international level to overcome regional and broader-scale environmental problems. By the early years of the twenty-first century all Western European nations had adopted legislation setting standards for the collection, treatment, and disposal of wastewater.

The stormwater policies of many Asian nations, including Japan and the People's Republic of China, are continually evolving. Australia, which has a well-developed stormwater policy, faces particular challenges because water resources are scarce on the Australian continent.

Stormwater management systems are generally much less advanced in developing nations than they are in the developed nations. In the cities of developing nations, the urban poor are most affected by inadequate stormwater management. Poor communities are often located on low-lying land, which is prone to flooding, or on steep hillsides, where heavy storms can wash away flimsy structures.

Robin L. Wulffson

FURTHER READING

Akan, A. Osman, and Robert J. Houghtalen. *Urban Hydrology, Hydraulics, and Stormwater Quality: Engineering Applications and Computer Modeling.* Hoboken, N.J.: John Wiley & Sons, 2003.

Committee on Reducing Stormwater Discharge Contributions to Water Pollution. *Urban Stormwater Management in the United States.* Washington, D.C.: National Academies Press, 2009.

Davis, Allen P. *Stormwater Management for Smart Growth.* New York: Springer, 2005.

Debo, Thomas N. *Municipal Stormwater Management.* 2d ed. Boca Raton, Fla.: CRC Press, 2002.

Gribbin, John E. *Introduction to Hydraulics and Hydrology with Applications for Stormwater Management.* 3d ed. Clifton Park, N.Y.: Thomson Delmar Learning, 2007.

Grigg, Neil S. *Water, Wastewater, and Stormwater Infrastructure Management.* Boca Raton, Fla.: CRC Press, 2002.

James, William. *Advances in Modeling the Management of Stormwater Impacts.* Boca Raton, Fla.: CRC Press, 1997.

Mays, Larry. *Stormwater Collection Systems Design Handbook.* New York: McGraw-Hill, 2001.

Sevbert, Thomas A. *Stormwater Management for Land Development: Methods and Calculations for Quantity Control.* Hoboken, N.J.: John Wiley & Sons, 2006.

Teton Dam collapse

CATEGORY: Disasters

THE EVENT: The catastrophic failure of a large earth-fill dam in Idaho, leading to the flooding of a town and the deaths of eleven people

DATE: June 5, 1976

SIGNIFICANCE: The failure and collapse of the Teton Dam prompted government examination of the procedures involved in the selection of dam sites and recommendations by experts regarding ways to minimize the risk of dam failure, which poses potential hazards to the public and associated damage to the environment.

The Teton Dam was located in a deep, narrow canyon on the Teton River, a tributary of the Snake River, in southeastern Idaho. It was 93 meters (305 feet) high and 975 meters (3,200 feet) long, forming a reservoir that extended 27 kilometers (17 miles) up the canyon. The U.S. Bureau of Reclamation used approximately 7.6 million cubic meters (10 million cubic yards) of clay, silt, sand, and gravel to build the multilayered structure, a construction technique that the bureau had previously used for approximately 250 other dams without a single failure. Extensive site investigations revealed that the fractured and porous bedrock of the area could be a problem, and in an attempt to produce a barrier impermeable to water seepage, grout (a cement-based filler) was pumped under high pressure into drill holes on both sides and across the floor of the canyon.

Construction was complete and the reservoir had been filled almost to capacity when two small springs were detected at 8:30 A.M. on June 5, 1976, in the lower wall of the canyon just below the dam. While attempts were being made to alleviate these flows, at 10:00 A.M. a large leak appeared in the dam itself, about one-quarter of the way up from the bottom and 4.6 meters (15 feet) from the canyon wall with the spring flow. This leak rapidly increased its discharge and began to erode material from the dam. Two 20-ton bulldozers were sent in to push boulders into the flow to stem it. By 11:00 A.M. the flow had become so rapid that a whirlpool developed on the upstream side of the dam, and the bulldozers had to be abandoned. At 11:57 the dam was breached, and a tremendous wall of water roared down the canyon. The flow was so powerful that one of the abandoned bulldozers was carried 11 kilometers (7 miles) downstream. The town of Rexburg and 777 square kilometers (300 square miles) of farmland were flooded. Eleven people were killed, and monetary estimates of the damage caused by the dam collapse were as high as $1 billion.

An independent panel of experts concluded that the failure of the dam was caused by water traveling through fissures in the canyon wall, penetrating the grout curtain, and then moving through and eroding the core of the dam, until it failed. The Bureau of Reclamation was criticized for poor design of the grout curtain and dam core and for overreliance on past design practice without giving sufficient consideration to the porous rock at the Teton Dam site. The bureau was also criticized for not including any way to collect and safely discharge leakage, which should have been anticipated because of the presence of porous bedrock.

Gene D. Robinson

FURTHER READING

Cech, Thomas V. "Dams." In *Principles of Water Resources: History, Development, Management, and Policy.* 3d ed. New York: John Wiley & Sons, 2010.
McDonald, Dylan J. *The Teton Dam Disaster.* Charleston, S.C.: Arcadia, 2006.

Tobago oil spill

CATEGORY: Disasters

THE EVENT: Collision of two oil tankers off the coast of Tobago in the Caribbean Sea that caused significant loss of human life and a large oil spill

DATE: July 19, 1979

SIGNIFICANCE: Because the oil carried by the tankers *Aegean Captain* and *Atlantic Empress* contained a high percentage of gasoline, the environmental damage of the spill was minimized.

On the evening of July 19, 1979, the weather off the northern tip of the Caribbean island of Tobago was rainy with gusty winds. The Liberian-registered *Aegean Captain*, weighing 210,257 tons, was bound from the Netherlands Antilles to Singapore with a cargo of transshipped Arabian crude oil. The *Atlantic Empress*, also Liberian-registered, was en route from the Persian Gulf to Beaumont, Texas, with a cargo of Arabian crude; this vessel was operating under charter to Mobil Oil. At 325 meters (1,066 feet) long and 292,666 tons, the *Atlantic Empress* was a very large vessel.

The two tankers were both using radar for collision avoidance, but, as they later reported, the pictures were "fuzzy" because of the rain. Each vessel was unaware of the other's presence until it was too late. They did not sight each other until they were approximately 183 meters (600 feet) apart. Because of their size, such vessels require miles to stop. The *Aegean Captain* was on an easterly heading and, upon sighting the *Atlantic Empress*, began a sharp left turn, although navigation rules allow for turns to the right only. The *Atlantic Empress* was northbound toward Texas, yet at the time of the collision it was on a southerly heading for unknown reasons. At 7:15 P.M., the two vessels collided 29 kilometers (18 miles) north of the northern tip of the island of Tobago.

The bow of the *Aegean Captain* struck the starboard (right) side of the *Atlantic Empress* and drove deep into the center of the other ship. The two vessels were locked together as fires broke out on both ships and oil began to spill into the sea. On the *Atlantic Empress* twenty-six crew members were killed in the collision; three crewmen died on the *Aegean Captain*. The captain of the *Aegean Captain* then backed his vessel away from the *Atlantic Empress* even though the *Atlantic Empress*'s captain had asked him not to, fearing his ship would sink.

Salvage tugs stationed nearby responded almost immediately to the collision. The *Atlantic Empress*, on fire and leaking oil badly, was taken in tow. The tugs applied for permission to bring the tanker into several local ports, where fighting the fires would have been more efficient, but in all cases permission was denied. The vessel was towed out into the Atlantic Ocean, where it was racked by several explosions and sank. The *Aegean Captain* remained afloat, and after the fires were put out and the oil leaks were stopped, it was taken to a local shipyard.

The fact that both vessels were carrying high-quality Arabian crude oil was actually a benefit in this case, as such oil is almost 25 percent gasoline. This meant that in the collision a large proportion of the oil burned rather than fouling local beaches and fishing areas. A large percentage of the remaining oil evaporated, and dispersants were used to treat the rest before it could come ashore. In total, 270,000 tons (2.14 million barrels) of oil were lost, and damage to the two vessels and the environment came to $54 million in insurance claims.

Robert J. Stewart

FURTHER READING

Fingas, Merv. *The Basics of Oil Spill Cleanup.* 2d ed. Boca Raton, Fla.: CRC Press, 2001.

Laws, Edward A. "Oil Pollution." In *Aquatic Pollution: An Introductory Text.* 3d ed. New York: John Wiley & Sons, 2000.

Torrey Canyon oil spill

CATEGORY: Disasters

THE EVENT: Grounding of the oil tanker *Torrey Canyon* off the coast of England, resulting in the spilling of tons of crude oil into the sea

DATE: March 18, 1967

SIGNIFICANCE: The *Torrey Canyon* spill resulted in the deaths of some 75,000 seabirds and countless other marine animals. Attempts to remove the oil that was deposited on beaches in England and France also caused great environmental harm, as many of the detergents used were toxic.

The *Torrey Canyon* was built at Newport News shipbuilding yards in Virginia in 1959 and was modified at Sasebo, Japan, in 1964. The ship was 297 meters (974 feet) long, 38 meters (125 feet) wide, and had a draft of 16 meters (52 feet), with eighteen cargo tanks capable of carrying 120,000 tons of oil. The vessel was owned by Union Oil Company of Los Angeles, California. It was chartered to British Petroleum and flew the Liberian flag while carrying predominantly Italian officers and crew.

When the *Torrey Canyon* departed Mina ala Ahmadi in the Persian Gulf in early 1967, it was loaded with 119,193 tons of Kuwaiti crude oil. It was bound for Milford Haven in Wales. The last leg of the voyage was to go past the Scilly Isles and into the Bristol Channel. The Scilly Isles lie about 34 kilometers (21 miles) off Land's End along the Cornwall coast of England. The Seven Stones Shoal lies in between the Scilly Isles and Land's End. The *Torrey Canyon* normally passed outside the Scilly Isles. On this voyage, however, the captain chose to pass between the islands and the shoal. The vessel ran aground on the Seven Stones Shoal on March 18.

Once the *Torrey Canyon* was aground, it began leaking oil. A salvage effort was quickly undertaken to try to refloat the vessel. At the same time, detergent was sprayed over the spilled oil to help disperse it. After one week of work, the vessel was broken into pieces while salvagers were attempting to tow it off the shoal. By this time the oil had blanketed the sea within an 80-kilometer (50-mile) radius of the vessel; on some of the beaches where it had begun to wash ashore, the oil was 46 centimeters (18 inches) thick.

The salvagers were not equipped to deal with the volume of oil spilled. After twelve days of salvage efforts, the British Royal Air Force began to drop explosive bombs and incendiary devices around the vessel in an attempt to burn the oil. Some small fires were started, but this technique failed. The oil continued to spread over the coasts of England and France. Both governments called in troops to help remove oil from the beaches. Pump trucks and boats were used to pump oil off the beaches, and bulldozers and other heavy equipment were used to remove contaminated sand and rock. The largest single environmental problem that arose was caused by the use of detergents to remove oil from rocky and hard-to-reach places on the beaches in both England and France. Many of these detergents were toxic and killed everything in their path.

Many effects from the spill continued to be felt long after the oil was gone. An estimated 75,000 seabirds died as a result of the spill, as did unknown numbers of other animals of all types. Some of these deaths were directly caused by the effects of the oil, while others were caused by the detergents and heavy equipment used to remove the oil.

Robert J. Stewart

FURTHER READING

Clark, R. B. *Marine Pollution.* 5th ed. New York: Oxford University Press, 2001.

Fingas, Merv. *The Basics of Oil Spill Cleanup.* 2d ed. Boca Raton, Fla.: CRC Press, 2001.

United Nations Convention on the Law of the Sea

CATEGORIES: Treaties, laws, and court cases; resources and resource management

THE CONVENTION: International agreement regarding all matters pertaining to international waters

DATE: Opened for signature on December 10, 1982

SIGNIFICANCE: The United Nations Convention on the Law of the Sea provides a legal framework over the world's oceans designed to protect the seas and clarify the responsibilities of signatory nations; however, it has not been endorsed by several major nations, including the United States.

Law of the sea is a distinct area of international law that outlines rules governing the exploitation of the world's oceans. It was the subject of the first attempt by the International Law Commission to place a large segment of international law on a multilateral treaty basis. Four conventions resulting from the commission's work were produced by the first and second Geneva Conferences in 1958 and 1960. The pressure leading to the law of the sea conference, which lasted between 1974 and 1982 and involved a very wide range of states and international organizations, included a variety of economic, political, and strategic factors and resulted in the adoption of the United Nations Convention on the Law of the Sea (UNCLOS), also known as the Law of the Sea Treaty. This convention, with 320 articles and 9 annexes, was adopted in 1982 by 130 votes to 4, with 17 abstentions. It came into force on November 16, 1994, and has been ratified by 156 nations.

The convention, which provides a legal framework and specific regime over each area of the sea, is often referred to as the constitution of the sea. Among the areas covered by UNCLOS are the territorial sea, international straits, continental shelves, the high seas, exclusive economic zones, innocent passage, nationality of ships, collisions at sea, pollution, the deep seabed, and settlements of disputes. UNCLOS covers all of the ground of the four 1958 conventions and quite a lot more. The preamble to the convention states that one of its key purposes is "to contribute to the realisation of a just and equitable international economic order which takes into account the interests and needs of mankind as a whole and, in particular, the special interests and needs of developing countries, whether coastal or landlocked." This theme underpins the convention's approach to dealing with exclusive economic zones, continental shelves, the deep seabed, and other issues.

Article 136 of the convention provides that both the area that includes the seabed, ocean floor, and subsoil thereof beyond the limits of national jurisdiction or economic zone and its resources are "the common heritage of mankind" and that no sovereign or other rights to this area and its resources may be recognized. The regulation of the seabed is an area of controversy, as the developed countries have the technologies and financial resources to exploit the natural resources found on and beneath the seabed, but the developing countries claim a share in those resources. Dissatisfaction with the deep-seabed regime in UNCLOS led the United States to vote against the convention's adoption. The United States, Germany, and the United Kingdom are not signatories to this convention.

Because of the negative impacts of the disposal of toxic and other noxious materials at sea, UNCLOS devotes about fifty articles to the protection of the marine environment. Signatory nations are responsible for the fulfillment of their international obligations concerning the protection and preservation of the marine environment and are liable in accordance with international law. For example, in the *Torrey Canyon* incident of 1967, a Liberian tanker that ran aground along the British coast was bombed by the British military as a necessary measure to protect the coastline and its marine life. Parties to the convention are required to have adequate provisions to compensate when those acting under their jurisdictions cause environmental damage and pollution. The convention's articles concerning protection of the marine environment also provide for global and regional cooperation, technical assistance, monitory and environmental assessment, and the development of the enforcement of international and domestic law aimed at preventing pollution.

Josephus J. Brimah

FURTHER READING

Anderson, David. *Modern Law of the Sea: Selected Essays.* Boston: Martinus Nijhoff, 2008.

Freestone, David, Richard Barnes, and David Ong, eds. *The Law of the Sea: Progress and Prospects.* New York: Oxford University Press, 2007.

Nelson, Jason C. "The Contemporary Seabed Mining Regime: A Critical Analysis of the Mining Regulations Promulgated by the International Seabed Authority." *Colorado Journal of International Environmental Law and Policy* 16, no. 1 (2005): 27-76.

Sohn, Louis B., et al. *The Law of the Sea in a Nutshell.* 2d ed. St. Paul, Minn.: West, 2010.

U.S. Geological Survey

CATEGORIES: Organizations and agencies; land and land use; resources and resource management

IDENTIFICATION: U.S. federal agency that provides scientific information on the conditions of the nation's natural resources

DATE: Established on March 3, 1879

SIGNIFICANCE: By providing scientific information on water, biological, energy, and mineral resources to the public, legislators, and policy makers, the U.S. Geological Survey carries out its mission of enhancing and protecting Americans' quality of life.

In 1879 President Rutherford B. Hayes signed the congressional bill providing funding for the establishment of the U.S. Geological Survey (USGS) within the Department of the Interior. Industrial growth in the years immediately following the Civil War had produced a significant strain on the nation's natural resources. In an 1866 report Joseph Wilson, commissioner of the General Land Office, indicated that proper management of mineral resources in the West was vital to further development of the United States. Following up on Wilson's recommendations, Congress authorized a geological survey of the West, largely following the path of the newly finished transcontinental railroad. Clarence King and Ferdinand Hayden were placed in charge of the project and by 1870 had presented a plan to Congress for the survey. Additional surveys were privately sponsored as well.

Downturns in the American economy resulted in Congress looking for more efficient alternatives for mapping the West. In 1878 Congress requested that the National Academy of Sciences, which had been established in 1863 by President Abraham Lincoln, develop a plan for surveying and mapping western territories. The academy's recommendations included the establishment of the USGS, the purpose of which would be to oversee the study of geological and mineral resources in the public domain.

King was appointed first director of the USGS, and in 1879 a comprehensive study of mining districts in Nevada and Colorado was begun, as well as similar studies of iron and copper resources in other parts of the country. The study was completed prior to King's resignation from the position of director in 1881.

The duties assigned to the USGS underwent significant expansion during subsequent decades. In 1882 Congress authorized the creation of a comprehensive geological map of the United States, with the result that topographic mapping became the largest program within the USGS. The agency's geological studies also benefited with the inclusion of scientific research into the origins of ore deposits as well as newly introduced fields such as glacial ecology and studies of rock classes. Western droughts during the 1880's resulted in the addition of research concerning irrigation and water utilization within the USGS before the beginning of the new century. By 1904 the USGS had completed topographic maps covering more than 25 percent of the United States and Alaska. That year Congress also authorized mapping of areas of potential fossil fuels, including both coal and oil deposits.

Although the divisions within the USGS have undergone changes over the years, the agency has remained largely unchanged in its focus. Its areas of responsibility have grown over time to include the monitoring of seismic and magnetic activity throughout the world and the examination of the geological features of worldwide earthquake zones and volcanoes.

Richard Adler

FURTHER READING

Cech, Thomas V. "Federal Water Agencies." In *Principles of Water Resources: History, Development, Manage-*

ment, and Policy. 3d ed. New York: John Wiley & Sons, 2010.

National Research Council. *Toward a Sustainable and Secure Water Future: A Leadership Role for the U.S. Geological Survey*. Washington, D.C.: National Academies Press, 2009.

_____. *Weaving a National Map: Review of the U.S. Geological Survey Concept of the National Map*. Washington, D.C.: National Academies Press, 2003.

Wastewater management

CATEGORY: Waste and waste management

DEFINITION: Treatment and discharge of water supplies that have been already used for consumption, bathing, washing, industrial processes, and irrigation

SIGNIFICANCE: Not enough fresh water is available on the planet to meet human water needs without the reuse of wastewater. Because human uses of water almost always result in its contamination, managing the treatment and discharge of wastewater is crucial for protecting this vital resource.

Water is arguably the single most important resource on the planet, and one for which there is no alternative. All life depends on water. Drinking water is a basic human necessity, yet more than one billion people do not have access to safe drinking water. Humans use about half the freshwater that is available for agricultural (about 70 percent), industrial (about 20 percent), and municipal (about 10 percent) purposes. Because these uses add contaminants such as nutrients, chemicals, and pathogens to water, managing the collection, use, treatment, and distribution of wastewater is of utmost importance. Additionally, healthy ecosystems depend on adequate supplies of clean water.

Wastewater management involves the rules, best practices, and technology of collecting, treating, and distributing wastewater. Wastewater is a major source of nutrient pollution, which leads to the eutrophication of aquatic ecosystems, harmful algal blooms, fish kills, and dead zones. Contaminants such as pesticides and hormones can interfere with the endocrine systems of animals, resulting in reproductive, developmental, and immunological problems observed in fish and amphibians. Some health experts are concerned that these contaminants are affecting humans, too.

MUNICIPAL WASTEWATER

Municipal wastewater contains a mixture of contaminants added to the water by every residence and business in the city. Common contaminants in municipal wastewater include detergents, urine, feces, pharmaceuticals, pesticides, food waste, fats, and chemicals from several kinds of personal care products. Gray water—wastewater from showers or laundry that does not contain human waste—is often combined with black water (water that comes from toilets containing urine and feces) and sent to a common sewage system or septic tank. It is becoming increasingly popular for gray water to be reused for applications that do not require potable water, such as irrigation and toilet flushing.

In settlements of low population density, domestic wastewater can be treated with septic systems. Household wastewater is collected in a tank, where anaerobic bacteria digest solid waste and the liquid component is released into a leach field, where water percolates into the soil or is transpired by plants. Water released from septic systems contains high concentrations of nitrogen and phosphorus, which contribute to eutrophication of aquatic ecosystems. Septic tanks must be periodically pumped to remove solids that are not decomposed by bacterial digestion.

In higher-density communities, domestic wastewater is collected in networks of pipes and transported to central wastewater treatment plants. Some collection systems combine stormwater with sewage for treatment. (Stormwater by itself is not considered wastewater, because it has not been used by people.) Municipal sewage comprises a complex mixture of contaminants, but the main contaminants that wastewater treatment plants remove include solids, wastes that impose a high biochemical oxygen demand (BOD), and nitrogenous waste. Municipal wastewater treatment includes physical separation (primary treatment) of large solids, such as rags, condoms, and tampon applicators, using a bar screen; the removal of grit; and gravity separation of smaller solids that sink and fats and oils that float. Biological removal (secondary treatment) of BOD wastes, ammonia, nitrates, and other nutrients takes place in aeration basins, trickle filters, and other kinds of bioreactors.

Although different secondary treatment processes are used, they all engage both aerobic bacteria, to metabolize organic material and carry out nitrification to reduce BOD and ammonia, and anaerobic denitrifying bacteria, to convert nitrates to harmless nitrogen gas and reduce BOD. Protozoans, fungi, and small animals such as rotifers and insects are found in these biological systems, further reducing the amount of waste solids in this bacteria-based food web. Solids and liquids are again separated by gravity in a clarifier. The solids are treated with aerobic or anaerobic digestion, and the resulting biosolid is incinerated, stored in a landfill, or used as a soil amendment. Anaerobic digestion produces methane gas, which can be used for power generation. The effluent is "polished" (a tertiary treatment) through processing that removes additional contaminants. Finally, disinfection is carried out before the treated water is discharged back into the environment. Many communities are increasingly using such "reclaimed water" for irrigation.

Municipal wastewater treatment plants do not remove all contaminants, and many of the chemical contaminants that remain in water discharged from wastewater treatment plants have negative environmental consequences. There is mounting evidence, for example, that treated effluent has endocrine-disrupting compounds that create reproductive problems in fishes. Caffeine is another compound that is not removed by standard wastewater treatment, making it a commonly used tracer compound for waters affected by human excrement.

AGRICULTURAL WASTEWATER

In the United States, raising animals such as cattle, pigs, chickens, and fish for human consumption creates more than three times as much urine and feces as are produced by humans. This type of agricultural wastewater is often retained in ponds, which allows for some settling of solids and microbial degradation of waste before it is released into the environment. During rainstorms, however, large amounts of this minimally treated wastewater can escape into the larger environment. The solids that are retained are typically composted and used as soil amendments. Although it is possible to treat this wastewater using the processes described above for municipal wastewater, such treatment rarely occurs.

Waste irrigation water is the largest source of wastewater. This wastewater is contaminated by whatever materials are applied to the land, such as fertilizers, insecticides, and herbicides. Irrigation wastewater gets contaminated by the 2.5 million tons of pesticides that are applied annually across the globe. One of the most effective "best practices" to protect aquatic ecosystems is to maintain a riparian buffer between crop fields and streams. Riparian vegetation slows the flow of runoff, trapping some of the sediment and contaminants in the irrigation wastewater. Nutrient farming is a growing practice of treating irrigation wastewater using the ecosystem service of nutrient removal. With this practice, coupled nitrification/denitrification is enhanced, removing nitrogen pollution from the water and lessening the problem of eutrophication.

INDUSTRIAL WASTEWATER

Industrial processes contaminate water with acids, bases, metals, solvents, oil, grease, organics, and BOD. Urban industries work closely with municipal wastewater treatment plants to devise plans to pretreat wastewater before it is discharged into sewage treatment systems designed to remove wastes, such as metals, that municipal treatment plants do not treat well.

Larger-scale industries, notably the mining industry, produce large amounts of metal-contaminated wastewater that cannot be combined with municipal wastewater. This wastewater is generally held in settling ponds before it is discharged into surface waters. Inadequate treatment can often lead to problems with acid mine drainage and therefore significant environmental impairment. Many Superfund sites (sites of abandoned or uncontrolled hazardous wastes that have been identified by the Environmental Protection Agency and placed on its National Priorities List for eventual cleanup) have had to be established because of inadequate treatment of mining wastes.

Mining operations constitute the largest single source of waste in the United States, estimated to total 50 billion tons located at more than 500,000 sites. Active treatment plants can remove metals from mining wastewater by adjusting the pH level of the waste to around 10, precipitating the metal hydroxides with polymers, separating the precipitates in a clarifier, filtering the water, and adjusting the pH back to neutral (about 7) for discharge into the environment. The metal hydroxides are dewatered and discarded. Passive treatment of mining and other wastewaters can be achieved with constructed wetlands, which carry out the ecosystem services that improve water quality. Passive treatment is cheaper than active treatment, making it more applicable for most contaminated sites in remote locations.

EMERGING TECHNOLOGIES

The diversity of materials that contaminate water presents a huge challenge for effective treatment. Advances are being made in wastewater treatment to help correct some of the shortcomings in current practices mentioned above. Removal of endocrine disrupters from municipal wastewater is being achieved using activated carbon, wetlands, reverse osmosis, and even aquaponic systems. Microbial fuel cells are being tested to convert organic waste in water directly to electricity. Some dairy farmers are generating methane from manure and using it to heat buildings or produce electricity. Wastewater effluent flows downgradient to surface waters in nearly all wastewater treatment plants. This hydraulic head can be used to drive turbines for electrical generation. When wastewater is viewed as a resource instead of an environmental hazard, wastewater treatment plants can become power plants.

Greg Cronin

FURTHER READING

Grigg, Neil S. *Water, Wastewater, and Stormwater Infrastructure Management.* Boca Raton, Fla.: CRC Press, 2002.

Hammer, Mark J. *Water and Wastewater Technology.* Upper Saddle River, N.J.: Pearson, 2004.

Miller, G. Tyler, Jr., and Scott Spoolman. "Water Pollution." In *Living in the Environment: Principles, Connections, and Solutions.* 16th ed. Belmont, Calif.: Brooks/Cole, 2009.

Qasim, Syed A. *Wastewater Treatment Plants: Planning, Design, and Operation.* 2d ed. Lancaster, Pa.: Technomic, 1999.

Roseland, Mark. "Water and Sewage." In *Toward Sustainable Communities: Resources for Citizens and Their Governments.* Rev. ed. Gabriola Island, B.C.: New Society, 2005.

U.S. Environmental Protection Agency. Office of Wastewater Management. *Primer for Municipal Wastewater Treatment Systems.* Washington, D.C.: Author, 2004.

Water conservation

CATEGORY: Resources and resource management

DEFINITION: Management of water consumption in ways that minimize waste, maximize efficiency, and help to maintain adequate supplies of high-quality water

SIGNIFICANCE: Water conservation is a comparatively simple and inexpensive means of addressing water shortages and making the most of existing water supplies. Effective conservation programs can postpone or prevent the need to construct additional water-supply infrastructure and can also reduce wastewater discharges. As the earth's population increases, conservation measures become an increasingly important tool for meeting society's water needs.

In 2010 the world population reached 6.9 billion and was projected to rise to 9.5 billion by the year 2050. Because water is a basic human necessity, it follows that the amount of water needed for human existence will increase by a factor of roughly 1.4 over this forty-year period. While such an expansion in water supply is theoretically possible to achieve, the likelihood that it can or will happen is low for several reasons. First, although there is enough water available globally, it is not uniformly distributed around the world when and where it is needed. Second, the costs involved in such an expansion would be astronomical. Third, even if all needed moneys were readily available, it would be difficult to build the necessary facilities and have them operational by the time they would be needed.

DOMESTIC, INDUSTRIAL, AND AGRICULTURAL MEASURES

The greatest potential for water conservation in residential settings is in bathrooms. Traditional toilets use 19 to 26 liters (5 to 7 gallons) per flush. However, low-flow toilets using 13 or fewer liters (3.5 gallons) per flush—and ultra-low-flush models using as little as 6.1 liters (1.6 gallons)—are increasingly being installed in new homes and as replacements for traditional toilets in older homes. Baths and showers also use large amounts of water, and low-flow showerheads can contribute to water conservation efforts.

A great deal of water is also wasted in kitchens. Water can be conserved at kitchen sinks through simple means such as collecting food scraps for compost piles rather than putting them through garbage disposals. Low-flow sink faucets are also available. Running automatic dishwashers only for full loads is another water conservation technique; the same is true for clothes washers. Older models of both types of washers can be replaced with newer, more water-efficient ones.

Another potential source of water conservation in residential areas is found outside the homes, in plant and lawn watering. Methods of saving water include decreasing lawn sizes, landscaping with plants that require low amounts of water, mulching to reduce moisture evaporation from the soil, minimizing the frequency of watering, and using drip systems instead of sprinklers.

Business and industrial settings use large amounts of water. In some cases, water conservation measures may involve simple changes in the way things are done, such as substituting sweeping for the washing down of floors. In most cases, however, in these settings water conservation on a noticeable scale results from process changes of some type. For example, by converting from a water-cooled ice machine to an air-cooled one, a restaurant may improve water efficiency in its ice making by 25 to 50 percent.

The largest amounts of water are used in agriculture for irrigation. In the United States, a history of relatively cheap and readily available water led farmers to waste great amounts through improper or excessive application. Water can be and has been saved through computerized timing of water application. Modifications of irrigation procedures have also helped. For example, drip irrigation, which applies water slowly and uniformly at or below soil level adjacent to plants through mechanical water outlets, has produced significant water savings over traditional methods of simply spraying water onto the soil.

OTHER WAYS OF CONSERVING

As is true of the consumption of other commodities, water usage can be affected by pricing. Water-conserving rates exhibit increasing unit costs as volume used increases. One simple model determines a certain rate for the average amount of water a household might be expected to use and a much higher rate for all water used over that average amount.

Yet another way in which municipalities as well as home and business owners can conserve water is by finding and repairing leaks that occur anywhere in water distribution systems; water audits—careful reviews of water usage over time—can help to identify leaks. In some water distribution systems, documented leakages have been found to amount to losses of more than 50 percent of the water sent through the systems.

Water reuse may be thought of as another form of water conservation. Ample opportunities for water reuse exist during industrial processes. For example, wastewaters that were being treated on-site and discharged into receiving streams might be reused as cooling water. Households might recycle water used for dishwashing or bathing as irrigation water for outdoor plants. While it is possible to treat sewage for reuse by households, most people are not yet ready to accept such a conservation measure.

The negative aspects of water conservation are generally related to monetary issues. For example, successful water conservation efforts can lead to reduced revenues for water utility companies, which may then be forced to increase their rates. Conserving water over the long term may also reduce the "slack" in the system, making short-term drought savings difficult to achieve and reducing the amount of water available for water rationing. Some water conservation efforts can be expensive to put in motion, while the actual savings from reduced water use are achieved more slowly, over a period of time. Such water conservation is not always cost-effective.

Jack B. Evett
Updated by Karen N. Kähler

FURTHER READING

American Water Works Association. *Water Conservation Programs: A Planning Manual.* Denver, Colo.: Author, 2006.

Asano, Takashi, et al. *Water Reuse: Issues, Technologies, and Applications.* New York: McGraw-Hill, 2007.

Chiras, Daniel D. "Water Resources: Preserving Our Liquid Assets and Protecting Aquatic Ecosystems." In *Environmental Science.* 8th ed. Sudbury, Mass.: Jones and Bartlett, 2010.

Glennon, Robert Jerome. *Unquenchable: America's Water Crisis and What to Do About It.* Washington, D.C.: Island Press, 2009.

Postel, Sandra. *Last Oasis: Facing Water Scarcity.* New York: W. W. Norton, 1992.

Unger, Paul W. *Soil and Water Conservation Handbook: Policies, Practices, Conditions, and Terms.* Binghamton, N.Y.: Haworth Press, 2006.

U.S. Environmental Protection Agency. *Cases in Water Conservation: How Efficiency Programs Help Water Utilities Save Water and Avoid Costs.* Washington, D.C.: Author, 2002.

Vickers, Amy. *Handbook of Water Use and Conservation: Homes, Landscapes, Businesses, Industries, Farms.* Amherst, Mass.: Waterplow Press, 2001.

Water pollution

CATEGORY: Water and water pollution

DEFINITION: Degradation of natural water as the result of human activities

SIGNIFICANCE: The pollution of water supplies, which can be caused by activities such as mining, agriculture, and improper waste disposal, can have negative health impacts on plant and animal life.

Before the Industrial Revolution in the nineteenth century, humans produced only minimal amounts of refined metals and organic materials. The production of various alloys of copper, tin, lead, and zinc by heating the mineral ores or by using natural copper metal was also minor. During the Industrial Revolution, however, people began to produce cast iron by burning charcoal to heat iron ores at high temperatures. They also used other methods to produce additional metals; for example, nickel, aluminum, titanium, cobalt, platinum, chromium, niobium, and molybdenum were discovered during this time. The extensive use of such metals resulted in massive increases in exploration, mining, and production, as well as increased use of energy, resulting in waste disposal problems and contamination of water supplies. In addition, growing urban populations produced concentrations of untreated human and animal wastes and associated disease-producing organisms in natural waters.

INORGANIC CONSTITUENTS

There are both natural and human sources of water contamination. Humans may increase natural contamination by, for example, mining natural resources and disposing of the waste, which may leach out dangerous constituents. Animal and plant health may be affected by enrichment or deficiency of certain dissolved constituents. Rocks and soils may have low concentrations of substances such as selenium, potassium, phosphorus, copper, cobalt, molybdenum, zinc, or iodine, which cause health problems in animals. Although humans may need to supplement their diets with these constituents for optimal health, substances such as selenium, radioactive elements, copper, and zinc can be concentrated enough in some drinking waters to be harmful.

Humans mine many elements and use them for manufacturing and other purposes faster than these elements weather out of natural rocks, producing a variety of atmospheric and water pollutants. For example, fertilizers have high concentrations of soluble nitrogen and phosphorus compounds, and animal wastes contain high nitrate. The use of fertilizers thus can produce high nitrate (a nitrogen-oxygen compound) and phosphate (a phosphorus-oxygen compound) in natural waters. Nitrate can combine with hemoglobin so that oxygen transport in the body is inhibited. This is a potentially serious threat to infants; they can literally turn blue, become sick, and die if they consume water high in nitrate over a long period of time. Water high in phosphorus can stimulate the growth of organisms such as algae. As the abundant algae die and drop to the bottom of a body of water, they may use up the dissolved oxygen in the water, which may, in turn, cause fish to die.

The use of table salt (sodium chloride) to melt the ice on roads in winter can result in high dissolved sodium and chloride concentrations in natural waters. In the past, deep groundwater with high salt concentrations that was brought up during petroleum extraction was placed in "evaporation pits" on the surface until the water evaporated. This would allow the salt to leak slowly into the water supply in the ground. Now petroleum companies are required to inject these salty waters back into the ground at the level from which they came.

Another major pollutant in water results from the acidity produced by acid mine drainage and acid rain. Acid mine drainage results from the chemical reaction of sulfide minerals such as pyrite (iron sulfide) with water and oxygen from the atmosphere to produce sulfuric acid and dissolved metals in water. Most acid mine drainage comes from small amounts of pyrite in coal mines or waste piles from coal miners. Some acid mine drainage results from metal mines and wastes such as those found in lead and zinc mines in southeastern Kansas. These acid waters can readily dissolve other metals, so acid mine waters may contain high concentrations of many poisonous metals.

Acid rain results from high concentrations of sulfur dioxide, carbon dioxide, and nitrogen oxide gases spewed out into the atmosphere by industry. These gases dissolve in the water in the atmosphere to produce acidity. The worst acid rain thus occurs in industrial areas. Acid rain produces acid lakes and streams in areas that have little natural capacity to neutralize the acid. This results in the destruction of organisms that cannot live in such acidic waters. In some areas that have abundant limestone (a rock composed of calcium carbonate), acid rain reacts with the limestone to neutralize the acidity, so there is little problem with acidity of the natural waters. Areas without rocks that can neutralize the acid continue to have problems with acidity.

ORGANIC COMPOUNDS

Organic compounds consist of carbon in chemical combination with hydrogen, oxygen, sulfur, chlorine, or nitrogen. Many thousands of organic compounds are currently manufactured, and their classification is complex, but they may be grouped simplistically as alkanes, benzene derivatives, chlorinated hydrocarbons, and pesticides. Alkanes are straight chains of carbon atoms combined with hydrogen. Benzene derivatives consist of six-membered rings of carbon combined with other constituents chemically attached to the carbon atoms. Alkanes and benzene derivatives with six to ten carbon atoms are the organic compounds found in gasoline, diesel fuel, and other fuels. Alkanes in gasoline are not very soluble in water, but benzene derivatives are. Alkanes are also more easily degraded by bacteria than are benzene derivatives. The leakage of gasoline into the groundwater system can be a major pollution problem in areas around gasoline stations.

The term "groundwater" refers to any water found under the earth's surface. The upper portions of groundwater contain both air and water in the pore space between mineral grains; the lower portions of groundwater contain only water in the pore space. The surface between the upper and lower zone is called the water table. Wells are usually drilled into the water table so some of the more soluble hydrocarbons of gasoline that has leaked into the groundwater system can dissolve in water and move in the saturated water zone. The insoluble alkanes and benzene derivatives of gasoline can also move as a separate fluid plume above the water table since they are lighter than water. The maximum allowable concentrations of these benzene derivatives in water are much lower than the allowable concentrations of the individual elements discussed previously.

Benzene derivatives are also fairly volatile. If they move in a liquid plume under buildings, they can move as vapors into basements or sewers, where they then may produce explosions or may cause illness in occupants of the affected buildings.

Chlorinated hydrocarbons contain the element chlorine in one or more parts of the compound. Many of these—such as dichloroethane, tetrachloroethane, and chloroform—are among the most common organic pollutants found in waste disposal sites in the United States. Many are carcinogens (cancer-producing substances), and they become increasingly toxic at higher concentrations.

PESTICIDES

Pesticides are complex organic compounds that kill unwanted organisms such as insects. Examples of pesticides include dichloro-diphenyl-trichloroethane (DDT), malathion, alachlor, atrazine, and chlordane. Pesticides may be carcinogenic, and some may not decompose readily in the food chain. DDT, for example, has long been banned in the United States because of its harmful effects and its slow decomposition in nature.

Pesticides vary greatly in the time it takes them to decompose naturally and move to the water table. At one extreme, pesticides such as prometon can last a long time and quickly move to the water table, thus rapidly contaminating the groundwater. At the other extreme, methyl parathion decomposes more readily and moves more slowly to the water table, and is thus less likely to contaminate the groundwater. Among the pesticides most often found in groundwater are dibromochloropropane (DBCP), aldicarb, carbofuran, chlordane, alachlor, and atrazine. In addition, a pesticide applied during times of high rainfall can rapidly move to streams, where the stream water can soak into the ground and contaminate the groundwater supply.

Another problem is that even if the original pesticide has been naturally destroyed by bacteria, the degradation products from the decomposition of the pesticide can be even more harmful to humans than the original pesticide. Few studies of these kinds of problems have been undertaken, and decay products from pesticides are often only poorly understood. The degradation products of a few pesticides, such as aldicarb, however, have been studied for a number of years. Such products may have entirely different movement and stability than the original pesticides.

RADIOACTIVITY AND HEAT POLLUTION

Humankind's use of radioactive materials has created special problems in the areas of waste disposal and water pollution, in particular because radiation cannot be detected by the senses and can be very damaging if ingested. At one extreme, the radioactive element plutonium has a half-life (the time it takes for one-half of the radioactivity to decay) of about twenty-four thousand years, and it concentrates in the bones of vertebrates. This means that plutonium that has leaked into groundwater must be removed for hundreds of thousands of years. At the other extreme, radioactive materials with short half-lives that do not concentrate in organisms may not be of much concern, since the radioactivity will decay before it can be ingested.

Radioactive wastes are divided into low-level, intermediate-level, and high-level wastes. High-level wastes may be more than one million times more radioactive than what is considered acceptable for human exposure. Low-level wastes may contain radioactivity up to one thousand times more radioactive than what is considered acceptable. Intermediate-level wastes have radioactivity between these ranges. A wide variety of low-level radioactive wastes are produced by hospitals, the nuclear industry, and research laboratories. These wastes are often sealed in drums and buried under a thin layer of soil or diluted in water to acceptable levels of radioactivity and flushed into sewer systems.

High-level radioactive wastes are produced by nuclear fuel generation in fairly small volumes and account for about 95 percent of radioactive waste materials. Many high-level wastes have been stored for decades in double-walled stainless-steel tanks that are air-conditioned because of the intense heat given off by the radioactivity. Some of these tanks have leaked, and radioactive fluids have moved into nearby groundwater systems.

Thermal pollution is the heating of natural waters caused by the activities of industry, the burning of fossil fuels, or nuclear power production. Dumping heated waters directly into a body of water can kill many temperature-sensitive organisms living there. One method of reducing thermal pollution is to allow heated water to cool in ponds before it is returned to the source body of water.

PREVENTION AND REMEDIATION

In the long run, it is easier and less expensive to prevent the pollution of natural waters than to try to clean a polluted water supply or remediate sources of pollution. Preventive approaches include keeping contaminants contained so they cannot escape into water systems and banning the production and use of dangerous substances such as certain pesticides. One way of disposing of potential polluting substances would be to transport them to an area with a dry cli-

mate and low population density and place them in geologic materials that are impermeable to water flow. This would minimize the chances that moving water would carry hazardous constituents to groundwater. The costs of transporting waste materials are high, however, and this means that municipal wastes are usually disposed of locally. In areas that have high rainfall, waste management facilities must be especially careful to keep the waste contained in geologic materials, such as unfractured mudstone, that are impermeable to movement of water.

The expense of both prevention and remediation of water pollution is a source of ongoing conflict between environmentalists and the industries that produce polluting materials. In general, industries are interested in avoiding the costs associated with proper waste disposal, whereas environmentalists' priority is to keep pollution to surface water and groundwater to a minimum.

Robert L. Cullers

FURTHER READING

Goudie, Andrew. "The Human Impact on the Waters." In *The Human Impact on the Natural Environment: Past, Present, and Future.* 6th ed. Malden, Mass.: Blackwell, 2005.

Hill, Marquita K. "Water Pollution." In *Understanding Environmental Pollution.* 3d ed. New York: Cambridge University Press, 2010.

Manahan, Stanley E. "Water Pollution." In *Fundamentals of Environmental Chemistry.* 2d ed. Boca Raton, Fla.: CRC Press, 2001.

Montgomery, Carla W. "Water Pollution." In *Environmental Geology.* 9th ed. New York: McGraw-Hill, 2010.

Smol, John P. *Pollution of Lakes and Rivers: A Paleoenvironmental Perspective.* 2d ed. Hoboken, N.J.: Wiley-Blackwell, 2008.

Spellman, Frank R. "Water Pollution." In *The Science of Water: Concepts and Applications.* 2d ed. Boca Raton, Fla.: CRC Press, 2008.

Thomas, Sarah V., ed. *Water Pollution Issues and Developments.* New York: Nova Science, 2008.

Viessman, Warren, et al. *Water Supply and Pollution Control.* 8th ed. Upper Saddle River, N.J.: Pearson/Prentice Hall, 2009.

Vigil, Kenneth M. *Clean Water: An Introduction to Water Quality and Water Pollution Control.* 2d ed. Corvallis: Oregon State University Press, 2003.

Water-pollution policy

CATEGORY: Water and water pollution

DEFINITION: High-level governmental plan of action for protecting waters from environmental degradation that would render them unfit for desired uses

SIGNIFICANCE: Water-pollution policy is determined by laws and regulatory agencies that deal with a society's interactions with waterborne contaminants, including infectious disease organisms. Included are policies that prevent the entry of these agents into or lower their levels in aquatic ecosystems. Two primary goals pervade such policies: protection of human health and protection of natural aquatic resources.

Water pollution can be defined as any physical, chemical, or biological change in water quality that adversely affects living organisms or makes water unsuitable for desired uses. There are natural sources of water contamination, such as oil seeps and toxic algal blooms, but water pollution is generally caused by human activities, and natural processes that produce contamination are often triggered or exacerbated by human actions. Categories of water pollutants include infectious agents such as bacteria and viruses; organic chemicals such as pesticides, plastics, and oil; inorganic chemicals such as acids, salts, and metals; radioactive materials; sediments; plant nutrients such as nitrates and phosphates; oxygen-demanding wastes such as manure and plant residues; and heat. Each of these categories presents unique scientific and technical problems that must be addressed through specific policies.

While the term "water pollution" evokes images of industrial or sewage discharge flowing into pristine waters, most pollution sources are not so easy to identify or control. Nonpoint sources—diffuse sources of a variety of contaminants—contribute substantially to pollution problems and pose a major challenge to pollution-control efforts. Wherever rainfall, snowmelt, and irrigation flow across the land or through the ground, they pick up contaminants. Ultimately, those contaminants migrate into rivers, lakes, coastal waters, and groundwater.

WATER QUALITY IN THE UNITED STATES

Since the 1970's water-pollution policy has been highly effective at increasing the quality of water in the United States. However, surveys indicate that a significant percentage of the surface waters and estuaries in the United States still do not meet water-quality goals. The National Water Quality Inventory Report is the primary method for informing Congress and the public about the conditions of water quality. The report, required under section 305(b) of the Clean Water Act, periodically characterizes the nation's water quality, identifies problem with water quality of national significance, and describes various programs implemented to restore and protect water. During 2004 a total of 16 percent—about 907,600 kilometers (564,000 miles)—of the river miles in the United States were surveyed for water quality. Of the surveyed miles, 56 percent had good water quality; 3 percent of these, however, were considered threatened. Some form of pollution affected the remaining miles. Pathogens, habitat alterations, and organic enrichment were cited as the leading pollutants entering rivers, with agricultural runoff, hydromodification (alterations such as dam construction and channelization), and unspecified nonpoint sources being the leading sources of the impairments.

The 2004 inventory assessed some 29 percent (approximately 65,780 square kilometers, or 25,400 square miles) of the nation's estuarine waters; of these, 70 percent were found to have good water quality. The 30 percent regarded as impaired were most affected by pathogens, organic enrichment, and mercury. Atmospheric deposition and unspecified nonpoint sources were major sources of pollutants. Despite the construction of new sewage treatment plants, improvements in older plants, and an increasing focus on improving the quality of stormwater runoff, municipal discharge was found to be another leading pollutant of estuaries.

In the same inventory, 39 percent of lake acreage in the United States was surveyed. Of this, 35 percent was reported to have good water quality, and an additional 1 percent was deemed good but threatened. The remaining 64 percent was impaired to the greatest extent by mercury, polychlorinated biphenyls, and nutrients (such as nitrogen and phosphorus). Atmospheric deposition, unspecified nonpoint sources, and agriculture were reported to be the leading sources of these pollutants.

U.S. WATER-POLLUTION LAWS

Numerous laws have been passed in the United States that have some influence on water quality in the

U.S. Drinking Water: Maximum Allowed Concentrations of Key Toxic Compounds

CONSTITUENT	MILLIGRAMS PER LITER
Arsenic	0.010
Atrazine (pesticide)	0.003
Benzene (volatile organic)	0.005
Cadmium	0.005
Chromium	0.1
Cyanide	0.2
Lead	0.015
Mercury	0.002
Pentachlorophenol	0.001
Selenium	0.05

country. In response to increasing public concern about water pollution, Congress passed the Federal Water Pollution Control Act (FWPCA) of 1948, the first federal legislation to deal directly with the issue. Its primary goal was to provide funding for the research and implementation of state programs to control water pollution. Additional legislation and funding occurred through a 1956 amendment to the FWPCA, which was drafted to combat water-quality problems associated with increasing industrialization. The early emphasis of state control of water quality was extended in a 1965 amendment to the FWPCA. Called the Federal Water Quality Act, it required states to adopt water-quality standards and implementation plans. However, this act did not provide for sufficient enforcement mechanisms, and by 1972 only about one-half of the states had set water-quality standards. Furthermore, many of the states did a poor job of enforcing the standards, particularly in the case of individual dischargers fouling state waters.

Congress passed the Federal Water Pollution Control Act Amendments of 1972 with the objective of restoring and maintaining the chemical, physical, and biological integrity of the nation's waters. Some of the specific goals of the act were to eliminate all discharges of pollutants into the navigable waters by 1985; protect fish, shellfish, and wildlife, and provide for recreation by 1983; prohibit the discharge of toxic pollutants in toxic amounts; and provide financial assistance for the construction of publicly owned waste treatment works. The amended act sought to accomplish these goals by combining state water-quality standards with the technology-based approach of setting effluent limitations. The Clean Water Act amendment of 1977, which addressed various technical issues that had become apparent since passage of the 1972 amendments, gave the legislation its current name.

In 1987 the Clean Water Act underwent further amendment. Congress recognized that, although significant progress had been made, substantial water-quality problems persisted. New provisions established a comprehensive program for controlling toxic pollutant discharges beyond that already provided in the act, added a program requiring states to develop and implement programs to control nonpoint sources of pollution, and authorized a total of $18 billion in aid for wastewater treatment assistance.

While the ambitious goals of the Clean Water Act have not been entirely met, there are many success stories. Notable among them is the improved management of the nation's municipal wastewater. The number of people in the United States served by sewage treatment plants increased from 85 million in 1972 to some 208 million by 2000. Discharges of untreated sewage were eliminated by 1996.

OTHER IMPORTANT POLICIES

In order to protect the environment and human health in the United States, Congress has passed a number of other water-quality bills. For example, in response to suggestions that drinking-water policies and enforcement of those policies were too lax, especially in rural water districts and small towns, the Safe Drinking Water Act of 1974 was passed. This law regulates water quality in commercial and municipal drinking-water systems by establishing minimum standards for drinking-water quality for every community. Among the contaminants regulated are bacteria; nitrates; metals such as arsenic, cadmium, chromium, lead, mercury, and silver; pesticides; radioactivity; and turbidity. The act also contains limited provisions for the protection of groundwater and aquifers.

In 1976 Congress passed the Toxic Substances Control Act, which categorizes toxic and hazardous substances, funds a research program, and regulates the use and disposal of poisonous chemicals. Before a new chemical can be manufactured in bulk, the manufacturer must submit a premanufacturing report to the Environmental Protection Agency (EPA) in which the environmental impacts are assessed, including those associated with disposal of the chemical.

Another important environmental protection law passed in 1976 was the Resource Conservation and Recovery Act (RCRA). The law, which regulates hazardous waste and nonhazardous solid waste, takes a "cradle-to-grave" approach to hazardous waste management. Under RCRA, once hazardous waste is generated, it must be tracked, handled, stored, transported, and disposed of responsibly. The law also encourages recycling and reuse as a means for reducing the volume of waste requiring disposal.

In response to water-quality problems associated with toxic waste dumps, Congress passed the Comprehensive Environmental Response, Compensation, and Liability Act (CERCLA) in 1980. This law is also known as the Superfund act because it established a fund that has provided billions of dollars toward cleaning abandoned toxic waste dump sites. Amendments to CERCLA include a 1986 act establishing a community's right to know about the presence of toxic materials in their area. Additional legislation, the Oil Pollution Act of 1990, was passed to toughen cleanup requirements and penalties for oil discharges after the highly publicized *Exxon Valdez* oil spill of 1989.

During the early twenty-first century, U.S. water-pollution policy under President George W. Bush's administration (2001-2009) relaxed to become more industry-friendly. Supreme Court decisions in 2001 and 2006 rolled back wetlands protections, funding lagged for wastewater treatment infrastructure, enforcement cases were stalled or dropped, and in a 2008 rule the transfer of contaminated water from one water body into a cleaner receiving water body was deregulated. Nine states sued the EPA over this water-transfer rule. During the presidency of Barack Obama in 2010 Congress began considering an amendment to the Clean Water Act that would restore protections to all natural water bodies put at risk by the Supreme Court decisions of 2001 and 2006.

INTERNATIONAL AGREEMENTS

The Convention on the Prevention of Marine Pollution by Dumping of Wastes and Other Matter, better known as the London Convention of 1972, is an international treaty ratified by the United States that calls for the cessation of the dumping of industrial wastes, effluents from cargo tank washing, and plastic trash into the world's oceans. The United States passed the Marine Protection, Research, and Sanctuaries Act in 1972 to support the provisions of the London Convention. Pollution from oceangoing vessels was ad-

dressed in another international agreement, the 1973 International Convention for the Prevention of Pollution from Ships, and a 1978 protocol that amended it. MARPOL 73/78, as the amended treaty is known, was further amended in 1988 to prohibit the dumping of plastics anywhere in the ocean.

Another key international agreement is the 1972 Great Lakes Water Quality Agreement between Canada and the United States. This agreement and subsequent amendments in 1978 and 1987 affirmed the two countries' determination to restore and enhance water quality in the Great Lakes system, which includes the entire lake basin and the St. Lawrence River. The initial agreement focused on the eutrophication of the Great Lakes and the need to reduce loadings of phosphorus. Since the signing of the agreement in 1972, additional objectives have focused on the virtual elimination of persistent and toxic substances.

Roy Darville
Updated by Karen N. Kähler

FURTHER READING

Copeland, Claudia. *Clean Water Act: A Summary of the Law.* Washington, D.C.: Congressional Research Service, 2008.

Finkmoore, Richard J. *Environmental Law and the Values of Nature.* Durham, N.C.: Carolina Academic Press, 2010.

Gross, Joel M., and Lynn Dodge. *Clean Water Act.* Chicago: American Bar Association, 2005.

Lazarus, Richard J. *The Making of Environmental Law.* Chicago: University of Chicago Press, 2004.

Milazzo, Paul Charles. *Unlikely Environmentalists: Congress and Clean Water, 1945-1972.* Lawrence: University Press of Kansas, 2006.

United States Environmental Protection Agency. *National Water Quality Inventory: Report to Congress, 2004 Reporting Cycle.* Washington, D.C.: Author, 2009.

Water quality

CATEGORY: Water and water pollution
DEFINITION: Characteristics of water as defined by the solutes and gases dissolved in it, as well as the matter suspended in it
SIGNIFICANCE: Because safe drinking water is crucial

to human and other animal life, scientists have developed methods for determining the quality of water supplies, and governments have established minimum standards for water quality.

Only a tiny fraction of the earth's abundant water supply is available as fresh water for consumption. Once a water source becomes contaminated or polluted, it must be restored before it can be returned to its original desired use. The U.S. government has passed laws to help ensure that natural water resources are protected from contamination and that water meets certain quality standards before it is consumed. The 1977 amendments to the Clean Water Act directed each state to establish water-quality standards for bodies of surface water. The Safe Drinking Water Act of 1974 mandated the U.S. Environmental Protection Agency (EPA) to establish drinking-water standards for all public water systems serving twenty-five or more people or having fifteen or more connections.

When contaminants enter a water supply, the quality of the water is often compromised. The contaminants affect the water in such a way as to alter one or more quality parameters. Several parameters are used to characterize a given body of water; these can be broadly classified into physical or chemical parameters. Physical parameters include turbidity, color, temperature, taste, odor, and amount of suspended solids. Chemical parameters include pH and hardness, as well as amount of dissolved solids, fluoride, metals, organics, nutrients, pathogens, and dissolved oxygen.

Water quality is perceived differently by different people. For example, public health officials are concerned with the viral and bacterial safety of water used for bathing and drinking, fishers are concerned that the quality of a body of water provides the best habitat for fish, and aquatic scientists are concerned about the habitats of all aquatic organisms. The state of the water and the nature of the concerned party will often determine which water-quality parameters must be measured. For instance, raw wastewater entering a wastewater treatment plant does not need to be tested for dissolved oxygen, but parameters such as amount of organics and metals are often important. In contrast, dissolved oxygen is extremely important for the health of rivers and lakes.

In an attempt to devise a standard system for comparing river water quality in various parts of the United States, the National Sanitation Foundation designed a water-quality index (WQI) in 1970 that became one of the most widely used tools of its kind. The WQI can be used to compare the water quality of different rivers, to monitor water-quality changes in a particular river section, or to compare the water quality of different sections within a river. To determine a WQI score, nine tests are performed. These include measures of dissolved oxygen, biochemical oxygen demand, pH, temperature, total solids, turbidity, nitrates, total phosphorus, and fecal coliform. The results from the tests are given numerical values, and the sum of the nine values yields the overall WQI score. Values range from 0 to 100: A score of 0-25 is very bad, 26-50 is bad, 51-70 is medium, 71-90 is good, and 91-100 is excellent.

POLLUTANTS

A host of different pollutants can enter a water body and affect its quality. The principal water pollut-

Concentrations of Main Constituents in Some Natural Waters
(milligrams per liter)

Constituent	Estimated Average World River Water	Average Seawater	Shallow Groundwater	Deep Groundwater, Midland, Michigan
Calcium	13.0	410	48.0	93,500
Magnesium	3.4	1,350	3.6	12,100
Sodium	5.2	10,500	1.0	28,100
Potassium	1.3	390	1.2	11,700
Bicarbonate	52.0	142	152.0	low
Sulfate	8.3	2,700	3.0	17
Chloride	5.8	19,000	8.0	255,000

ants include disease-causing agents (pathogens), oxygen-demanding wastes, inorganic chemicals, organic chemicals, and sediment or suspended matter. The disease-causing agents include bacteria, viruses, protozoa, and parasitic worms. These pathogens enter the water from domestic sewage and animal wastes. They can cause a variety of diseases, including cholera, dysentery, giardiasis, hepatitis, and typhoid fever.

Oxygen-demanding wastes are organic wastes capable of being decomposed by aerobic (oxygen-requiring) bacteria. In the process of decomposing this waste, the bacteria consume oxygen. If aquatic plants and contact with air do not replenish the oxygen at a rate that is equal to or greater than the rate at which it is depleted, then the oxygen level will drop. This can be measured by a decrease in the dissolved oxygen content. If the level drops low enough, it will affect all aquatic organisms that depend on oxygen. The quantity of oxygen-demanding wastes can be determined through measurement of the biochemical oxygen demand, or the amount of oxygen needed by aerobic bacteria to decompose the organic materials over a five-day period at 20 degrees Celsius (68 degrees Fahrenheit).

Inorganic chemicals that may pollute water include toxic metals, such as mercury and lead, and plant nutrients, such as nitrates and phosphates. When nutrients enter the water, they can cause extensive algal growth. When the algae die and decay, oxygen is depleted, and aquatic organisms are killed. This process is known as eutrophication. The source of these nutrients is often agricultural runoff containing fertilizers. Water-polluting organic chemicals include pesticides and petroleum products. These threaten human health as well as aquatic life. They are often resistant to microbial decomposition and can persist within the environment for long periods of time. Sediment and suspended matter are insoluble particles of soil and other solids that become suspended in water. By weight, such particles—which enter bodies of water most often as the result of soil erosion of land—are by far the largest water pollutant; they cloud the water, disrupt food chains, and often contain substances harmful to plant and animal life.

John P. DiVincenzo

FURTHER READING

Cech, Thomas V. "Water Quality." In *Principles of Water Resources: History, Development, Management, and Policy.* 3d ed. New York: John Wiley & Sons, 2010.

Gray, N. F. *Drinking Water Quality: Problems and Solutions.* 2d ed. New York: Cambridge University Press, 2008.

Udeh, Patrick J. *A Guide to Healthy Drinking Water: All You Need to Know About the Water You Drink.* Lincoln, Nebr.: iUniverse, 2004.

Vigil, Kenneth M. *Clean Water: An Introduction to Water Quality and Water Pollution Control.* 2d ed. Corvallis: Oregon State University Press, 2003.

Water rights

CATEGORY: Water and water pollution

DEFINITION: Legal interests regarding the use of water resources

SIGNIFICANCE: Laws concerning water rights are generally intended to safeguard the use, quality, availability, and enjoyment of water found underground and in streams, rivers, lakes, and ponds.

In the early years after the establishment of the United States, most Americans considered water to be an abundant resource that needed scant government regulation. As the population of the nation grew, however, this view changed. Growing numbers of disputes over access to fresh water prompted lawmakers and courts to establish various doctrines of water rights to protect water as a precious and limited resource.

English common law provided the legal foundation for decisions about water rights in the eastern states. One of its chief provisions recognized riparian, or riverside, rights. These rights entitled landowners whose lands abutted natural, free-flowing streams and rivers to use the water from those sources for ordinary purposes such as bathing and drinking. They did not have the right to pollute, stem, or divert waters from their natural paths in ways that would interfere with the water rights of other landowners downstream. With the arrival of the Industrial Revolution, riparian rights came under attack as factory owners tried to divert water from rivers for industrial purposes. Though many courts struck down such attempts, others rendered legal decisions that allowed riparian owners "reasonable use" of water for industrial purposes, providing it did not excessively harm the rights of other riparians.

Even more radical changes took place in the American West during the late nineteenth century, when growing numbers of miners, farmers, and ranchers competed for scarce water sources with little regard for riparian rights as recognized in the East. As a result, disputes over water rights multiplied. One of the more famous feuds took place along the Poudre River in Colorado when one group of settlers diverted water for irrigation purposes and deprived others downstream of sufficient water. The Colorado state legislature took up the matter in 1876 and established the Colorado doctrine, also known as the prior appropriation doctrine, which held that all water rights belonged to the first user to claim them.

Other western states quickly adopted versions of Colorado's "first in time, first in right" approach. Eventually, however, state courts modified the doctrine by applying a "reasonable use" standard test to water disputes. Under this provision, senior water users could be forced to reduce their water consumption if a challenger proved the senior user took more than a reasonable share of water. Unlike in the East, western laws concerning water rights hold that water is a thing separate from the soil rather than an ingredient of it. This principle permits western landowners to remove water from their land and sell it as a commodity. In 1982 the U.S. Supreme Court ruled in *Sporhase v. Nebraska* that an individual even has the right to export water from one state to another.

Though water rights exist in many—and often conflicting—forms across the United States, they are all subject to state and federal authority. Laws concerning water rights have increasingly needed to address water disputes arising from water shortages. While most of the feuds over water rights in the United States still take place in the semiarid West, conflicts have also occurred in water-rich states with fast-growing populations, such as Florida and Georgia.

Water shortages are not unique to the United States. In 1997 the United Nations reported the results of a study that found that one-fifth of the world's population lacked clean drinking water. In many developing nations, people face daily water rations and have no running potable water. The growing water scarcity is a result of human population growth, increasing agricultural demands, industrialization, urbanization, and the continuous degradation of a finite reserve of fresh water. The United Nations has predicted that if present trends continue, two-thirds of the world's population will face critical water shortages by the year 2025.

Sovereign nations have the legal means and the authority to resolve disputes over water rights within their own borders. Such conflicts are harder to settle when several countries share a given body of water, however. Serious international quarrels arose among riparian nations along the Ganges, Niger, Mekong, and several other river basins during the late twentieth century. Squabbles over access to the Jordan River in the parched Middle East have, on some occasions, provoked talk of war. International law offers only limited help in solving these problems. For example, nations have the right to exercise authority over any resources under their immediate control, but a United Nations convention of 1972 and the Helsinki Rules of 1966 oblige countries to share water rights with other riparians as long as they show regard for the needs of local populations and traditional water consumption practices. Generally, riparian nations rely on international treaties and agreements to establish water rights. Without effective enforcement powers, however, they have few options other than persuasion, sanctions, and even military force to ensure treaty compliance.

Proposed solutions to the world's growing water shortage include improved water conservation and pollution reduction efforts, a community approach among riparian nations to establish equitable water rights, and the privatization of water delivery systems that are currently under government control. Water experts at the World Bank and the United Nations have called upon nations to abandon the concept of water as an abundant and cheap resource to be subsidized by governments. Instead, they suggest, water should be viewed as an "economic good," much like oil or gold, that is subject to free market mechanisms. They assert that under such an approach water's proper price would match its value and assure its own protection. Critics, however, contend that water is too precious to be turned over to commerce. All humans, they argue, have a right to a fair share of this scarce resource that bestows life.

John M. Dunn

FURTHER READING

Andrews, Richard N. L. *Managing the Environment, Managing Ourselves: A History of American Environmental Policy.* 2d ed. New Haven, Conn.: Yale University Press, 2006.

Cech, Thomas V. "Water Allocation Law." In *Principles of Water Resources: History, Development, Management, and Policy.* 3d ed. New York: John Wiley & Sons, 2010.

Ferrey, Steven. "Rights to Use Water." In *Environmental Law: Examples and Explanations*. 5th ed. New York: Aspen, 2010.

Hodgson, Stephen. *Modern Water Rights: Theory and Practice*. Rome: Food and Agriculture Organization of the United Nations, 2006.

Water-saving toilets

CATEGORY: Water and water pollution

DEFINITION: Toilets designed to use minimal amounts of water to move human waste products into sewer lines or septic tanks

SIGNIFICANCE: Because flush toilets account for the greatest amount of water used by residences in industrialized nations, toilets designed to minimize the water needed for each flush offer excellent opportunities for water conservation.

It has been estimated that an average family of four in the United States uses 340,000 liters (90,000 gallons) of water per year. Modest but conscious changes in water use and modifications of plumbing fixtures in and around homes can save thousands of gallons each year. Such savings reduce water and energy costs in individual homes and also help protect water resources for future generations.

Toilets are made to suit a wide range of budgets, decors, and functions, and choosing the right toilet involves informed decision making. Among the characteristics of toilets that consumers should consider are trap size, bowl-water surface, tank lining, and toilet footprint. Sufficient trap size ensures the ability of a toilet to flush well without clogging; larger traps are less likely to clog. The amount of bowl-water surface influences how well a toilet remains clean between regular scrubbings; toilets with larger bowl-water surface areas generally require cleaning less often. Whether or not a toilet's tank is lined can be particularly important in a bathroom that is not adequately air-conditioned; lined tanks do not "sweat" during hot weather. The toilet footprint is the space that the toilet pedestal takes up on the floor.

A further consideration in selecting a toilet is how much water it uses. The toilet in a residence housing four people is flushed, on average, thirty times per day. Toilet flushing is generally considered to be the single largest source of water loss in the home because it accounts for about 38 percent of the water used each day.

The amount of water used by a toilet is called the flush rate, which is measured in gallons per flush (gpf) in the United States and liters per flush (lpf) in most other parts of the world. Typical toilets rate at 3.5 gpf (13 lpf) or higher. However, designs have been introduced that rate at 1.6 gpf (6 lpf). Some of the best available rate at 1.5 gpf (5.7 lpf). Toilets that perform at these levels are called low-consumption, low-flush, ultra-low-flush, or water-saving toilets. They come in a variety of engineering designs. The four designs that are the most common are gravity-tank, flushometer, pressurized-tank, and vacuum-assist toilets.

It has been estimated that water consumption in the home can be cut by 25 percent or more through the replacement of an old-style toilet with a low-consumption model. This reduction is both automatic and permanent. In order to achieve these savings on a larger scale, some communities in Canada and the United States now require that all new or replacement installations of two-piece tank-type and floor-mounted flushing toilets rate at no more than 1.6 gpf. Water management officials in these communities also provide incentives to owners of existing homes to install low-flush toilets.

Josué Njock Libii

FURTHER READING

Cech, Thomas V. *Principles of Water Resources: History, Development, Management, and Policy*. 3d ed. New York: John Wiley & Sons, 2010.

George, Rose. *The Big Necessity: The Unmentionable World of Human Waste and Why It Matters*. New York: Henry Holt, 2008.

Water treatment

CATEGORY: Water and water pollution

DEFINITION: Processing of raw water to make it safe for drinking

SIGNIFICANCE: To be safe for drinking, water must be free of disease-producing bacteria, undesirable tastes and odors, color, turbidity, and harmful chemicals. The proper treatment of water supplies addresses all such possible problems and is thus essential to providing the safe drinking water that is necessary to human health and welfare.

Many substances may occur naturally in raw water that are either harmful or unpalatable to people. Human discharge of many substances into the environment also contaminates water supplies. Contaminants, either natural or anthropogenic (human-caused) in origin, can be divided into three groups: organoleptic substances that pertain to the senses of vision, taste, and odor; inorganic and organic chemical substances, which could be toxic or aesthetically undesirable, or could interfere with water treatment processes; and harmful microorganisms, which usually result from human and animal wastes.

The organoleptic parameters must be reduced to very low levels for drinking water to be acceptable for public use. Color, turbidity, and particulate matter represent visual problems. Color results from organic matter that leaches from soil or decaying vegetation. Turbidity results from suspended clay or organic matter that imparts a muddy and therefore undesirable appearance to the water. Particulate matter floating in water is not only aesthetically undesirable but also may provide food for certain organisms. Decomposed organic material and volatile chemicals result in unpleasant tastes and odors in water.

Iron, manganese, and aluminum are metals that are commonly found in water. Other metals such as lead, copper, cadmium, and silver are occasionally present, as are the nonmetals nitrate, fluoride, and phenols. These chemicals have both natural and anthropogenic origins. Chemically synthesized compounds such as pesticides, herbicides, and polychlorinated biphenyls (PCBs) are particularly dangerous as they can enter the food chain and accumulate in animal tissue.

Although most bacteria are harmless and indeed essential to life, some varieties (pathogens) can cause illness and death. These waterborne diseases include cholera, typhoid, and bacillary dysentery, all of which are common in areas without properly treated water. Viruses are pathogenic organisms that are much smaller and much harder to control than bacteria. Common viral diseases include poliomyelitis and infectious hepatitis. *Cryptosporidium* and *Giardia* are protozoan waterborne parasites that are found in surface waters. They cause severe forms of gastroenteritis that can be deadly in people who have immune-suppressed systems, such as those living with acquired immunodeficiency syndrome (AIDS).

The origin and characteristics of the raw water source govern the type of treatment necessary to provide safe drinking water. For example, groundwater may require only pH adjustment and minor disinfection if the source is relatively pristine. In heavily fertilized agricultural areas and locations where soluble iron and manganese are naturally present, however, ion exchange for nitrate removal and chemical treatment for iron and manganese removal may be needed.

Surface water generally requires many more types of treatment, such as screening, sedimentation, chemical treatment, clarification, filtration, and disinfection. Installation of bar screens to block fish and debris is a standard first step in treating raw surface water. The screens must be strong enough to prevent wood, game fish, and even shopping carts from getting into the treatment plant and damaging the machinery. The next step is usually a sedimentation basin, where the larger suspended particles can settle out by gravity. This process may be accelerated through the mixing of chemicals with the water to form a flocculate precipitate, which helps settle the suspended particles. The chemical coagulation process removes natural color originating from peat, animal and vegetable debris, plankton, and other organic substances.

Even after sedimentation, some of the finer particles in the water may still be in suspension and have to be removed by filtration. Sand filters provide an inexpensive and effective medium for the removal of fine solids in either raw water or partially treated water. Many facilities in the United States have replaced sand filters with granular activated carbon (GAC) filters because these can remove a wide variety of undesirable organic compounds such as herbicides, pesticides, and chemical compounds that form naturally. They are also useful in the treatment of taste and odor. Indeed, many beverage manufacturers that make products (such as soda or beer) in which water is a major component use GAC filters. Residential point-of-use kitchen filters for drinking water incorporate GAC filters as the major treatment technique.

The final treatment process is disinfection, since pathogenic bacteria can pass through both the sedimentation basin and filtration. Government-set standards for drinking-water quality in the United States require the absence of the indicator organisms fecal streptococci and the coliform group of bacteria, specifically fecal *Escherichia coli*, in the distributed water. Disinfection, which is the killing of harmful bacteria, is usually accomplished through chlorination. Chlorine is a very effective biocide, but one major disadvantage of its use is that it is very reactive and can produce compounds, such as trihalomethanes, that are potentially carcinogenic. Other compounds produced by chlorine have taste and odor problems. Ozone and ultraviolet light are also powerful disinfectants, but they do not have the residual properties of chlorine, which protects water from contamination as it travels through the distribution system.

Some water treatment plants built since the late twentieth century use a combination of ozonation for its effectiveness against *Cryptosporidium, Giardia,* and viruses; GAC filters for taste and odor control; and small amounts of chlorine as a residual biocide for the treated water in the distribution system.

Robert M. Hordon

Further Reading

Ford, Tim. "Water and Health." In *Environmental Health: From Global to Local,* edited by Howard Frumkin. 2d ed. Hoboken, N.J.: John Wiley & Sons, 2010.

McKinney, Michael L., Robert M. Schoch, and Logan Yonavjak. "Water Pollution." In *Environmental Science: Systems and Solutions.* 4th ed. Sudbury, Mass.: Jones and Bartlett, 2007.

Manahan, Stanley E. "Water Treatment." In *Fundamentals of Environmental Chemistry.* 2d ed. Boca Raton, Fla.: CRC Press, 2001.

Sullivan, Patrick J., Franklin J. Agardy, and James J. Clark. "Water Protection." In *The Environmental Science of Drinking Water.* Burlington, Mass.: Elsevier Butterworth-Heinemann, 2005.

Water use

CATEGORY: Resources and resource management

DEFINITION: Consumption of fresh water by residences, businesses, industries, governments, and food-production interests in support of human populations

SIGNIFICANCE: Human beings' use of fresh water has numerous impacts on the environment, in part because available freshwater resources, like mineral resources, are unevenly distributed, necessitating the transport of water over long distances.

Although water is the earth's most abundant liquid and can be found almost everywhere, 97 percent of it is too salty for human use. Of the remainder, about 68.7 percent is frozen in icecaps and glaciers. Raw fresh water can come from either surface or ground sources. Surface sources include river systems, lakes, and reservoirs. Groundwater sources vary from unconsolidated materials, such as the sandy deposits along the Atlantic and Gulf Coastal Plain and the stratified sands and gravels of glaciated areas, to consolidated rocks, such as sandstone and shale, where water is obtained from the fractures within the formations. Water-supply systems that rely on groundwater can vary in size from a few wells serving a small community to a network of many wells serving a larger area, such as the Suffolk County Water Authority in Long Island, New York.

Types of Water Uses

Water for public supply needs is defined as water that is delivered to multiple users for domestic, commercial, and industrial purposes, as well as for firefighting, street washing, municipal parks, and public swimming pools. The purveyor may be either public, such as a city-run utility, or private (an example is American Water, an investor-owned company that serves communities in several states). In the United States public systems that deliver potable water to a variety of users must comply with federal and state standards for safe drinking water. In public systems, the water's source and quality are subject to routine tests to ensure regulatory compliance.

Domestic water use is defined as the use of water for normal household purposes, such as drinking, food preparation, bathing, washing dishes and clothes, toilet flushing, lawn and garden watering, and home car washing. Households that obtain their water from on-site wells are not part of the public potable water system infrastructure. The number of households in the United States that fall into this self-supplied category is substantial. The federal Environmental Protection Agency (EPA) reports that approximately 15 percent of the U.S. population—more than 15.8 million housing units, according to 2009 census data—are served by their own private drinking-water supplies. Although these supplies are not regulated by the EPA, some state and local governments set standards for private wells. Self-supplied domestic water systems are rarely metered, and minimal data exist as to the amounts withdrawn.

Industrial water use includes the use of water necessary for processing, washing, diluting, cooling, and sanitation in factories that make a variety of products. In-

U.S. Daily Water Use, 1940-2000
(billions of gallons)

YEAR	TOTAL	PER CAPITA (GALLONS)	IRRIGATION	PUBLIC SUPPLY	RURAL	INDUSTRIAL & MISC.	STEAM ELECTRIC UTILITIES
1940	140	1,027	71	10	3.1	29	23
1950	180	1,185	89	14	3.6	37	40
1960	270	1,500	110	21	3.6	38	100
1970	370	1,815	130	27	4.5	47	170
1980	440	1,953	150	34	5.6	45	210
1990	408	1,620	137	41	7.9	30	195
1995	402	1,500	134	40	8.9	29	190
2000	408	1,430	137	43	9.2	23	196

Source: U.S. Department of Commerce, *Statistical Abstract of the United States, 2004*, 2004.
Note: Per capita figures are gallons; all other values are in billions of gallons.

dustries that use large amounts of water include the steel, chemical, paper, and petroleum-refining industries. Of the industrial uses of water, thermoelectric power constitutes a substantial water-use category in itself. It includes water used for electric power generation from fossil-fuel, nuclear, or renewable energy sources. Most of the water used by thermoelectric plants goes for condenser and reactor cooling. Only a small fraction of the water used in this category comes from public water systems. Another industry, mining, is also in a category by itself. Mining water use includes quarrying, crushing, washing, and other activities associated with mineral extraction operations.

Irrigation water use includes water employed to sustain plant growth in agriculture and horticulture. It encompasses the use of water not only for watering plants but also for applying agricultural chemicals, controlling weeds, preparing fields, cooling crops, suppressing dust, protecting against frost, and harvesting. Larger-scale nonagricultural irrigation—of golf courses, parks, nurseries, cemeteries, and the like—are included in this category.

Livestock water use is that associated with the farming of dairy and beef cattle, sheep and lambs, goats, hogs and pigs, horses, and poultry. It includes water devoted to livestock watering, feedlots, dairy operations, cooling of animal facilities, facility sanitation and washdown, and animal waste disposal systems. Similarly, aquaculture water use is that associated with sustaining organisms that live in water, notably finfish

and shellfish. Aquaculture, which involves controlled feeding, sanitation, and harvesting of aquatic organisms, may be conducted for food, restoration, conservation, or sport purposes.

According to the U.S. Geological Survey, the estimated percentage distribution for total water withdrawals in the United States in 2005 was as follows: 49 percent thermoelectric power, 31 percent irrigation, 11 percent public supply, 4 percent self-supplied (not public supply) industrial, 2 percent aquaculture, 1 percent self-supplied domestic, 1 percent mining, and less than 1 percent livestock. (These percentages include water lost through system leakage.) Some 1.552 billion cubic meters (410 billion gallons) per day were withdrawn in 2005 for all these categories.

WATER CONSUMPTION TRENDS AND CONFLICTS

In the United States, more than one-fourth of the total water used in 2005 was withdrawn in California, Texas, Idaho, and Florida. California alone was responsible for 11 percent of all the nation's withdrawals that year. Thermoelectric power and irrigation were the largest water-use categories; along with public supply, they accounted for more than 90 percent of the nation's withdrawals. Generally, per-capita water consumption in the United States tends to be highest in the West, presumably reflecting the region's lower precipitation and higher evapotranspiration rates in comparison with other regions.

Water use in most countries is a function of population served. Consequently, as the population increases, water consumption also increases, which means that water purveyors continually need to expand their water-supply sources. The need for additional supplies of water has resulted in innumerable sociopolitical disputes over the years. In arid areas such as the Middle East, water is crucial for general use and irrigation; thus the decision by Turkey in the late twentieth century to build large reservoirs in the headwaters of the Tigris and Euphrates rivers caused friction between that nation and the downstream states of Syria and Iraq, which objected to the prospect of being deprived of a portion of the flow on which they had historically depended. The allocation of the Jordan River among Israel, Jordan, Syria, and Lebanon in another politically sensitive arid area is intimately related to the possibility of sustained peace in the region. Egypt is totally dependent on the Nile River, which originates in Ethiopia and Lakes Albert and Victoria in East-Central Africa. Thus, when upstream African countries began negotiating a cooperative framework to revise water-sharing arrangements in 2010, concerns over the impact of major irrigation and hydropower projects upstream caused Egypt to oppose the agreement.

Balancing water use and the availability of water requires serious and sustained effort at local, state, national, and international levels. Even with prudent planning and cooperation among parties, drought, desertification, water pollution, and population expansion increase the likelihood that water-use conflicts will arise.

Robert M. Hordon
Updated by Karen N. Kähler

FURTHER READING

Chiras, Daniel D. "Water Resources: Preserving Our Liquid Assets and Protecting Aquatic Ecosystems." In *Environmental Science*. 8th ed. Sudbury, Mass.: Jones and Bartlett, 2010.

Correljé, Aad, and Thorsten Schuetze. *Every Drop Counts: Environmentally Sound Technologies for Urban and Domestic Water Use Efficiency.* Nairobi: United Nations Environment Programme, 2008.

Dzurik, Andrew Albert. *Water Resources Planning.* 3d ed. Lanham, Md.: Rowman & Littlefield, 2003.

Gleick, Peter H., et al. *The World's Water, 2008-2009: The Biennial Report on Freshwater Resources.* Washington, D.C.: Island Press, 2009.

Glennon, Robert Jerome. *Water Follies: Groundwater Pumping and the Fate of America's Fresh Waters.* Washington, D.C.: Island Press, 2002.

Kenny, Joan F., et al. *Estimated Use of Water in the United States in 2005.* Reston, Va.: U.S. Geological Survey, 2009.

Shiklomanov, I. A., ed. *World Water Resources at the Beginning of the Twenty-first Century.* New York: Cambridge University Press, 2003.

Vickers, Amy. *Handbook of Water Use and Conservation: Homes, Landscapes, Businesses, Industries, Farms.* Amherst, Mass.: Waterplow Press, 2001.

Watershed management

CATEGORY: Land and land use
DEFINITION: Policies governing the use of land areas bounded by drainage divides within which precipitation drains to particular watercourses or bodies of water
SIGNIFICANCE: Human activity can cause unanticipated changes in watersheds, affecting the hydrologic balance. Careful management of watersheds is important because land use alters the balance between storage and dispersal of precipitation, in many cases increasing erosion, stream sedimentation, and flooding hazards.

Watersheds are defined at many scales: The Mississippi River watershed contains the Ohio River watershed, which in turn contains smaller watersheds. A fundamental part of the hydrologic cycle, the watershed collects and stores precipitation in soils, lakes, wetlands, or aquifers and disperses water by evaporation, plant transpiration, surface runoff, springs, and base flow to streams. Watersheds of different geographic regions have distinctive characteristics based on climate, topography, and soil type; therefore, the natural variability among watersheds is predictably large. In arid regions, precipitation occurs as intense, infrequent storms, with most of the water rapidly running off and eroding soil with little protective vegetation. Watersheds in humid areas are characterized by frequent, usually gentle rain that replenishes aquifers and sustains streams, springs, and wetlands.

Ecologically, the watershed provides habitat and nutrients for plants and animals, including humans. Land use can disrupt a watershed's ecology by disturbing habitat and nutrient cycling through soil loss and removal of native vegetation. The role of the watershed in environmental problems such as flooding, erosion, sedimentation, and ecological disruption has led to increased emphasis on the watershed as the basic unit for environmental management, rather than political units such as states or counties.

The 1954 Watershed Protection and Flood Prevention Act authorized the secretary of the U.S. Department of Agriculture (USDA) to manage watersheds in cooperation with states and local organizations, such as soil and water conservation districts. The driving idea behind the act is that floods are better controlled through management of runoff upstream in the watershed than through downstream engineering projects. The act requires local interests to contribute up to 50 percent of the costs to ensure local support for watershed projects. In contrast, Army Corps of Engineers flood-control projects originally were funded entirely by the federal government. The Watershed Protection and Flood Prevention Act is generally administered through the USDA's Natural Resources Conservation Service, formerly the Soil Conservation Service.

Recognizing the need for basinwide planning, the federal government created the Water Resources Council through the 1965 Water Resources Planning Act. This council created river basin planning commissions but fell into disfavor and lost funding because the river basins were too large for effective planning.

A major step in watershed management was taken with the 1972 Clean Water Act. With this act, land management began to include water-quality control. Nonpoint sources of pollution were targeted, among them agriculture, forestry, mining, and waste disposal. Most states passed laws directing the use of certain widely accepted methods of preventing soil and water problems (known as best management practices, or BMPs) to protect or rehabilitate watershed functions. The Clean Water Act provided for regulation of land use, initially through incentives. The 1985 Food Security Act provided incentives for landowners to control erosion on highly erodible croplands. The act's "swampbuster" provisions directed protection of existing wetlands and also provided incentives for wetlands restoration. The 1986 amendments to the 1974 Safe Drinking Water Act encouraged public suppliers of drinking water to protect wellheads. The 1987 amendments to the Clean Water Act encouraged states to address nonpoint source pollution.

State regulations on nonpoint source pollution range from voluntary compliance with BMPs to strict enforcement of BMPs with fines for noncompliance. In general, however, such regulations have become increasingly detailed and comprehensive. The concept of the total maximum daily load (TMDL) permissible for nonpoint source pollutants has been intro-

Characteristics of Selected Major Drainage Basins

River	Continent	Outflow	Length	Area	Average Annual Suspended Load
Amazon	South America	180.0	6,300	5,800	360
Congo	Africa	39.0	4,700	3,700	—
Yangtze	Asia	22.0	5,800	1,900	500
Mississippi	North America	18.0	6,000	3,300	296
Irawaddy	Asia	14.0	2,300	430	300
Brahmaputra	Asia	12.0	2,900	670	730
Ganges	Asia	12.0	2,500	960	1,450
Mekong	Asia	11.0	4,200	800	170
Nile	Africa	2.8	6,700	3,000	110
Colorado	North America	0.2	2,300	640	140
Ching	Asia	0.06	320	57	410

Note: Rivers are ordered by outflow; outflow is multiplied by 1,000 cumecs (cubic meters of water per second); length is measured in kilometers; area is measured in square kilometers multiplied by 1,000; average annual suspended load is measured in millions of metric tons.

duced, but determining TMDL is costly and difficult because appropriate loads vary with land use and with watershed.

Over time, Americans' perspectives on land and water management have broadened. Whereas management initially focused on single farms or individual fields, the watershed view has come to be widely accepted. This change has been influenced in part by concerns about the greenhouse effect, in which atmosphere-biosphere-hydrosphere-terrasphere interactions are critical. The term "ecosystem management" may better reflect watershed management focus in the future.

Watersheds are managed for a spectrum of land uses, including water supply, settlement, grazing, crop production, forestry, and recreation. Management focuses on water, sediment, and wastes. Water management generally seeks to reduce runoff; exceptions are landfills and mine spoils in which infiltration is minimized. Sediment management seeks to prevent soil erosion or to trap eroded sediment. Waste management seeks to distribute the waste load properly and to prevent it from reaching water. The appropriate strategies for achieving these management goals vary from problem to problem.

For example, in forestry one strategy might include revegetating logged areas, diverting water from logging roads, and closing logging roads after use. The overall approach to watershed management is to identify the problem and its source and then select and implement BMPs. While the law requires that BMPs be considered, no definitive catalog of such practices exists. Many state agencies have written and assembled their own collections of BMPs for various land uses, which are available to the public. Public education and public participation in decision making have played increasingly important roles in sustainable watershed management in the United States.

Mary W. Stoertz

FURTHER READING

Black, Peter E. *Watershed Hydrology.* 2d ed. Chelsea, Mich.: Ann Arbor Press, 1996.
France, Robert L., ed. *Facilitating Watershed Management: Fostering Awareness and Stewardship.* Lanham, Md.: Rowman & Littlefield, 2005.
Heathcote, Isobel W. *Integrated Watershed Management: Principles and Practice.* 2d ed. Hoboken, N.J.: John Wiley & Sons, 2009.
Newson, Malcolm. *Land, Water, and Development: Sustainable and Adaptive Management of Rivers.* 3d ed. New York: Routledge, 2009.
Satterlund, Donald R., and Paul W. Adams. *Wildland Watershed Management.* 2d ed. New York: John Wiley & Sons, 1992.

Wells

CATEGORY: Water and water pollution
DEFINITION: Holes bored into the ground to extract or inject fluid
SIGNIFICANCE: Wells serve an important purpose in enabling the extraction of fluids from beneath the earth's surface, but sometimes the processes involved in boring wells can contribute to environmental degradation, such as through habitat destruction and water pollution.

The earliest wells were excavated by hand, and over time various mechanical methods have been developed for boring into the ground. The machinery used to create wells in the modern world depends on the depth desired and the types of rock through which the drill must bore. The borehole is cased with plastic pipe in shallow wells and steel pipe in deep wells to prevent caving of the walls. The casing is perforated at the depth from which production occurs. This section, called a screen, allows an exchange of fluid between the casing and surrounding rock. The space between the screen and the surrounding rock is filled with gravel to allow fluid to flow freely between the well and the aquifer. The space between the casing and the exposed rock in the upper part of the well is tightly sealed with impermeable grout to prevent contaminants from entering the bore from the surface.

Wells were originally used only to extract underground water. Today they serve many purposes, including extraction, injection, and monitoring of fluid below the surface. Water wells and oil wells are examples of producing wells that extract fluids from the subsurface. A typical water well draws water either from the surface aquifer or from deeper, confined aquifers. Oil and gas wells produce from deep rock strata. Wells are also used to remove contaminated groundwater and dewater saturated zones in which construction or other activity extends below the water table.

Injection wells are used to introduce fluids into the

subsurface. They are used as a way to store water that could otherwise be lost to high evaporation rates or runoff. Oil is occasionally pumped into subsurface, impermeable salt caverns for storage. To increase production in an oil well, water or gas may be pumped into oil-bearing strata to displace the oil. One means of disposal of hazardous wastes is to inject them into deep levels of the earth's crust. Monitoring wells are used to determine variations in depth to the water table and to provide early warning of the migration of hazardous fluids. Frequent tests of monitoring wells are required around sites of potential groundwater contamination.

Groundwater is a major source of water for domestic, agricultural, and industrial use. It exists in the subsurface, filling pores and cracks in consolidated rocks and loose, unconsolidated sand, gravel, clays, and mixtures of these materials. The surface aquifer is the saturated zone that receives water by percolation down from the surface. This is the zone most susceptible to contamination by toxic substances from industrial and municipal wastes, feedlots, septic tanks, crop fertilizers, pesticides, and herbicides. Confined aquifers are less susceptible to contamination because they are sealed from surface percolation by overlying impermeable beds. Confined aquifers can be contaminated when they are exposed to direct recharge or by boreholes that reach them from the surface. Disposal wells with corroded casings may serve as conduits for hazardous waste into subsurface water supplies. Improperly grouted wells may allow surface contamination to infiltrate water supplies through seepage along the outside of the casing.

René A. De Hon

FURTHER READING

Misstear, Bruce, David Banks, and Lewis Clark. *Water Wells and Boreholes.* Hoboken, N.J.: John Wiley & Sons, 2006.

Sipes, James L. *Sustainable Solutions for Water Resources: Policies, Planning, Design, and Implementation.* Hoboken, N.J.: John Wiley & Sons, 2010.

Wolman, Abel

CATEGORIES: Activism and advocacy; urban environments

IDENTIFICATION: American sanitary engineer

BORN: June 10, 1892; Baltimore, Maryland
DIED: February 22, 1989; Baltimore, Maryland
SIGNIFICANCE: Wolman was a pioneer in the field of sanitary engineering. His innovations and advocacy influenced the establishment of sound water-resource management strategies by American cities during the twentieth century.

Abel Wolman graduated from Baltimore's well-known high school Baltimore City College in 1909. He earned a bachelor of arts degree from The Johns Hopkins University in 1913 and then completed a bachelor of science degree in engineering at Johns Hopkins two years later. While he was working toward his second degree in 1914, he took a job as an engineer with the Maryland State Department of Health.

While working in the health department, Wolman began to pioneer the use of engineering methods to improve public health. He was specifically concerned with water supplies, wastewater treatment, and sewage disposal, addressing the dangers of such waterborne diseases as typhoid. In 1919 Wolman worked with chemist Linn Enslow to standardize techniques to chlorinate municipal drinking-water supplies. Many people believed that chlorine in any amount was poisonous, but Wolman convinced officials to adopt the procedure by explaining the disinfectant benefits of chlorination. His efforts in this area are considered to be among the most influential improvements in water management for public health, resulting in decreased death rates from waterborne diseases.

Promoting a regional approach to water supply and sewage disposal, Wolman helped consolidate the Baltimore area into one water-supply region. Named chief engineer for the Maryland State Department of Health in 1922, he analyzed municipal water-supply needs and evaluated how best to recycle wastewater. In 1935 U.S. president Franklin D. Roosevelt appointed Wolman as chairman of the Water Resources Committee of the Natural Resources Planning Board, which was in charge of managing the federal government's water resources projects.

During the 1950's Wolman predicted possible environmental problems from unsafe disposal of nuclear wastes when private companies were granted access to nuclear energy through the Atoms for Peace program. During his service on the Reactor Licensing Board of the Atomic Energy Commission, Wolman insisted that concrete containment structures be built for the first commercial nuclear power plants in the

United States. During the 1960's Wolman stressed the dangers of nonorganic environmental hazards to public health, noting that new technologically produced chemicals and contaminants had been introduced to water sources. He warned that humans must be held accountable for how they alter the environment and must envision how to protect resources.

Wolman served as editor in chief of the *Journal of the American Water Works Association* (1921-1937) and the journal *Municipal Sanitation* (1929-1935) and as associate editor of the *American Journal of Public Health* (1923-1927). The Johns Hopkins University presented Wolman with an honorary doctorate in 1937 when he established a Department of Sanitary Engineering at the university; he held the position of department chairman until he retired in 1962. Wolman received numerous awards, including the Tyler Prize for Environmental Achievement. He was a prolific author, and his major articles were collected in *Water, Health, and Society: Selected Papers*, edited by Gilbert F. White, in 1969.

Wolman offered his environmental engineering expertise worldwide as a consultant, and he emphasized the responsibility of engineers to protect environmental quality. An advocate for the poor, Wolman testified against landlords who did not provide clean water for tenants. The *Baltimore Evening Sun* promoted environmental engineering during the International Drinking Water Supply and Sanitation Decade in the 1980's by eulogizing Wolman: "[He] envisioned a world in which the most basic of necessities, water to drink, would be safe and plentiful to all peoples of the world."

Elizabeth D. Schafer

FURTHER READING

Melosi, Martin V. *Effluent America: Cities, Industry, Energy, and the Environment.* Pittsburgh: University of Pittsburgh Press, 2001.

Rogers, Jerry R., ed. *Environmental and Water Resources: Milestones in Engineering History.* Reston, Va.: American Society of Civil Engineers, 2007.

Zebra mussels

CATEGORY: Animals and endangered species

DEFINITION: Endemic European freshwater bivalves that occur in North America as an exotic species

SIGNIFICANCE: Zebra mussels are a source of concern in North America, where they are an invasive or exotic species, because of the mussels' potential influence on aquatic systems. When zebra mussels colonize a body of water, they reduce the abundance and species diversity of native mussels, and they also reproduce in such density that they restrict water flow in pipes.

The zebra mussel (*Dreissena polymorpha*) is native to southern Russia and is thought to have been introduced into Lake Saint Clair—which lies between Michigan and Ontario, Canada—in 1986 via discharged ballast water. Since its introduction, the zebra mussel has become widely dispersed, occurring in all of the Great Lakes by 1990; by 1994 it had appeared in or adjacent to nineteen U.S. states. This rapid dispersal is largely the result of the mussels' ability to attach to boats that navigate these waters, as well as their ability at all life stages to survive overland transport (for example, living on the hulls of boats as the boats are transported between lakes). It is expected that the species will continue to disperse and increasingly colonize North American inland lakes.

The shell sizes of zebra mussels average 25 to 35 millimeters (1 to 1.4 inches). Zebra mussels typically live three to five years, and females usually reproduce during their second year; each female can produce more than forty thousand eggs in one reproductive cycle. After fertilization, veliger larvae emerge within three to five days and are free-swimming for up to one month. Dispersal during this time is primarily caused by water currents. Larvae then settle to the bottom, where they crawl via a foot, looking for suitable substrate (preferred to be hard or rocky). To attach themselves to the substrate, they secrete proteinaceous byssal threads from a byssal gland located in the foot.

From an ecological and environmental perspective, one of the most important concerns related to zebra mussel colonization of a body of water is that it reduces the abundance and species diversity of native unionid mussels. Because native unionid mussel beds provide the type of hard substrate that zebra mussels prefer, zebra mussels readily colonize such areas, negatively influencing feeding, growth, locomotion, respiration, and reproduction of native unionids.

In addition, zebra mussels have an important influence on the environment because of their role as biofoulers. When they colonize pipes they can restrict water flow, negatively affecting water supply to hydro-

A native fatmucket mussel is encrusted by invasive zebra mussels. (USFWS)

electric facilities, nuclear power plants, and public water supply plants. Zebra mussels can also attach to the hulls of boats, leading to increased drag, and their weight can sink navigational buoys. Because zebra mussel densities have been measured as high as 700,000 mussels per 1 square meter (10.8 square feet), they clearly can cause serious problems.

Despite their negative effects on aquatic systems, zebra mussels can have positive effects on water quality through their role as biofilters. An adult zebra mussel can filter the phytoplankton from as much as 1 liter of water per day and can significantly alter water quality. However, even this influence has potential negative consequences in that it reduces the amount of food available for zooplankton and eventually for recruiting fishes. This can also lead to a change in food webs

from phytoplankton-dominated systems to macrophyte-dominated systems. Given their filtering ability, zebra mussels also tend to bioaccumulate substances, possibly increasing the concentration of toxic substances that are passed up the food web.

Dennis R. DeVries

FURTHER READING

Pimentel, David, ed. *Biological Invasions: Economic and Environmental Costs of Alien Plant, Animal, and Microbe Species.* Boca Raton, Fla.: CRC Press, 2002.

Van Driesche, Jason, and Roy Van Driesche. "Refuge for the Mussels: Biotic Integrity and Zebra Mussel Invasion in the Ohio River Basin." In *Nature Out of Place: Biological Invasions in the Global Age.* Washington, D.C.: Island Press, 2000.

Bibliography

Allsopp, Michelle, et al. *State of the World's Oceans.* New York: Springer, 2009.

Asano, Takashi, et al. *Water Reuse: Issues, Technologies, and Applications.* New York: McGraw-Hill, 2007.

Copeland, Claudia. *Clean Water Act: A Summary of the Law.* Washington, D.C.: Congressional Research Service, 2008.

Field, John G., Gotthilf Hempel, and Colin P. Summerhayes, eds. *Oceans 2020: Science, Trends, and the Challenge of Sustainability.* Washington, D.C.: Island Press, 2002.

Gleick, Peter H., et al. *The World's Water, 2008-2009: The Biennial Report on Freshwater Resources.* Washington, D.C.: Island Press, 2009.

Glennon, Robert Jerome. *Unquenchable: America's Water Crisis and What to Do About It.* Washington, D.C.: Island Press, 2009.

Kenny, Joan F., et al. *Estimated Use of Water in the United States in 2005.* Reston, Va.: U.S. Geological Survey, 2009.

Pearce, Fred. *When the Rivers Run Dry: Water, the Defining Crisis of the Twenty-first Century.* Boston: Beacon Press, 2006.

Ryan, Mark. *The Clean Water Act Handbook.* 2d ed. Chicago: American Bar Association, 2003.

Shiklomanov, I. A., ed. *World Water Resources at the Beginning of the Twenty-first Century.* New York: Cambridge University Press, 2003.

U.S. Environmental Protection Agency. *National Water Quality Inventory: Report to Congress, 2004 Reporting Cycle.* Washington, D.C.: Author, 2009.

Vickers, Amy. *Handbook of Water Use and Conservation: Homes, Landscapes, Businesses, Industries, Farms.* Amherst, Mass.: Waterplow Press, 2001.

CATEGORY INDEX

ACTIVISM AND ADVOCACY
Brent Spar occupation, 13
Wolman, Abel, 134

AGRICULTURE AND FOOD
Irrigation, 52
Soil salinization, 106

ANIMALS AND ENDANGERED SPECIES
Kesterson Reservoir, 54
Klamath River, 55
Zebra mussels, 135

ATMOSPHERE AND AIR POLLUTION
Best available technologies, 7
Environment Canada, 31
Environmental Protection Agency, 32
Externalities, 38
Gulf War oil burning, 50
North American Free Trade Agreement, 72
Polluter pays principle, 87

DISASTERS
Amoco Cadiz oil spill, 1
Argo Merchant oil spill, 5
BP *Deepwater Horizon* oil spill, 9
Braer oil spill, 12
Cuyahoga River fires, 22
Exxon Valdez oil spill, 38
Gulf War oil burning, 50
Monongahela River tank collapse, 69
PEMEX oil well leak, 86
Sacramento River pesticide spill, 97
Santa Barbara oil spill, 99
Sea Empress oil spill, 100
Teton Dam collapse, 109
Tobago oil spill, 110
Torrey Canyon oil spill, 111

ECOLOGY AND ECOSYSTEMS
Black Sea, 8
Chesapeake Bay, 14
Continental shelves, 20
Lake Baikal, 56
Mississippi River, 65

Mono Lake, 68
Nile River, 71

HUMAN HEALTH AND THE ENVIRONMENT
Ashio, Japan, copper mine, 6
Environment Canada, 31
Environmental Protection Agency, 32

LAND AND LAND USE
Coastal Zone Management Act, 18
Floodplains, 41
U.S. Geological Survey, 113
Watershed management, 131

NUCLEAR POWER AND RADIATION
Rocky Flats, Colorado, nuclear plant releases, 92

ORGANIZATIONS AND AGENCIES
Environment Canada, 31
Environmental Protection Agency, 32
Great Lakes International Joint Commission, 48
U.S. Geological Survey, 113

PLACES
Black Sea, 8
Chesapeake Bay, 14
Colorado River, 18
Danube River, 27
Ganges River, 47
Klamath River, 55
Lake Baikal, 56
Lake Erie, 58
Mississippi River, 65
Mono Lake, 68
Nile River, 71
Pacific Islands, 84
Rhine River, 91

POLLUTANTS AND TOXINS
Leachates, 59

PRESERVATION AND WILDERNESS ISSUES
Dams and reservoirs, 23
Los Angeles Aqueduct, 62

RESOURCES AND RESOURCE MANAGEMENT
    Flood Control Act, 40
    Klamath River, 55
    Pacific Islands, 84
    Rainwater harvesting, 89
    United Nations Convention on the Law of the
        Sea, 112
    U.S. Geological Survey, 113
    Water conservation, 116
    Water use, 129

TREATIES, LAWS, AND COURT CASES
    Clean Water Act and amendments, 16
    Coastal Zone Management Act, 18
    Flood Control Act, 40
    London Convention on the Prevention of Marine
        Pollution, 61
    North American Free Trade Agreement, 72
    Polluter pays principle, 87

Safe Drinking Water Act, 98
United Nations Convention on the Law of the
    Sea, 112

URBAN ENVIRONMENTS
    Rain gardens, 88
    Wolman, Abel, 134

WASTE AND WASTE MANAGEMENT
    Leachates, 59
    Ocean dumping, 76
    Seabed disposal, 103
    Sludge treatment and disposal, 105
    Wastewater management, 114

WEATHER AND CLIMATE
    Floods, 43
    Ocean currents, 74
    Sea-level changes, 101

INDEX

Acid mine drainage, 1, 118
Acid rain, 118
Acidification, lakes, 36
Africa, Nile River, 71-72
Agenda 21, 81
Agriculture
    irrigation, 52-54
    runoff, 94-95
Air pollution, 34
Algal blooms, 22, 36, 80, 118
All-American Canal, 52
Amoco Cadiz oil spill, 1-2
Aquaculture, 130
Aqueducts, 2-4
    Los Angeles, 62-64
Aquifers, 4-5, 134
    pollution, 49-50
Argo Merchant oil spill, 5-6
Ashio, Japan, copper mine, 6-7
Ashland Oil, 69
Aswan High Dam, 26, 71
Atomic weapons. *See* Nuclear weapons

Beaches
    erosion, 86
    rejuvenation, 105
Benefit-cost analysis, 7-8
Best available technologies, 7-8, 17
Bioaccumulation, 55, 58, 80
Biodiversity losses, 86
Biological pump, 75
Biomagnification, 58, 80
Bioremediation, 40, 83, 106
Black Sea, 8-9
Black water, 114
BP *Deepwater Horizon* oil spill, 9-12, 21
Braer oil spill, 12-13
Brent Spar occupation, 13-14
Buffer lands, 95

Canada
    Environment Canada, 31-32
    Experimental Lakes Area, 36-37
    International Joint Commission, 48-49
Cantara pesticide spill, 97-98

Carbon dioxide, 80, 118
    and oceans, 75
Central Arizona Project, 3
Chesapeake Bay, 14-15, 22
Chlorinated compounds, 15-16
Chlorinated hydrocarbons, 60, 119
Chlorination, 15-16, 30, 128, 134
Chloroform, 15
Clean Water Act (1972), 16-18, 94, 108, 122, 124
    watershed management, 132
Climate change, sea-level changes, 101-103

Coastal Zone Management Act (1972), 18
Coffman, Larry, 88
Colorado River, 18-20
Commission for Environmental Cooperation, 73
Comprehensive Environmental Response,
    Compensation, and Liability Act (1980), 34, 123
Conservation, water, 31, 116-117, 127
Continental shelves, 20-21
Convention on the Prevention of Marine Pollution.
    See London Convention on the Prevention of
    Marine Pollution
Copper mining, Ashio, Japan, 6-7
Coral reefs, 20, 85
Cuyahoga River fires, 22-23

Dams, 23-27, 45
    Colorado River, 19
    and earthquakes, 26
    Klamath River, 56
    Missouri River, 41
    Nile River, 71
    Teton, 109-110
Danube River, 27-28
DDT. *See* Dichloro-diphenyl-trichloroethane
Dead zones, 8, 15, 20, 36, 67
Deepwater Horizon oil spill, 9-12, 21
Deforestation, 6
Desalination, 28-30
Dichloro-diphenyl-trichloroethane, 20
Dioxins, 60
Dredging, 29-30
    continental shelves, 21
    marine pollution, 79

Drinking water, 30-31
    chlorination, 15-16
    fluoridation, 45-47
    safety standards, 98-99, 122
    treatment, 127-129

Earthquakes, 26
Echo Park Dam opposition, 26
Economics, externalities, 38
Ecosystem services, 115
Ecosystems, riparian, 42, 115
Endangered species
    Klamath River basin, 55
    snail darter, 26
Endocrine disrupters, 114
Environment Canada, 31-32
Environmental cleanup
    oil spills, 39, 52, 83, 100, 111
    polluter pays principle, 87-88
    Rocky Flats nuclear weapons plant, 93
    Superfund, 34
Environmental law, oceans, 112-113
Environmental policy, water quality, 121-123
Environmental Protection Agency, 17, 32-35
Erosion, 29
    beaches, 86
Escherichia coli, 128
Europe, Rhine River, 91
Eutrophication, 8, 35-37, 58, 94, 108
    cultural, 22
Exotic species, 8
    zebra mussels, 135-136
Experimental Lakes Area, 36-37
Externalities, 38, 87
Exxon Valdez oil spill, 38-40

Farming. See Agriculture
Federal Insecticide, Fungicide, and Rodenticide Act
    (1947), 34
Federal Water Pollution Control Act (1948), 16,
    122
Federal Water Quality Act (1965), 16, 122
Fertilizers, 20, 50, 78, 94-95, 118
Fish farming. See Aquaculture
Fisheries, Great Lakes, 59
Fishing, commercial, 74
Flood Control Act (1944), 40-41
Floodplains, 26, 41-43
    rejuvenation, 105
Floods, 26, 42-45, 108

Mississippi River, 67
Nile River, 71
Watarase Valley, 6
Fluoridation, 45-47
Food Security Act (1985), 132
Foul Area, 103

Ganges River, 47-48
Garbage. See Solid waste
Gardening, naturescaping, 97
Gardens, rain, 88-89, 108
Gasoline, 50, 119
Glen Canyon Dam, 26
Global warming, 20. See also Climate change
    sea-level changes, 101-103
Gorbachev, Mikhail, 58
Gray water, 114
Great Lakes, 22
    zebra mussels, 135
Great Lakes International Joint Commission, 48-49,
    59

Great Lakes Toxic Substances Control Agreement
    (1986), 59
Great Lakes Water Quality Agreement (1972), 48,
    59, 108, 123
Great Pacific Garbage Patch, 77
Greenhouse effect, 133
Greenpeace, Brent Spar occupation, 13-14
Groundwater, 4-5, 30, 119, 129, 134
    pollution, 1, 49-50, 81
Gulf of Mexico, oil spills, 9-12, 21, 86-87
Gulf War oil burning, 50-52, 81

Hazardous waste. See also Industrial waste
    management, 123
    ocean dumping, 103
    petroleum products, 82
Heavy metals, 50
Hetch Hetchy Dam, 26
Hydrologic cycle, 131
Imperial Valley, 52

India, Ganges River, 47-48
Industrial Revolution, 118
Industrial waste, 58, 104, 115
    Mississippi River, 67
    ocean dumping, 76, 78, 103
    treatment, 105-106. See also Hazardous waste
Insecticides. See Pesticides

International Commission for the Protection of the Danube River, 27
International Convention for the Prevention of Pollution from Ships (1973), 77, 81, 103, 123
International Joint Commission, 48-49, 59
International Maritime Organization, 61
Introduced species. *See* Exotic species
Invasive species. *See* Exotic species
Irrigation, 52-54, 115, 117, 130
    runoff, 95
    and soil salinization, 107

Japan, copper mining, 6-7

Kesterson Reservoir, 54-55, 107
Klamath River, 55-56
Kuwait oil fields burning, 50-52, 81

Lake Baikal, 56-58
Lake Erie, 22, 58-59, 94, 108
Lake Shasta, 97
Land pollution, 81
    nuclear waste, 93
    oil, 51
Land use, watersheds, 133
Landfills, leachates, 59-61
Law of the Sea Treaty (1982), 80, 112-113
Leachates, 59-61
London Convention on the Prevention of Marine Pollution (1972), 61-62, 77, 80, 103, 123
Los Angeles Aqueduct, 3, 62-64, 68

Marine pollution, 13, 76-81, 103-104, 112
    London Convention, 61-62
    oil, 82
Marine Protection, Research, and Sanctuaries Act (1972), 21, 123
MARPOL. *See* International Convention for the Prevention of Pollution from Ships
Massachusetts Bay Industrial Waste Site, 103
Mediterranean Blue Plan, 64-65
Mediterranean Sea, pollution, 64-65
Mercury, 37
Metam sodium, 97
Methane from reservoirs, 26
Methylmercury, 37
Middle East
    desalination plants, 28
    water rights, 131
Mining. *See also* Copper mining, Seabed mining

methods, 29
Pacific Islands, 86
wastes, 115
water pollution, 1, 6-7
Mississippi River, 65-68
Missouri River, 40
Mono Lake, 62, 68-69
Monongahela River oil spill, 69-71
Mulholland, William, 62
Municipal solid waste. *See* Solid waste

National Coastal Zone Management Program, 18
National Environmental Policy Act (1970), 32
National Estuarine Research Reserve System, 18
National Oceanic and Atmospheric Administration, 18
National Pollutant Discharge Elimination System, 16, 109
National Water-Quality Assessment program, 94
National Water Quality Inventory Report, 121
Nile River, 71-72, 131
Nitrates, 50, 78, 98, 118
Nixon, Richard, 16, 32
NOAA. *See* National Oceanic and Atmospheric Administration
North American Agreement on Environmental Cooperation (1992), 73
North American Free Trade Agreement (1992), 72-74
Nuclear waste, 120, 134
    ocean dumping, 103
    Rocky Flats plant, 92-94
Nuclear weapons, Rocky Flats plant, 92-94

Ocean Dumping Act. *See* Marine Protection, Research, and Sanctuaries Act
Oceans
    acidity, 80
    continental shelves, 20-21
    currents, 74-76
    global warming, 101-103
    Law of the Sea Treaty, 112-113
    pollution, 20, 78-82
    waste dumping, 21, 61-62, 76-78, 103-104
Oil Pollution Act (1990), 17, 123
Oil spills, 81-84
    Amoco Cadiz, 1-2
    Argo Merchant, 5-6
    Braer, 12-13
    continental shelves, 21

Exxon Valdez, 38-40
Gulf of Mexico, 9-12, 86-87
marine pollution, 79-80
Monongahela River, 69-71
Santa Barbara, 99-100
Sea Empress, 100-101
Tobago, 110-111
Torrey Canyon, 111-112
Olmsted, Frederick Law, 96
Organic farming, 95
O'Shaughnessy Dam. *See* Hetch Hetchy Dam
Overfishing, 74

Pacific Islands, environmental overview, 84-86
PCBs. *See* Polychlorinated biphenyls
PEMEX oil spill, 21, 86-87
Persian Gulf War oil burning, 50-52, 81
Pesticides, 94-95, 119
Sacramento River spill, 97-98
Petroleum pipelines, 81
Phosphorus, 108, 118
Pick-Sloan Act (1944), 40
Plastics, marine pollution, 77, 80, 103
Plutonium, 93
Polluter pays principle, 87-88
Pollution. *See* Air pollution, Marine pollution, Water
pollution
Polychlorinated biphenyls, 58
Population growth and water supplies, 30
Prior appropriation doctrine, 92, 126

Radiation in groundwater, 119
Rain gardens, 88-89, 108
Rainwater harvesting, 89-90
Reagan, Ronald, 17
Reservoirs, 23-27, 36
methane, 26
Resource Conservation and Recovery Act (1976),
34, 123
Rhine River, 91
Rio Declaration on Environment and Development
(1992), 87
Riparian rights, 91-92, 125
Rocky Flats nuclear weapons plant, 92-94
Roosevelt, Theodore, 62
Royal Dutch Shell, 13
Runoff, agricultural, 20, 54, 78, 94-95, 115
urban, 78, 88, 95-97, 107-109

Sacramento River pesticide spill, 97-98
Safe Drinking Water Act (1974), 30, 98-99, 122, 124,
132
Salinization, soil, 53, 106-107
Salmon
Klamath River, 55
Rhine River, 91
Sanitary engineering, 134
Santa Barbara oil spill, 99-100
Sea Empress oil spill, 100-101
Sea-level changes, 101-103
Pacific Islands, 85
Seabed disposal, 13, 76, 79, 103-104
Seabed mining, 112
Seafood farming. *See* Aquaculture
Sedimentation, 29, 104-105
Selenium, 54, 107
Septic systems, 114
Sewage treatment, 59, 79, 105-106, 114, 134
Sierra Club, 26
Sludge treatment, 79, 105-106
Snail darter, 26
Soil
contamination, 81
salinization, 53, 106-107
Solid waste management, 60
Soviet Union, Lake Baikal, 56-58
Sporhase v. Nebraska (1982), 126
Stormwater management, 59, 95-97, 107-109, 121
rain gardens, 88-89
rainwater harvesting, 89-90
Sulfur dioxide and acid rain, 118
Superfund (1980), 34, 123
Superfund Amendments and Reauthorization Act
(1986), 35

Taiga, 56
Tellico Dam, 26
Teton Dam collapse, 109-110
Thermal pollution, 120
Thermohaline circulation, 75
Tobago oil spill, 110-111
Toilets, low-flush, 116, 127
Torrey Canyon oil spill, 6, 111-112
Tourism and environmental impacts, 86
Toxic Substances Control Act (1976), 34, 122
Tragedy of the commons, 92
Trash. *See* Solid waste
Trihalomethanes, 15, 129

Union Oil Company, 99, 111
United Nations Convention on the Law of the Sea
    (1982), 80, 112-113
United Nations Environment Programme, 64
U.S. Army Corps of Engineers, 17, 41
U.S. Geological Survey, 113-114

War, environmental effects, 51
Waste. *See* Hazardous waste, Industrial waste,
    Nuclear waste, Solid waste
Waste management, ocean dumping, 76-81,
    103-104
Wastewater treatment, 114-117, 134
Watarase River, 6
Water conservation, toilets, 127
Water cycle. *See* Hydrologic cycle
Water distribution, aqueducts, 2-4, 62-64
Water pollution, 49-50, 118-120, 124
    acidification, 36
    agricultural runoff, 94-95
    Chesapeake Bay, 14-15
    Clean Water Act, 34
    Cuyahoga River fires, 22-23
    Danube River, 27-28
    dredging, 29-30
    eutrophication, 22, 35-36
    Kesterson Reservoir, 54-55
    Lake Baikal, 57
    Lake Erie, 58-59
    Mediterranean Sea, 64-65
    mining, 1, 6-7
    Mississippi River, 67
    nitrates, 50, 78, 98, 118
    Pacific Islands, 86
    policy making, 121-123

Rhine River, 91
    urban runoff, 88-89, 95-97, 107-109
Water quality, 121-125, 134
    safety standards, 16-18, 30-31, 98-99
    sedimentation, 104-105
    treatment, 15-16, 45-47, 127-129
Water Quality Improvement Act (1970), 16
Water resources
    aquifers, 4-5
    rainwater harvesting, 89-90
Water rights, 91-92, 125-127, 131
    Colorado River, 19
Water treatment, 127-129
    chlorination, 15-16, 134
    desalination, 28-29
    drinking water, 30
    wastewater, 114-116
Water use, 129-131
    conservation, 116-117
    irrigation, 54
Watershed Protection and Flood Prevention Act
    (1954), 132
Watersheds
    agricultural runoff, 95
    management, 131-133
Wells, 133-134
Wetlands, 17
Wildlife refuges, Kesterson, 54-55
Wolman, Abel, 134-135
World Heritage Sites, Lake Baikal, 58

Yiamouyiannis, John, 46

Zebra mussels, 135-136